WINDS OF DOCTRINE

and

PLATONISM
AND THE SPIRITUAL LIFE

HARPER TORCHBOOKS

———— ★ ————

George Santayana

WINDS of DOCTRINE

and

PLATONISM AND THE SPIRITUAL LIFE

HARPER TORCHBOOKS

HARPER & BROTHERS PUBLISHERS
New York

WINDS OF DOCTRINE
Reprinted by arrangement with J. M. Dent & Sons, London

PLATONISM AND THE SPIRITUAL LIFE
Reprinted by arrangement with Constable and Company, London

First HARPER TORCHBOOK edition published 1957

Printed in the United States of America

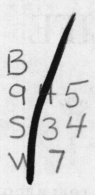
Library of Congress catalogue card number: 57–10533

CONTENTS

WINDS OF DOCTRINE

I

THE INTELLECTUAL TEMPER OF THE AGE

THE present age is a critical one and interesting to live in. The civilisation characteristic of Christendom has not disappeared, yet another civilisation has begun to take its place. We still understand the value of religious faith; we still appreciate the pompous arts of our forefathers; we are brought up on academic architecture, sculpture, painting, poetry, and music. We still love monarchy and aristocracy, together with that picturesque and dutiful order which rested on local institutions, class privileges, and the authority of the family. We may even feel an organic need for all these things, cling to them tenaciously, and dream of rejuvenating them. On the other hand the shell of Christendom is broken. The unconquerable mind of the East, the pagan past, the industrial socialistic future confront it with their equal authority. Our whole life and mind is saturated with the slow upward filtration of a new spirit—that of an emancipated, atheistic, international democracy.

These epithets may make us shudder; but what they describe is something positive and self-justified, something deeply rooted in our animal nature and inspiring to our hearts, something which, like every vital impulse, is pregnant with a morality of its own. In vain do we deprecate it; it has possession of us already through our propensities, fashions, and language. Our very plutocrats and monarchs are at ease only when they are vulgar. Even prelates and missionaries are hardly sincere or conscious of an honest function, save as they devote themselves to social work; for willy-nilly the new spirit has hold of our consciences as well. This spirit is amiable as well as disquieting, liberating as well as barbaric; and a philosopher in our day, conscious both of the old life and of the new, might repeat what Goethe said of his successive love affairs—that it is sweet to see the moon rise while the sun is still mildly shining.

Meantime our bodies in this generation are generally safe, and often comfortable; and for those who can suspend their irrational labours long enough to look about them, the spectacle of the world, if not particularly beautiful or touching, presents a rapid and crowded drama and (what here concerns me most) one unusually intelligible. The nations, parties, and movements that divide the scene have a known history. We are not condemned, as most generations have been, to fight and believe without an inkling of the cause. The past lies before us; the history of everything is published. Every one records his opinion, and loudly proclaims what he wants. In this Babel of ideals few demands are ever literally satisfied; but many evaporate, merge together, and reach an unintended issue, with which they are content. The whole drift of things presents a huge, good-natured comedy to the observer. It stirs not unpleasantly a certain sturdy animality and hearty self-trust which lie at the base of human nature.

A chief characteristic of the situation is that moral confusion is not limited to the world at large, always the scene of profound conflicts, but that it has penetrated to the mind and heart of the average individual. Never perhaps were men so like one another and so divided within themselves. In other ages, even more than at present, different classes of men have stood at different levels of culture, with a magnificent readiness to persecute and to be martyred for their respective principles. These militant believers have been keenly conscious that they had enemies; but their enemies were strangers to them, whom they could think of merely as such, regarding them as blank negative forces, hateful black devils, whose existence might make life difficult but could not confuse the ideal of life. No one sought to understand these enemies of his, nor even to conciliate them, unless under compulsion or out of insidious policy, to convert them against their will; he merely pelted them with blind refutations and clumsy blows. Every one sincerely felt that the right was entirely on his side, a proof that such intelligence as he had moved freely and exclusively within the lines of his faith. The result of this was that his faith was intelligent, I mean, that he understood it, and had a clear, almost instinctive perception of what was compatible or incompatible with it. He defended his walls and he cultivated his garden. His position and his possessions were unmistakable.

When men and minds were so distinct it was possible to describe and to count them. During the Reformation, when external confusion was at its height, you might have ascertained almost statistically what persons and what regions each side snatched from the other; it was not doubtful which was which. The history of their respective victories and defeats could consequently be written. So in the eighteenth century it was easy to perceive how many people Voltaire and Rousseau might be alienating from Bossuet and Fénelon. But how shall we satisfy ourselves now whether, for instance, Christianity is holding its own? Who can tell what vagary or what compromise may not be calling itself Christianity? A bishop may be a modernist, a chemist may be a mystical theologian, a psychologist may be a believer in ghosts. For science, too, which had promised to supply a new and solid foundation for philosophy, has allowed philosophy rather to undermine its foundation, and is seen eating its own words, through the mouths of some of its accredited spokesmen, and reducing itself to something utterly conventional and insecure. It is characteristic of human nature to be as impatient of ignorance regarding what is not known as lazy in acquiring such knowledge as is at hand; and even those who have not been lazy sometimes take it into their heads to disparage their science and to outdo the professional philosophers in psychological scepticism, in order to plunge with them into the most vapid speculation. Nor is this insecurity about first principles limited to abstract subjects. It reigns in politics as well. Liberalism had been supposed to advocate liberty; but what the advanced parties that still call themselves liberal now advocate is control, control over property, trade, wages, hours of work, meat and drink, amusements, and in a truly advanced country like France control over education and religion; and it is only on the subject of marriage (if we ignore eugenics) that liberalism is growing more and more liberal. Those who speak most of progress measure it by quantity and not by quality; how many people read and write, or how many people there are, or what is the annual value of their trade; whereas true progress would rather lie in reading or writing fewer and better things, and being fewer and better men, and enjoying life more. But the philanthropists are now preparing an absolute subjection of the individual, in soul and body, to the instincts of the majority—the most cruel and unprogressive of masters; and I am not sure that the liberal maxim, " the greatest happiness of the greatest number," has not lost whatever was just or generous in its intent and come to mean the greatest idleness of the largest possible population.

Nationality offers another occasion for strange moral confusion. It had seemed that an age that was levelling and connecting all nations, an age whose real achievements were of international application, was destined to establish the solidarity of mankind as a sort of axiom. The idea of solidarity is indeed often invoked in speeches, and there is an extreme socialistic party that—when a wave of national passion does not carry it the other way —believes in international brotherhood. But even here, black men and yellow men are generally excluded; and in higher circles, where history, literature, and political ambition dominate men's minds, nationalism has become of late an omnivorous all-permeating passion. Local parliaments must be everywhere established, extinct or

provincial dialects must be galvanised into national
languages, philosophy must be made racial, religion must
be fostered where it emphasises nationality and denounced
where it transcends it.   Man is certainly an animal that,
when he lives at all, lives for ideals.   Something must be
found to occupy his imagination, to raise pleasure and
pain into love and hatred, and change the prosaic alternative between comfort and discomfort into the tragic one
between happiness and sorrow.   Now that the hue of
daily adventure is so dull, when religion for the most
part is so vague and accommodating, when even war is
a vast impersonal business, nationality seems to have
slipped into the place of honour.   It has become the one
eloquent, public, intrepid illusion.   Illusion, I mean,
when it is taken for an ultimate good or a mystical essence,
for of course nationality is a fact.   People speak some
particular language and are very uncomfortable where
another is spoken or where their own is spoken differently.
They have habits, judgments, assumptions to which they
are wedded, and a society where all this is unheard of
shocks them and puts them at a galling disadvantage.
To ignorant people the foreigner as such is ridiculous,
unless he is superior to them in numbers or prestige,
when he becomes hateful.   It is natural for a man to
like to live at home, and to live long elsewhere without a
sense of exile is not good for his moral integrity.   It is
right to feel a greater kinship and affection for what lies
nearest to oneself.   But this necessary fact and even
duty of nationality is accidental; like age or sex it is a
physical fatality which can be made the basis of specific
and comely virtues; but it is not an end to pursue or a

flag to flaunt or a privilege not balanced by a thousand incapacities. Yet of this distinction our contemporaries tend to make an idol, perhaps because it is the only distinction they feel they have left.

Anomalies of this sort will never be properly understood until people accustom themselves to a theory to which they have always turned a deaf ear, because, though simple and true, it is materialistic: namely, that mind is not the cause of our actions but an effect, collateral with our actions, of bodily growth and organisation. It may therefore easily come about that the thoughts of men, tested by the principles that seem to rule their conduct, may be belated, or irrelevant, or premonitory; for the living organism has many strata, on any of which, at a given moment, activities may exist perfect enough to involve consciousness, yet too weak and isolated to control the organs of outer expression; so that (to speak geologically) our practice may be historic, our manners glacial, and our religion palæozoic. The ideals of the nineteenth century may be said to have been all belated; the age still yearned with Rousseau or speculated with Kant, while it moved with Darwin, Bismarck, and Nietzsche: and to-day, in the half-educated classes, among the religious or revolutionary sects, we may observe quite modern methods of work allied with a somewhat antiquated mentality. The whole nineteenth century might well cry with Faust: " Two souls, alas, dwell in my bosom! " The revolutions it witnessed filled it with horror and made it fall in love romantically with the past and dote on ruins, because they were ruins; and the best learning and fiction of the time were historical, inspired by an unprecedented effort to understand remote forms of life and feeling, to appreciate exotic arts and religions, and to rethink the blameless thoughts of savages and criminals. This sympathetic labour and retrospect, however, was far from being merely sentimental; for the other half of this divided soul was looking ahead. Those same revolutions, often so destructive, stupid, and bloody, filled it with pride, and prompted it to invent several incompatible theories concerning a steady and inevitable progress in the world. In the study of the past, side by side with romantic sympathy, there was a sort of realistic, scholarly intelligence and an adventurous love of truth; kindness too was often mingled with dramatic curiosity. The pathologists were usually healers, the philosophers of evolution were inventors or humanitarians or at least idealists: the historians of art (though optimism was impossible here) were also guides to taste, quickeners of moral sensibility, like Ruskin, or enthusiasts for the irresponsibly beautiful, like Pater and Oscar Wilde. Everywhere in the nineteenth century we find a double preoccupation with the past and with the future, a longing to know what all experience might have been hitherto, and on the other hand to hasten to some wholly different experience, to be contrived immediately with a beating heart and with flying banners. The imagination of the age was intent on history; its conscience was intent on reform.

Reform! This magic word itself covers a great equivocation. To reform means to shatter one form and to create another; but the two sides of the act are not always equally intended nor equally successful. Usually the movement starts from the mere sense of oppression, and people break down some established form, without any qualms about the capacity of their freed instincts to generate the new forms that may be needed. So the Reformation, in destroying the traditional order, intended to secure truth, spontaneity, and profuseness of religious forms; the danger of course being that each form might become meagre and the sum of them chaotic. If the accent, however, could only be laid on the second phase of the transformation, reform might mean the creation of order where it did not sufficiently appear, so that diffuse life should be concentrated into a congenial form that should render it strong and self-conscious. In this sense, if we may trust Mr. Gilbert Murray, it was a great wave of reform that created Greece, or at least all that was characteristic and admirable in it — an effort to organise, train, simplify, purify, and make beautiful the chaos of barbaric customs and passions that had preceded. The danger here, a danger to which Greece actually succumbed, is that so refined an organism may be too fragile, not inclusive enough within, and not buttressed strongly enough without against the flux of the uncivilised world. Christianity also, in the first formative centuries of its existence, was an integrating reform of the same sort, on a different scale and in a different sphere; but here too an enslaved rabble within the soul claiming the suffrage, and better equipped intellectual empires rising round about, seem to prove that the harmony which the Christian system made for a moment out of nature and life was partial and insecure. It is a terrible dilemma in the life of reason whether it will sacrifice natural abundance to moral order, or moral order to natural abundance. Whatever compromise we choose proves unstable, and forces us to a new experiment.

Perhaps in the century that has elapsed since the French Revolution the pendulum has had time to swing as far as it will in the direction of negative reform, and may now begin to move towards that sort of reform which is integrating and creative. The veering of the advanced political parties from liberalism to socialism would seem to be a clear indication of this new tendency. It is manifest also in the love of nature, in athletics, in the new woman, and in a friendly medical attitude towards all the passions.

In the fine arts, however, and in religion and philosophy, we are still in full career towards disintegration. It might have been thought that a germ of rational order would by this time have penetrated into fine art and speculation from the prosperous constructive arts that touch the one, and the prosperous natural and mathematical sciences that touch the other. But as yet there is little sign of it. Since the beginning of the nineteenth century painting and sculpture have passed through several phases, representatives of each naturally surviving after the next had appeared. Romanticism, half lurid, half effeminate, yielded to a brutal pursuit of material truth, and a pious preference for modern and humble sentiment. This realism had a romantic vein in it, and studied vice and crime, tedium and despair, with a very genuine horrified sympathy. Some went in for a display of archæological lore or for exotic *motifs ;* others gave all their attention to rediscovering and emphasising abstract problems of execution, the highway of technical tradition having long been abandoned. Beginners are still supposed to study their art, but they have no masters from whom to learn it. Thus, when there seemed to be some danger that art should be drowned in science and history, the artists deftly eluded it by becoming amateurs. One gave himself to religious archaism, another to Japanese composition, a third to barbaric symphonies of colour; sculptors tried to express dramatic climaxes, or inarticulate lyrical passion, such as music might better convey; and the latest whims are apparently to abandon painful observation altogether, to be merely decorative or frankly mystical, and to be satisfied with the childishness of hieroglyphics or the crudity of caricature. The arts are like truant children who think their life will be glorious if they only run away and play for ever; no need is felt of a dominant ideal passion and theme, nor of any moral interest in the interpretation of nature. Artists have no less talent than ever; their taste, their vision, their sentiment are often interesting; they are mighty in their independence and feeble only in their works.

In philosophy there are always the professors, as in art there are always the portrait painters and the makers of official sculpture; and both sorts of academicians are often very expert and well-educated. Yet in philosophy, besides the survival of all the official and endowed systems, there has been of late a very interesting fresh movement, largely among the professors themselves, which in its various hues may be called irrationalism, vitalism, pragmatism, or pure empiricism. But this movement, far from being a reawakening of any organising instinct, is simply an extreme expression of romantic anarchy. It is in essence but a franker confession of the principle upon which modern philosophy has been building—or unbuilding—for these three hundred years, I mean the principle of subjectivity. Berkeley and Hume, the first prophets of the school, taught that experience is not a partial discovery of other things but is itself the only possible object of experience. Therefore, said Kant and the second generation of prophets, any world we may seem to live in, even those worlds of theology or of history which Berkeley or Hume had inadvertently left standing, must be an idea which our present experience suggests to us and which we frame as the principles of our mind allow and dictate that we should. But then, say the latest prophets—Avenarius, William James, M. Bergson —these mental principles are no antecedent necessities or duties imposed on our imagination; they are simply parts of flying experience itself, and the ideas—say of God or of matter—which they lead us to frame have nothing compulsory or fixed about them. Their sole authority lies in the fact that they may be more or less congenial or convenient, by enriching the flying moment æsthetically, or helping it to slip prosperously into the next moment. Immediate feeling, pure experience, is the only reality, the only *fact :* if notions which do not reproduce it fully as it flows are still called true (and they evidently ought not to be) it is only in a pragmatic sense of the word, in that while they present a false and heterogeneous image of reality they are not practically misleading; as, for instance, the letters on this page are no true image of the sounds they call up, nor the sounds

of the thoughts, yet both may be correct enough if they
lead the reader in the end to the things they symbolise.
It is M. Bergson, the most circumspect and best equipped
thinker of this often scatter-brained school, who has put
this view in a frank and tenable form, avoiding the
bungling it has sometimes led to about the " meaning of
truth." Truth, according to M. Bergson, is given only
in intuitions which prolong experience just as it occurs,
in its full immediacy; on the other hand, all representation, thought, theory, calculation, or discourse is so much
mutilation of the truth, excusable only because imposed
upon us by practical exigences. The world, being a
feeling, must be felt to be known, and then the world
and the knowledge of it are identical; but if it is talked
about or thought about it is denaturalised, although
convention and utility may compel the poor human being
to talk and to think, exiled as he is from reality in his
Babylon of abstractions. Life, like the porcupine when
not ruffled by practical alarms, can let its fretful quills
subside. The mystic can live happy in the droning consciousness of his own heart-beats and those of the universe.

With this we seem to have reached the extreme of self-
concentration and self-expansion, the perfect identity and
involution of everything in oneself. And such indeed is
the inevitable goal of the malicious theory of knowledge,
to which this school is committed, remote as that goal
may be from the boyish naturalism and innocent intent of
many of its pupils. If all knowledge is of experience and
experience cannot be knowledge of anything else, knowledge proper is evidently impossible. There can be only
feeling; and the least self-transcendence, even in memory,

must be an illusion. You may have the most complex images you will; but nothing pictured there can exist outside, not even past or alien experience, if you picture it.[1] Solipsism has always been the evident implication of idealism; but the idealists, when confronted with this consequence, which is dialectically inconvenient, have never been troubled at heart by it, for at heart they accept it. To the uninitiated they have merely murmured, with a pitying smile and a wave of the hand: What! are you still troubled by that? Or if compelled to be so scholastic as to labour the point they have explained, as usual, that oneself cannot be the absolute because the *idea* of oneself, to arise, must be contrasted with other ideas. Therefore, you cannot well have the idea of a world in which nothing appears but the *idea* of yourself.

[1] Perhaps some unsophisticated reader may wonder if I am not trying to mislead him, or if any mortal ever really maintained anything so absurd. Strictly the idealistic principle does not justify a denial that independent things, by chance resembling my ideas, may actually exist; but it justifies the denial that these things, if they existed, could be those I know. My past would not be my past if I did not appropriate it; my ideas would not refer to their objects unless both were ideas identified in my mind. In practice, therefore, idealists feel free to ignore the gratuitous possibility of existences lying outside the circle of objects knowable to the thinker, which, according to them, is the circle of his ideas. In this way they turn a human method of approach into a charter for existence and non-existence, and their point of view becomes the creative power. When the idealist studies astronomy, does he learn anything about the stars that God made? Far from him so naïve a thought! His astronomy consists of two activities of his own (and he is very fond of activity): star-gazing and calculation. When he has become quite proficient he knows all about star-gazing and calculation; but he knows nothing of any stars that God made; for there are no stars except his visual images of stars, and there is no God but himself. It is true that to soften this hard saying a little he would correct me and say his *higher* self; but as his lower self is only the idea of himself which he may have framed, it is his higher self that is himself simply: although whether he or his idea of himself is really the higher might seem doubtful to an outsider.

This explanation, in pretending to refute solipsism, of course assumes and confirms it; for all these *cans* and *musts* touch only your idea of yourself, not your actual being, and there is no thinkable world that is not within you, as you exist really. Thus idealists are wedded to solipsism irrevocably; and it is a happy marriage, only the name of the lady has to be changed.

Nevertheless, lest peace should come (and peace nowadays is neither possible nor desired), a counter-current at once overtakes the philosophy of the immediate and carries it violently to the opposite pole of speculation—from mystic intuition to a commercial cult of action and a materialisation of the mind such as no materialist had ever dreamt of. The tenderness which the pragmatists feel for life in general, and especially for an accelerated modern life, has doubtless contributed to this revulsion, but the speculative consideration of the immediate might have led to it independently. For in the immediate there is marked expectancy, craving, prayer; nothing absorbs consciousness so much as what is not quite given. Therefore it is a good reading of the immediate, as well as a congenial thing to say to the contemporary world, that reality is change, growth, action, creation. Similarly the sudden materialisation of mind, the unlooked-for assertion that consciousness does not exist, has its justification in the same quarter. In the immediate what appears is the thing, not the mind to which the thing appears. Even in the passions, when closely scanned introspectively, you will find a new sensitiveness or ebullition of the body, or a rush of images and words; you will hardly find a separate object called anger or

love. The passions, therefore, when their moral essence
is forgotten, may be said to be literally nothing but a
movement of their organs and their objects, just as ideas
may be said to be nothing but fragments or cross-threads
of the material world. Thus the mind and the object
are rolled into one moving mass; motions are identified
with passions, things are perceptions extended, perceptions are things cut down. And, by a curious revolution in sentiment, it is things and motions that are
reputed to have the fuller and the nobler reality. Under
cover of a fusion or neutrality between idealism and
realism, moral materialism, the reverence for mere existence and power, takes possession of the heart, and ethics
becomes idolatrous. Idolatry, however, is hardly possible
if you have a cold and clear idea of blocks and stones,
attributing to them only the motions they are capable of;
and accordingly idealism, by way of compensation, has
to take possession of physics. The idol begins to wink
and drop tears under the wistful gaze of the worshipper.
Matter is felt to yearn, and evolution is held to be more
divinely inspired than policy or reason could ever be.

Extremes meet, and the tendency to practical
materialism was never wholly absent from the idealism
of the moderns. Certainly, the tumid respectability of
Anglo-German philosophy had somehow to be left
behind; and Darwinian England and Bismarckian
Germany had another inspiration as well to guide them,
if it could only come to consciousness in the professors.
The worship of power is an old religion, and Hegel, to go
no farther back, is full of it; but like traditional religion
his system qualified its veneration for success by attribut-

ing success, in the future at least, to what could really inspire veneration; and such a master in equivocation could have no difficulty in convincing himself that the good must conquer in the end if whatever conquers in the end is the good. Among the pragmatists the worship of power is also optimistic, but it is not to logic that power is attributed. Science, they say, is good as a help to industry, and philosophy is good for correcting whatever in science might disturb religious faith, which in turn is helpful in living. What industry or life are good for it would be unsympathetic to inquire: the stream is mighty, and we must swim with the stream. Concern for survival, however, which seems to be the pragmatic principle in morals, does not afford a remedy for moral anarchy. To take firm hold on life, according to Nietzsche, we should be imperious, poetical, atheistic; but according to William James we should be democratic, concrete, and credulous. It is hard to say whether pragmatism is come to emancipate the individual spirit and make it lord over things, or on the contrary to declare the spirit a mere instrument for the survival of the flesh. In Italy, the mind seems to be raised deliriously into an absolute creator, evoking at will, at each moment, a new past, a new future, a new earth, and a new God. In America, however, the mind is recommended rather as an un-patented device for oiling the engine of the body and making it do double work.

Trustful faith in evolution and a longing for intense life are characteristic of contemporary sentiment; but they do not appear to be consistent with that contempt for the intellect which is no less characteristic of it.

Human intelligence is certainly a product, and a late
and highly organised product, of evolution; it ought
apparently to be as much admired as the eyes of molluscs
or the antennæ of ants. And if life is better the more
intense and concentrated it is, intelligence would seem
to be the best form of life. But the degree of intelligence
which this age possesses makes it so very uncomfortable
that, in this instance, it asks for something less vital, and
sighs for what evolution has left behind. In the presence
of such cruelly distinct things as astronomy or such
cruelly confused things as theology it feels *la nostalgie de
la boue*. It was only, M. Bergson tells us, where dead
matter oppressed life that life was forced to become
intelligence; for this reason intelligence kills whatever it
touches; it is the tribute that life pays to death. Life
would find it sweet to throw off that painful subjection to
circumstance and bloom in some more congenial direction.
M. Bergson's own philosophy is an effort to realise this
revulsion, to disintegrate intelligence and stimulate
sympathetic experience. Its charm lies in the relief
which it brings to a stale imagination, an imagination
from which religion has vanished and which is kept
stretched on the machinery of business and society, or on
small half-borrowed passions which we clothe in a mean
rhetoric and dot with vulgar pleasures. Finding their
intelligence enslaved, our contemporaries suppose that
intelligence is essentially servile; instead of freeing it,
they try to elude it. Not free enough themselves
morally, but bound to the world partly by piety and
partly by industrialism, they cannot think of rising to a
detached contemplation of earthly things, and of life

itself and evolution; they revert rather to sensibility, and seek some by-path of instinct or dramatic sympathy in which to wander. Having no stomach for the ultimate, they burrow downwards towards the primitive. But the longing to be primitive is a disease of culture; it is archaism in morals. To be so preoccupied with vitality is a symptom of anæmia. When life was really vigorous and young, in Homeric times for instance, no one seemed to fear that it might be squeezed out of existence either by the incubus of matter or by the petrifying blight of intelligence. Life was like the light of day, something to use, or to waste, or to enjoy. It was not a thing to worship; and often the chief luxury of living consisted in dealing death about vigorously. Life indeed was loved, and the beauty and pathos of it were felt exquisitely; but its beauty and pathos lay in the divineness of its model and in its own fragility. No one paid it the equivocal compliment of thinking it a substance or a material force. Nobility was not then impossible in sentiment, because there were ideals in life higher and more indestructible than life itself, which life might illustrate and to which it might fitly be sacrificed. Nothing can be meaner than the anxiety to live on, to live on anyhow and in any shape; a spirit with any honour is not willing to live except in its own way, and a spirit with any wisdom is not over-eager to live at all. In those days men recognised immortal gods and resigned themselves to being mortal. Yet those were the truly vital and instinctive days of the human spirit. Only when vitality is low do people find material things oppressive and ideal things unsubstantial. Now there is more motion than life, and more haste than force; we are driven to distraction by the ticking of the tiresome clocks, material and social, by which we are obliged to regulate our existence. We need ministering angels to fly to us from somewhere, even if it be from the depths of protoplasm. We must bathe in the currents of some nonhuman vital flood, like consumptives in their last extremity who must bask in the sunshine and breathe the mountain air; and our disease is not without its sophistry to convince us that we were never so well before, or so mightily conscious of being alive.

When chaos has penetrated so far into the moral being of nations they can hardly be expected to produce great men. A great man need not be virtuous, nor his opinions right, but he must have a firm mind, a distinctive, luminous character; if he is to dominate things, something must be dominant in him. We feel him to be great in that he clarifies and brings to expression something which was potential in the rest of us, but which with our burden of flesh and circumstance we were too torpid to utter. The great man is a spontaneous variation in humanity; but not in any direction. A spontaneous variation might be a mere madness or mutilation or monstrosity; in finding the variation admirable we evidently invoke some principle of order to which it conforms. Perhaps it makes explicit what was preformed in us also; as when a poet finds the absolutely right phrase for a feeling, or when nature suddenly astonishes us with a form of absolute beauty. Or perhaps it makes an unprecedented harmony out of things existing before, but jangled and detached. The first man was a great man for this latter reason; having been an ape perplexed and corrupted by his multiplying instincts, he suddenly found a new way of being decent, by harnessing all those instincts together, through memory and imagination, and giving each in turn a measure of its due; which is what we call being rational. It is a new road to happiness, if you have strength enough to castigate a little the various impulses that sway you in turn. Why then is the martyr, who sacrifices everything to one attraction, distinguished from the criminal or the fool, who do the same thing? Evidently because the spirit that in the martyr destroys the body is the very spirit which the body is stifling in the rest of us; and although his private inspiration may be irrational, the tendency of it is not, but reduces the public conscience to act before any one else has had the courage to do so. Greatness is spontaneous; simplicity, trust in some one clear instinct, are essential to it; but the spontaneous variation must be in the direction of some possible sort of order; it must exclude and leave behind what is incapable of being moralised. How, then, should there be any great heroes, saints, artists, philosophers, or legislators in an age when nobody trusts himself, or feels any confidence in reason, in an age when the word *dogmatic* is a term of reproach? Greatness has character and severity, it is deep and sane, it is distinct and perfect. For this reason there is none of it to-day.

There is indeed another kind of greatness, or rather largeness of mind, which consists in being a synthesis of humanity in its current phases, even if without prophetic emphasis or direction: the breadth of a Goethe, rather than the fineness of a Shelley or a Leopardi. But such largeness of mind, not to be vulgar, must be impartial, comprehensive, Olympian; it would not be greatness if its miscellany were not dominated by a clear genius and if before the confusion of things the poet or philosopher were not himself delighted, exalted, and by no means confused. Nor does this presume omniscience on his part. It is not necessary to fathom the ground or the structure of everything in order to know what to make of it. Stones do not disconcert a builder because he may not happen to know what they are chemically; and so the unsolved problems of life and nature, and the Babel of society, need not disturb the genial observer, though he may be incapable of unravelling them. He may set these dark spots down in their places, like so many caves or wells in a landscape, without feeling bound to scrutinise their depths simply because their depths are obscure. Unexplored they may have a sort of lustre, explored they might merely make him blind, and it may be a sufficient understanding of them to know that they are not worth investigating. In this way the most chaotic age and the most motley horrors might be mirrored limpidly in a great mind, as the Renaissance was mirrored in the works of Raphael and Shakespeare; but the master's eye itself must be single, his style unmistakable, his visionary interest in what he depicts frank and supreme. Hence this comprehensive sort of greatness too is impossible in an age when moral confusion is pervasive, when characters are complex, undecided, troubled by the mere existence of what is not congenial to them, eager to be not themselves; when, in a word, thought is weak and the flux of things overwhelms it.

Without great men and without clear convictions this age is nevertheless very active intellectually; it is studious, empirical, inventive, sympathetic. Its wisdom consists in a certain contrite openness of mind; it flounders, but at least in floundering it has gained a sense of possible depths in all directions. Under these circumstances, some triviality and great confusion in its positive achievements are not unpromising things, nor even unamiable. These are the *Wanderjahre* of faith; it looks smilingly at every new face, which might perhaps be that of a predestined friend; it chases after any engaging stranger; it even turns up again from time to time at home, full of a new tenderness for all it had abandoned there. But to settle down would be impossible now. The intellect, the judgment are in abeyance. Life is running turbid and full; and it is no marvel that reason, after vainly supposing that it ruled the world, should abdicate as gracefully as possible, when the world is so obviously the sport of cruder powers—vested interests, tribal passions, stock sentiments, and chance majorities. Having no responsibility laid upon it, reason has become irresponsible. Many critics and philosophers seem to conceive that thinking aloud is itself literature. Sometimes reason tries to lend some moral authority to its present masters, by proving how superior they are to itself; it worships evolution, instinct, novelty, action, as it does in modernism, pragmatism, and the philosophy of M. Bergson. At other times it retires into the freehold of those temperaments whom this world has ostracised, the region of the non-existent, and comforts itself with its indubitable conquests there. This happened earlier to the romanticists (in a way which I have tried to describe in the subjoined paper on Shelley) although their poetic and political illusions did not suffer them to perceive it. It is happening now, after disillusion, to some radicals and mathematicians like Mr. Bertrand Russell, and to others of us who, perhaps without being mathematicians or even radicals, feel that the sphere of what happens to exist is too alien and accidental to absorb all the play of a free mind, whose function, after it has come to clearness and made its peace with things, is to touch them with its own moral and intellectual light, and to exist for its own sake.

These are but gusts of doctrine; yet they prove that the spirit is not dead in the lull between its seasons of steady blowing. Who knows which of them may not gather force presently and carry the mind of the coming age steadily before it?

II

MODERNISM AND CHRISTIANITY

PREVALENT winds of doctrine must needs penetrate at
last into the cloister. Social instability and moral
confusion, reconstructions of history and efforts after
reform, are things characteristic of the present age; and
under the name of modernism they have made their
appearance even in that institution which is constitutionally the most stable, of most explicit mind, least
inclined to revise its collective memory or established
usages—I mean the Catholic church. Even after this
church was constituted by the fusion of many influences
and by the gradual exclusion of those heresies—some of
them older than explicit orthodoxy—which seemed to
misrepresent its implications or spirit, there still remained
an inevitable propensity among Catholics to share the
moods of their respective ages and countries, and to reconcile them if possible with their professed faith. Often
these cross influences were so strong that the profession
of faith was changed frankly to suit them, and Catholicism
was openly abandoned; but even where this did not
occur we may detect in the Catholic minds of each age
some strange conjunctions and compromises with the
Zeitgeist. Thus the morality of chivalry and war, the
ideals of foppishness and honour, have been long maintained side by side with the maxims of the gospel, which
they entirely contradict. Later the system of Copernicus,

incompatible at heart with the anthropocentric and moralistic view of the world which Christianity implies, was accepted by the church with some lame attempt to render it innocuous; but it remains an alien and hostile element, like a spent bullet lodged in the flesh. In more recent times we have heard of liberal Catholicism, the attitude assumed by some generous but divided minds, too much attached to their traditional religion to abandon it, but too weak and too hopeful not to glow also with enthusiasm for modern liberty and progress. Had those minds been, I will not say intelligently Catholic but radically Christian, they would have felt that this liberty was simply liberty to be damned, and this progress not an advance towards the true good of man, but a lapse into endless and heathen wanderings. For Christianity, in its essence and origin, was an urgent summons to repent and come out of just such a worldly life as modern liberty and progress hold up as an ideal to the nations. In the Roman empire, as in the promised land of liberalism, each man sought to get and to enjoy as much as he could, and supported a ponderous government neutral as to religion and moral traditions, but favourable to the accumulation of riches; so that a certain enlightenment and cosmopolitanism were made possible, and private passions and tastes could be gratified without encountering persecution or public obloquy, though not without a general relaxation of society and a vulgarising of arts and manners. That something so self-indulgent and worldly as this ideal of liberalism could have been thought compatible with Christianity, the first initiation into which, in baptism, involves renouncing the world, might well astonish us, had we not been rendered deaf to moral discords by the very din which from our birth they have been making in our ears.

But this is not all. Primitive Christianity was not only a summons to turn one's heart and mind away from a corrupt world; it was a summons to do so under pain of instant and terrible punishment. It was the conviction of pious Jews since the days of the Prophets that mercilessness, avarice, and disobedience to revealed law were the direct path to ruin; a world so wicked as the liberal world against which St. John the Baptist thundered was necessarily on the verge of destruction. Sin, although we moderns may not think so, seemed to the ancient Jews a fearful imprudence. The hand of the Lord would descend on it heavily, and very soon. The whole Roman civilisation was to be overthrown in the twinkling of an eye. Those who hoped to be of the remnant and to be saved, so as to lead a clarified and heavenly life in the New Jerusalem, must hasten to put on sackcloth and ashes, to fast and to pray, to watch with girded loins for the coming of the kingdom; it was superfluous for them to study the dead past or to take thought for the morrow. The cataclysm was at hand; a new heaven and a new earth—far more worthy of study—would be unrolled before that very generation.

There was indeed something terribly levelling, revolutionary, serious, and expectant about that primitive gospel; and in so far as liberalism possessed similar qualities, in so far as it was moved by indignation, pity, and fervent hope, it could well preach on early Christian texts. But the liberal Catholics were liberals of the

polite and governmental sort; they were shocked at
suffering rather than at sin, and they feared not the Lord
but the movement of public opinion. Some of them
were vaguely pious men, whose conservativism in social
and moral matters forbade them to acquiesce in the dis-
appearance of the church altogether, and they thought
it might be preserved, as the English church is, by
making opportune concessions. Others were simply
aristocrats, desirous that the pacifying influence of
religion should remain strong over the masses. The
clergy was not, in any considerable measure, tossed by
these opposing currents; the few priests who were
liberals were themselves men of the world, patriots, and
orators. Such persons could not look forward to a
fierce sifting of the wheat from the tares, or to any burn-
ing of whole bundles of nations, for they were nothing if
not romantic nationalists, and the idea of faggots of any
sort was most painful to their minds. They longed
rather for a sweet cohabitation with everybody, and a
mild tolerance of almost everything. A war for religion
seemed to them a crime, but a war for nationality glorious
and holy. No wonder that their work in nation-building
has endured, while their sentiments in religion are
scattered to the winds. The liberalism for the sake of
which they were willing to eviscerate their Christianity
has already lost its vitality; it survives as a pale parlia-
mentary tradition, impotent before the tide of socialism
rising behind its back. The Catholicism which they
wished to see gently lingering is being driven out of
national life by official spoliations and popular mockeries.
It is fast becoming what it was in the beginning, a sect

with more or less power to alienate the few who genuinely adhere to it from the pagan society in which they are forced to live.

The question what is true or essential Christianity is a thorny one, because each party gives the name of genuine Christianity to what it happens to believe. Thus Professor Harnack, not to mention less distinguished historians, makes the original essence of Christianity coincide—what a miracle!—with his own Lutheran and Kantian sentiments. But the essence of Christianity, as of everything else, is the whole of it; and the genuine nature of a seed is at least as well expressed by what it becomes in contact with the earth and air as by what it seems in its primitive minuteness. It is quite true, as the modernists tell us, that in the beginning Christian faith was not a matter of scholastic definitions, nor even of intellectual dogmas. Religions seldom begin in that form, and paganism was even less intellectual and less dogmatic than early Christianity. The most primitive Christian faith consisted in a conversion of the whole man—intellect, habits, and affections—from the life of the world to a new mystical life, in answer to a moral summons and a prophecy about destiny. The moral summons was to renounce home, kindred, possessions, the respect of men, the hypocrisies of the synagogue, and to devote oneself to a wandering and begging life, healing, praying, and preaching. And preaching what? Preaching the prophecy about destiny which justified that conversion and renunciation; preaching that the world, in its present constitution, was about to be destroyed on account of its wickedness, and that the

ignorant, the poor, and the down-trodden, if they trusted
this prophecy, and turned their backs at once on all the
world pursues, would be saved in the new deluge, and
would form a new society, of a more or less supernatural
kind, to be raised on the ruins of all present institutions.
The poor were called, but the rich were called also, and
perhaps even the heathen; for there was in all men, even
in all nature (this is the one touch of speculative feeling
in the gospel), a precious potentiality of goodness. All
were essentially amiable, though accidentally wretched
and depraved; and by the magic of a new faith and hope
this soul of goodness in all living things might be freed
from the hideous incubus of circumstance that now
oppresses it, and might come to bloom openly as the
penetrating eye of the lover, even now, sees that it could
bloom. Love, then, and sympathy, particularly towards
the sinful and diseased, a love relieved of sentimentality
by the deliberate practice of healing, warning, and
comforting; a complete aversion from all the interests
of political society, and a confident expectation of a
cataclysm that should suddenly transfigure the world—
such was Christian religion in its origin. The primitive
Christian was filled with the sense of a special election
and responsibility, and of a special hope. He was serene,
abstracted, incorruptible, his inward eye fixed on a
wonderful revelation. He was as incapable of attacking
as of serving the state; he despised or ignored everything
for which the state exists, labour, wealth, power, felicity,
splendour, and learning. With Christ the natural man
in him had been crucified, and in Christ he had risen
again a spiritual man, to walk the earth, as a messenger

from heaven, for a few more years. His whole life was an experience of perpetual graces and miracles.

The prophecy about the speedy end of this wicked world was not fulfilled as the early Christians expected; but this fact is less disconcerting to the Christian than one would suppose. The spontaneous or instinctive Christian — and there is such a type of mind, quite apart from any affiliation to historic Christianity—takes a personal and dramatic view of the world; its values and even its reality are the values and reality which it may have for him. It would profit him nothing to win it, if he lost his own soul. That prophecy about the destruction of nature springs from this attitude; nature must be subservient to the human conscience; it must satisfy the hopes of the prophet and vindicate the saints. That the years should pass and nothing should seem to happen need not shatter the force of this prophecy for those whose imagination it excites. This world must actually vanish very soon for each of us; and this is the point of view that counts with the Christian mind. Even if we consider posterity, the kingdoms and arts and philosophies of this world are short lived; they shift their aims continually and shift their substance. The prophecy of their destruction is therefore being fulfilled continually; the need of repentance, if one would be saved, is truly urgent; and the means of that salvation cannot be an operation upon this world, but faith in another world that, in the experience of each soul, is to follow upon it. Thus the summons to repent and the prophecy about destiny which were the root of Christianity, can fully retain their spirit when for " this wicked world " we read " this transitory life " and for " the coming of the Kingdom " we read " life everlasting." The change is important, but it affects the application rather than the nature of the gospel. Morally there is a loss, because men will never take so hotly what concerns another life as what affects this one; speculatively, on the other hand, there is a gain, for the expectation of total transformations and millenniums on earth is a very crude illusion, while the relation of the soul to nature is an open question in philosophy, and there will always be a great loftiness and poetic sincerity in the feeling that the soul is a stranger in this world and has other destinies in store.

What would make the preaching of the gospel utterly impossible would be the admission that it had no authority to proclaim what has happened or what is going to happen, either in this world or in another. A prophecy about destiny is an account, however vague, of events to be actually experienced, and of their causes. The whole inspiration of Hebraic religion lies in that. It was not metaphorically that Sodom and Gomorrah were destroyed. The promised land was a piece of earth. The kingdom was an historical fact. It was not symbolically that Israel was led into captivity, or that it returned and restored the Temple. It was not ideally that a Messiah was to come. Memory of such events is in the same field as history; prophecy is in the same field as natural science. Natural science too is an account of what will happen, and under what conditions. It too is a prophecy about destiny. Accordingly, while it is quite true that speculations about nature and history are not contained explicitly in the religion of the gospel, yet

the message of this religion is one which speculations
about nature and reconstructions of history may extend
congruously, or may contradict and totally annul. If
physical science should remove those threats of destruction to follow upon sin which Christian prophecy contains,
or if it should prove that what brings destruction is
just that unworldly, prayerful, all-forgiving, idle, and
revolutionary attitude which the gospel enjoins, then
physical science would be incompatible with Christianity;
not with this or that text of the Bible merely, about the
sun standing still or the dead rising again, but with the
whole foundation of what Christ himself, with John the
Baptist, St. Paul, St. James, and St. John, preached to
the world.

Even the pagan poets, when they devised a myth, half
believed in it for a fact. What really lent some truth—
moral truth only—to their imaginations was indeed the
beauty of nature, the comedy of life, or the groans of
mankind, crushed between the upper and the nether
millstones; but being scientifically ignorant they allowed
their pictorial wisdom to pass for a revealed science, for
a physics of the unseen. If even among the pagans the
poetic expression of human experience could be mistaken
in this way for knowledge of occult existences, how much
more must this have been the case among a more ignorant
and a more intense nation like the Jews? Indeed,
events are what the Jews have always remembered and
hoped for; if their religion was not a guide to events,
an assured means towards a positive and experimental
salvation, it was nothing. Their theology was meagre in
the description of the Lord's nature, but rich in the

description of his ways. Indeed, their belief in the existence and power of the Lord, if we take it pragmatically and not imaginatively, was simply the belief in certain moral harmonies in destiny, in the sufficiency of conduct of a certain sort to secure success and good fortune, both national and personal. This faith was partly an experience and partly a demand; it turned on history and prophecy. History was interpreted by a prophetic insight into the moral principle, believed to govern it; and prophecy was a passionate demonstration of the same principles, at work in the catastrophes of the day or of the morrow.

There is no doubt a Platonic sort of religion, a worship of the ideal apart from its power to realise itself, which has entered largely into the life of Christians; and the more mystical and disinterested they were, the more it has tended to take the place of Hebraism. But the Platonists, too, when left to their instincts, follow their master in attributing power and existence, by a sort of cumulative worship and imaginative hyperbole, to what in the first place they worship because it is good. To divorce, then, as the modernists do, the history of the world from the story of salvation, and God's government and the sanctions of religion from the operation of matter, is a *fundamental apostasy* from Christianity. Christianity, being a practical and living faith in a possible eventual redemption from sin, from the punishment for sin, from the thousand circumstances that make the most brilliant worldly life a sham and a failure, essentially involves a faith in a supernatural physics, in such an economy of forces, behind, within, and around the discoverable forces

of nature, that the destiny which nature seems to prepare
for us may be reversed, that failures may be turned into
successes, ignominy into glory, and humble faith into
triumphant vision: and this not merely by a change in
our point of view or estimation of things, but by an
actual historical, physical transformation in the things
themselves. To believe this in our day may require
courage, even a certain childish simplicity; but were not
courage and a certain childish simplicity always requisite
for Christian faith? It never was a religion for the
rationalist and the worldling; it was based on alienation
from the world, from the intellectual world no less than
from the economic and political. It flourished in the
Oriental imagination that is able to treat all existence
with disdain and to hold it superbly at arm's length, and
at the same time is subject to visions and false memories,
is swayed by the eloquence of private passion, and raises
confidently to heaven the cry of the poor, the bereaved,
and the distressed. Its daily bread, from the beginning,
was hope for a miraculous change of scene, for prison-
walls falling to the ground about it, for a heart inwardly
comforted, and a shower of good things from the sky.

It is clear that a supernaturalistic faith of this sort,
which might wholly inspire some revolutionary sect, can
never wholly inspire human society. Whenever a nation
is converted to Christianity, its Christianity, in practice,
must be largely converted into paganism. The true
Christian is in all countries a pilgrim and a stranger; not
his kinsmen, but whoever does the will of his Father who
is in heaven is his brother and sister and mother and his
real compatriot. In a nation that calls itself Christian

every child may be pledged, at baptism, to renounce the world, the flesh, and the devil; but the flesh will assert itself notwithstanding, the devil will have his due, and the nominal Christian, become a man of business and the head of a family, will form an integral part of that very world which he will pledge his children to renounce in turn as he holds them over the font. The lips, even the intellect, may continue to profess the Christian ideal; but public and social life will be guided by quite another. The ages of faith, the ages of Christian unity, were such only superficially. When all men are Christians only a small element can be Christian in the average man. The thirteenth century, for instance, is supposed to be the golden age of Catholicism; but what seems to have filled it, if we may judge by the witness of Dante? Little but bitter conflicts, racial and religious; faithless rebellions, both in states and in individuals, against the Christian regimen; worldliness in the church, barbarism in the people, and a dawning of all sorts of scientific and æsthetic passions, in themselves quite pagan and contrary to the spirit of the gospel. Christendom at that time was by no means a kingdom of God on earth; it was a conglomeration of incorrigible rascals, intellectually more or less Christian. We may see the same thing under different circumstances in the Spain of Philip II. Here was a government consciously labouring in the service of the church, to resist Turks, convert pagans, banish Moslems, and crush Protestants. Yet the very forces engaged in defending the church, the army and the Inquisition, were alien to the Christian life; they were fit embodiments rather of chivalry and greed, or of policy and jealous dominion. The ecclesiastical forces also, theology, ritual, and hierarchy, employed in spreading the gospel were themselves alien to the gospel. An anti-worldly religion finds itself in fact in this dilemma: if it remains merely spiritual, developing no material organs, it cannot affect the world; while if it develops organs with which to operate on the world, these organs become a part of the world from which it is trying to wean the individual spirit, so that the moment it is armed for conflict such a religion has two enemies on its hands. It is stifled by its necessary armour, and adds treason in its members to hostility in its foes. The passions and arts it uses against its opponents are as fatal to itself as those which its opponents array against it.

In every age in which a supernaturalistic system is preached we must accordingly expect to find the world standing up stubbornly against it, essentially unconverted and hostile, whatever name it may have been christened with; and we may expect the spirit of the world to find expression, not only in overt opposition to the supernaturalistic system, but also in the surviving or supervening worldliness of the faithful. Such an insidious revulsion of the natural man against a religion he does not openly discard is what, in modern Christendom, we call the Renaissance. No less than the Revolution (which is the later open rebellion against the same traditions) the Renaissance is radically inimical to Christianity. To say that Christianity survives, even if weakened or disestablished, is to say that the Renaissance and the Revolution are still incomplete. Far from being past events they are living programmes. The ideal of

the Renaissance is to restore pagan standards in polite
learning, in philosophy, in sentiment, and in morals.   It
is to abandon and exactly reverse one's baptismal vows.
Instead of forsaking this wicked world, the men of the
Renaissance accept, love, and cultivate the world, with
all its pomp and vanities; they believe in the blameless-
ness of natural life and in its perfectibility; or they
cling at least to a noble ambition to perfect it and a
glorious ability to enjoy it.   Instead of renouncing the
flesh, they feed, refine, and adorn it; their arts glorify
its beauty and its passions.   And far from renouncing
the devil—if we understand by the devil the proud
assertion on the part of the finite of its autonomy,
autonomy of the intellect in science, autonomy of the
heart and will in morals—the men of the Renaissance
are possessed by the devil altogether.   They worship
nothing and acknowledge authority in nothing save in
their own spirit.   No opposition could be more radical
and complete than that between the Renaissance and
the anti-worldly religion of the gospel.

" I see a vision," Nietzsche says somewhere, " so full
of meaning, yet so wonderfully strange—Cæsar Borgia
become pope! Do you understand?   Ah, that would
verily have been the triumph for which I am longing
to-day.   Then Christianity would have been done for."
And Nietzsche goes on to accuse Luther of having spoiled
this lovely possibility, which was about to be realised, by
frightening the papacy out of its mellow paganism into
something like a restoration of the old acrid Christianity.
A dream of this sort, even if less melodramatic than
Nietzsche's, has visited the mind of many a neo-Catholic

or neo-pagan. If the humanistic tendencies of the Renaissance could have worked on unimpeded, might not a revolution from above, a gradual rationalisation, have transformed the church? Its dogma might have been insensibly understood to be nothing but myth, its miracles nothing but legend, its sacraments mere symbols, its Bible pure literature, its liturgy just poetry, its hierarchy an administrative convenience, its ethics an historical accident, and its whole function simply to lend a warm mystical aureole to human culture and ignorance. The Reformation prevented this euthanasia of Christianity. It re-expressed the unenlightened absolutism of the old religion; it insisted that dogma was scientifically true, that salvation was urgent and fearfully doubtful, that the world, and the worldly paganised church, were as Sodom and Gomorrah, and that sin, though natural to man, was to God an abomination. In fighting this movement, which soon became heretical, the Catholic church had to fight it with its own weapons, and thereby reawakened in its own bosom the same sinister convictions. It did not have to dig deep to find them. Even without Luther, convinced Catholics would have appeared in plenty to prevent Cæsar Borgia, had he secured the tiara, from being pope in any novel fashion or with any revolutionary result. The supernaturalism, the literal realism, the other-worldliness of the Catholic church are too much the soul of it to depart without causing its dissolution. While the church lives at all, it must live on the strength which these principles can lend it. And they are not altogether weak. Persons who feel themselves to be exiles in this world—and what noble mind, from Empedocles down, has not had that feeling?—are mightily inclined to believe themselves citizens of another. There will always be spontaneous, instinctive Christians; and when, under the oppression of sin, salvation is looked for and miracles are expected, the supernatural scheme of salvation which historical Christianity offers will not always be despised. The modernists think the church is doomed if it turns a deaf ear to the higher criticism or ignores the philosophy of M. Bergson. But it has outlived greater storms. A moment when any exotic superstition can find excitable minds to welcome it, when new and grotesque forms of faith can spread among the people, when the ultimate impotence of science is the theme of every cheap philosopher, when constructive philology is reefing its sails, when the judicious grieve at the portentous metaphysical shams of yesterday and smile at those of to-day—such a moment is rather ill chosen for prophesying the extinction of a deep-rooted system of religion because your own studies make it seem to you incredible; especially if you hold a theory of knowledge that regards all opinions as arbitrary postulates, which it may become convenient to abandon at any moment.

Modernism is the infiltration into minds that begin by being Catholic and wish to remain so of two contemporary influences: one the rationalistic study of the Bible and of church history, the other modern philosophy, especially in its mystical and idealistic forms. The sensitiveness of the modernists to these two influences is creditable to them as men, however perturbing it may be to them as Catholics; for what makes them adopt the views of rationalistic historians is simply the fact that those views seem, in substance, convincingly true; and what makes them wander into transcendental speculations is the warmth of their souls, needing to express their faith anew, and to follow their inmost inspiration, wherever it may lead them. A scrupulous honesty in admitting the probable facts of history, and a fresh up-welling of mystical experience, these are the motives, creditable to any spiritual man, that have made modernists of so many. But these excellent things appear in the modernists under rather unfortunate circumstances. For the modernists to begin with are Catholics, and usually priests; they are pledged to a fixed creed, touching matters both of history and of philosophy; and it would be a marvel if rationalistic criticism of the Bible and rationalistic church history confirmed that creed on its historical side, or if irresponsible personal speculations, in the manner of Ritschl or of M. Bergson, confirmed its metaphysics.

I am far from wishing to suggest that an orthodox Christian cannot be scrupulously honest in admitting the probable facts, or cannot have a fresh spiritual experience, or frame an original philosophy. But what we think probable hangs on our standard of probability and of evidence; the spiritual experiences that come to us are according to our disposition and affections; and any new philosophy we frame will be an answer to the particular problems that beset us, and an expression of the solutions we hope for. Now this standard of probability, this disposition, and these problems and hopes may be those of a Christian or they may not. The true Christian, for instance, will begin by regarding miracles as probable; he will either believe he has experienced them in his own person, or hope for them earnestly; nothing will seem to him more natural, more in consonance with the actual texture of life, than that they should have occurred abundantly and continuously in the past. When he finds the record of one he will not inquire, like the rationalist, how that false record could have been concocted; but rather he will ask how the rationalist, in spite of so many witnesses to the contrary, has acquired his fixed assurance of the universality of the commonplace. An answer perhaps could be offered of which the rationalist need not be ashamed. We might say that faith in the universality of the commonplace (in its origin, no doubt, simply an imaginative presumption) is justified by our systematic mastery of matter in the arts. The rejection of miracles *a priori* expresses a conviction that the laws by which we can always control or predict the movement of matter govern that movement universally; and evidently, if the material course of history is fixed mechanically, the mental and moral course of it is thereby fixed on the same plan; for a mind not expressed somehow in matter cannot be revealed to the historian. This may be good philosophy, but we could not think so if we were good Christians. We should then expect to move matter by prayer. Rationalistic history and criticism are therefore based, as Pius X. most accurately observed in his Encyclical on modernism, on rationalistic philosophy; and we might add that rationalistic philosophy is based on practical art, and that practical art, by which we help ourselves, like Prometheus, and make instruments of what religion worships, when this art is carried beyond the narrowest bounds, is the essence of pride and irreligion. Miners, machinists, and artisans are irreligious by trade. Religion is the love of life in the consciousness of impotence.

Similarly, the spontaneous insight of Christians and their new philosophies will express a Christian disposition. The chief problems in them will be sin and redemption; the conclusion will be some fresh intuition of divine love and heavenly beatitude. It would be no sign of originality in a Christian to begin discoursing on love like Ovid or on heaven like Mohammed, or stop discoursing on them at all; it would be a sign of apostasy.

Now the modernists' criterion of probability in history or of worthiness in philosophy is not the Christian criterion. It is that of their contemporaries outside the church, who are rationalists in history and egotists or voluntarists in philosophy. The biblical criticism and mystical speculations of the modernists call for no special remark; they are such as any studious or spiritual person, with no inherited religion, might compose in our day. But what is remarkable and well-nigh incredible is that even for a moment they should have supposed this non-Christian criterion in history and this non-Christian direction in metaphysics compatible with adherence to the Catholic church. That seems to presuppose, in men who in fact are particularly thoughtful and learned, an inexplicable ignorance of history, of theology, and of the world.

Everything, however, has its explanation. In a Catholic seminary, as the modernists bitterly complain, very little is heard of the views held in the learned world outside. It is not taught there that the Christian religion is only one of many, some of them older and superior to it in certain respects; that it itself is eclectic and contains inward contradictions; that it is and always has been divided into rancorous sects; that its position in the world is precarious and its future hopeless. On the contrary, everything is so presented as to persuade the innocent student that all that is good or true anywhere is founded on the faith he is preparing to preach, that the historical evidences of its truth are irrefragable, that it is logically perfect and spiritually all-sufficing. These convictions, which no breath from the outside is allowed to ruffle, are deepened in the case of pensive and studious minds, like those of the leading modernists, by their own religious experience. They understand in what they are taught more, perhaps, than their teachers intend. They understand how those ideas originated, they can trace a similar revelation in their own lives. This (which a cynic might expect would be the beginning of disillusion) only deepens their religious faith and gives it a wider basis; report and experience seem to conspire. But trouble is brewing here; for a report that can be confirmed by experience can also be enlarged by it, and it is easy to see in traditional revelation itself many diverse sources; different temperaments and different types of thought have left their impress upon it. Yet other temperaments and other types of thought might continue the task. Revelation seems to be progressive; a part may fall to us also to furnish.

This insight, for a Christian, has its dangers. No

doubt it gives him a key to the understanding and therefore, in one sense, to the acceptance of many a dogma.
Christian dogmas were not pieces of wanton information
fallen from heaven; they were imaginative views, expressing now some primordial instinct in all men, now
the national hopes and struggles of Israel, now the moral
or dialectical philosophy of the later Jews and Greeks.
Such a derivation does not, of itself, render these dogmas
necessarily mythical. They might be ideal expressions
of human experience and yet be literally true as well,
provided we assume (what is assumed throughout in
Christianity) that the world is made for man, and that
even God is just such a God as man would have wished
him to be, the existent ideal of human nature and the
foregone solution to all human problems. Nevertheless,
Christian dogmas are definite,[1] while human inspirations
are potentially limitless; and if the object of the two is
identical either the dogmas must be stretched and
ultimately abandoned, or inspiration which does not
conform to them must be denounced as illusory or
diabolical.

At this point the modernist first chooses the path
which must lead him away, steadily and for ever, from

[1] At least in their devotional and moral import. I suggest this
qualification in deference to M. Le Roy's interesting theory of dogma,
viz., that the verbal or intellectual definition of a dogma may be
changed without changing the dogma itself (as a sentence might be
translated into a new language without altering the meaning) provided
the suggested conduct and feeling in the presence of the mystery
remained the same. Thus the definition of transubstantiation might
be modified to suit an idealistic philosophy, but the new definition
would be no less orthodox than the old if it did not discourage the
worship of the consecrated elements or the sense of mystical union
with Christ in the sacrament.

the church which he did not think to desert. He
chooses a personal, psychological, variable standard of
inspiration; he becomes, in principle, a Protestant.
Why does he not become one in name also? Because, as
one of the most distinguished modernists has said, the
age of partial heresy is past. It is suicidal to make one
part of an organic system the instrument for attacking
another part; and it is also comic. What you appeal
to and stand firmly rooted in is no more credible, no more
authoritative, than what you challenge in its name. In
vain will you pit the church against the pope; at once
you will have to pit the Bible against the church, and
then the New Testament against the Old, or the genuine
Jesus against the New Testament, or God revealed in
nature against God revealed in the Bible, or God revealed
in your own conscience or transcendental self against
God revealed in nature; and you will be lucky if your
conscience and transcendental self can long hold their
own against the flux of immediate experience. Religion,
the modernists feel, must be taken broadly and sympathetically, as a great human historical symbol for the
truth. At least in Christianity you should aspire to
embrace and express the whole; to seize it in its deep
inward sources and follow it on all sides in its vital
development. But if the age of partial heresy is past,
has not the age of total heresy succeeded? What is this
whole phenomenon of religion but human experience
interpreted by human imagination? And what is the
modernist, who would embrace it all, but a freethinker,
with a sympathetic interest in religious illusions? Of
course, that is just what he is; but it takes him a

strangely long time to discover it. He fondly supposes
(such is the prejudice imbibed by him in the cradle and
in the seminary) that all human inspirations are necessarily similar and concurrent, that by trusting an inward
light he cannot be led away from his particular religion,
but on the contrary can only find confirmation for it,
together with fresh spiritual energies. He has been
reared in profound ignorance of other religions, which
were presented to him, if at all, only in grotesque caricature; or if anything good had to be admitted in them,
it was set down to a premonition of his own system or
a derivation from it — a curious conceit, which seems
somehow not to have wholly disappeared from the
minds of Protestants, or even of professors of philosophy. I need not observe how completely the secret
of each alien religion is thereby missed and its native
accent outraged: the most serious consequence, for the
modernist, of this unconsciousness of whatever is not
Christian is an unconsciousness of what, in contrast to
other religions, Christianity itself is. He feels himself
full of love—except for the pope—of mysticism, and of
a sort of archæological piety. He is learned and eloquent
and wistful. Why should he not remain in the church?
Why should he not bring all its cold and recalcitrant
members up to his own level of insight?

The modernist, like the Protestants before him, is
certainly justified in contrasting a certain essence or true
life of religion with the formulas and practices, not all
equally well-chosen, which have crystallised round it.
In the routine of Catholic teaching and worship there
is notoriously a deal of mummery: phrases and cere-

monies abound that have lost their meaning, and that
people run through without even that general devout
attitude and unction which, after all, is all that can be
asked for in the presence of mysteries. Not only is all
sense of the historical or moral basis of dogma wanting,
but the dogma itself is hardly conceived explicitly; all
is despatched with a stock phrase, or a quotation from
some theological compendium. Ecclesiastical authority
acts as if it felt that more profundity would be confusing
and that more play of mind might be dangerous. This
is that "Scholasticism" and "Mediævalism" against
which the modernists inveigh or under which they groan;
and to this intellectual barrenness may be added the
offences against taste, verisimilitude, and justice which
their more critical minds may discern in many an act
and pronouncement of their official superiors. Thus
both their sense for historical truth and their spontaneous
mysticism drive the modernists to contrast with the
official religion what was pure and vital in the religion
of their fathers. Like the early Protestants, they wish
to revert to a more genuine Christianity; but while their
historical imagination is much more accurate and well-
fed than that of any one in the sixteenth century could
be, they have no hold on the Protestant principle of
faith. The Protestants, taking the Bible as an oracle
which personal inspiration was to interpret, could reform
tradition in any way and to any extent which their
reason or feeling happened to prompt. But so long as
their Christianity was a positive faith, the residue, when
all the dross had been criticised and burned away, was
of divine authority. The Bible never became for them

merely an ancient Jewish encyclopædia, often eloquent, often curious, and often barbarous. God never became a literary symbol, covering some problematical cosmic force, or some ideal of the conscience. But for the modernist this total transformation takes place at once. He keeps the whole Catholic system, but he believes in no part of it as it demands to be believed. He understands and shares the moral experience that it enshrines; but the bubble has been pricked, the painted world has been discovered to be but painted. He has ceased to be a Christian to become an amateur, or if you will a connoisseur, of Christianity. He believes — and this unquestioningly, for he is a child of his age—in history, in philology, in evolution, perhaps in German idealism; he does not believe in sin, nor in salvation, nor in revelation. His study of history has disclosed Christianity to him in its evolution and in its character of a myth; he wishes to keep it in its entirety precisely because he regards it as a convention, like a language or a school of art; whereas the Protestants wished, on the contrary, to reduce it to its original substance, because they fondly supposed that that original substance was so much literal truth. Modernism is accordingly an ambiguous and unstable thing. It is the love of all Christianity in those who perceive that it is all a fable. It is the historic attachment to his church of a Catholic who has discovered that he is a pagan.

When the modernists are pressed to explain their apparently double allegiance, they end by saying that what historical and philological criticism conjectures to be the facts must be accepted as such; while the Christian dogmas touching these things — the incarnation and resurrection of Christ, for instance—must be taken in a purely symbolic or moral sense. In saying this they may be entirely right; it seems to many of us that Christianity is indeed a fable, yet full of meaning if you take it as such; for what scraps of historical truth there may be in the Bible or of metaphysical truth in theology are of little importance; whilst the true greatness and beauty of this, as of all religions, is to be found in its *moral idealism*, I mean, in the expression it gives, under cover of legends, prophecies, or mysteries, of the effort, the tragedy, and the consolations of human life. Such a moral fable is what Christianity is in fact; but it is far from what it is in intention. The modernist view, the view of a sympathetic rationalism, revokes the whole Jewish tradition on which Christianity is grafted; it takes the seriousness out of religion; it sweetens the pang of sin, which becomes misfortune; it removes the urgency of salvation; it steals empirical reality away from the last judgment, from hell, and from heaven; it steals historical reality away from the Christ of religious tradition and personal devotion. The moral summons and the prophecy about destiny which were the soul of the gospel have lost all force for it and become fables.

The modernist, then, starts with the orthodox but untenable persuasion that Catholicism comprehends all that is good; he adds the heterodox though amiable sentiment that any well-meaning ambition of the mind, any hope, any illumination, any science, must be good, and therefore compatible with Catholicism. He bathes himself in idealistic philosophy, he dabbles in liberal politics, he accepts and emulates rationalistic exegesis and anti-clerical church history. Soon he finds himself, on every particular point, out of sympathy with the acts and tendencies of the church to which he belongs; and then he yields to the most pathetic of his many illusions—he sets about to purge this church, so as not to be compelled to abandon it; to purge it of its first principles, of its whole history, and of its sublime if chimerical ideal.

The modernist wishes to reconcile the church and the world. Therein he forgets what Christianity came into the world to announce and why its message was believed. It came to announce salvation from the world; there should be no more need of just those things which the modernist so deeply loves and respects and blushes that his church should not be adorned with—emancipated science, free poetic religion, optimistic politics, and dissolute art. These things, according to the Christian conscience, were all vanity and vexation of spirit, and the pagan world itself almost confessed as much. They were vexatious and vain because they were bred out of sin, out of ignoring the inward and the revealed law of God; and they would lead surely and quickly to destruction. The needful salvation from these follies, Christianity went on to announce, had come through the cross of Christ; whose grace, together with admission to his future heavenly kingdom, was offered freely to such as believed in him, separated themselves from the world, and lived in charity, humility, and innocence, waiting lamp in hand for the celestial bridegroom. These abstracted and elected spirits were the true disciples of Christ and the church itself.

Having no ears for this essential message of Christianity, the modernist also has no eyes for its history. The church converted the world only partially and inessentially; yet Christianity was outwardly established as the traditional religion of many nations. And why? Because, although the prophecies it relied on were strained and its miracles dubious, it furnished a needful sanctuary from the shames, sorrows, injustices, violence, and gathering darkness of earth; and not only a sanctuary one might fly to, but a holy precinct where one might live, where there was sacred learning, based on revelation and tradition, to occupy the inquisitive, and sacred philosophy to occupy the speculative; where there might be religious art, ministering to the faith, and a new life in the family or in the cloister, transformed by a permeating spirit of charity, sacrifice, soberness, and prayer. These principles by their very nature could not become those of the world, but they could remain in it as a leaven and an ideal. As such they remain to this day, and very efficaciously, in the Catholic church. The modernists talk a great deal of development, and they do not see that what they detest in the church is a perfect development of its original essence; that monachism, scholasticism, Jesuitism, ultramontanism, and Vaticanism are all thoroughly apostolic; beneath the overtones imposed by a series of ages they give out the full and exact note of the New Testament. Much has been added, but nothing has been lost. Development (though those who talk most of it seem to forget it) is not the same as flux and dissolution. It is not a continuity through changes of any sort, but the evolution of something latent and preformed, or else the creation of new instruments of defence for the same original life. In this sense there was an immense development of Christianity during the first three centuries, and this development has continued, more slowly, ever since, but only in the Roman church; for the Eastern churches have refused themselves all new expressions, while the Protestant churches have eaten more and more into the core. It is a striking proof of the preservative power of readjustment that the Roman church, in the midst of so many external transformations as it has undergone, still demands the same kind of faith that John the Baptist demanded, I mean faith in another world. The *mise-en-scène* has changed immensely. The gospel has been encased in theology, in ritual, in ecclesiastical authority, in conventional forms of charity, like some small bone of a saint in a gilded reliquary; but the relic for once is genuine, and the gospel has been preserved by those thick incrustations. Many an isolated fanatic or evangelical missionary in the slums shows a greater resemblance to the apostles in his outer situation than the pope does; but what mind-healer or revivalist nowadays preaches the doom of the natural world and its vanity, or the reversal of animal values, or the blessedness of poverty and chastity, or the inferiority of natural human bonds, or a contempt for lay philosophy? Yet in his palace full of pagan marbles the pope actually preaches all this. It is here, and certainly not among the modernists, that the gospel is still believed.

Of course, it is open to any one to say that there is a nobler religion possible without these trammels and this officialdom, that there is a deeper philosophy than this supernaturalistic rationalism, that there is a sweeter life than this legal piety. Perhaps: I think the pagan Greeks, the Buddhists, the Mohammedans would have much to say for themselves before the impartial tribunal of human nature and reason. But they are not Christians and do not wish to be. No more, in their hearts, are the modernists, and they should feel it beneath their dignity to pose as such; indeed the more sensitive of them already feel it. To say they are not Christians at heart, but diametrically opposed to the fundamental faith and purpose of Christianity, is not to say they may not be profound mystics (as many Hindus, Jews, and pagan Greeks have been), or excellent scholars, or generous philanthropists. But the very motive that attaches them to Christianity is worldly and un-Christian. They wish to preserve the continuity of moral traditions; they wish the poetry of life to flow down to them uninterruptedly and copiously from all the ages. It is an amiable and wise desire; but it shows that they are men of the Renaissance, pagan and pantheistic in their profounder sentiment, to whom the hard and narrow realism of official Christianity is offensive just because it presupposes that Christianity is true.

Yet even in this historical and poetical allegiance to Christianity I suspect the modernists suffer from a serious illusion. They think the weakness of the church lies in its not following the inspirations of the age. But when this age is past, might not that weakness be a source

of strength again? For an idea ever to be fashionable
is ominous, since it must afterwards be always old-
fashioned. No doubt it would be dishonest in any of us
now, who see clearly that Noah surely did not lead all
the animals two by two into the Ark, to say that we
believe he did so, on the ground that stories of that kind
are rather favourable to the spread of religion. No
doubt such a story, and even the fables essential to
Christian theology, are now incredible to most of us.
But on the other hand it would be stupid to assume that
what is incredible to you or me now must always be
incredible to mankind. What was foolishness to the
Greeks of St. Paul's day spread mightily among them
one or two hundred years later; and what is foolishness
to the modernist of to-day may edify future generations.
The imagination is suggestible and there is nothing men
will not believe in matters of religion. These rational
persuasions by which we are swayed, the conventions of
unbelieving science and unbelieving history, are superficial growths; yesterday they did not exist, to-morrow
they may have disappeared. This is a doctrine which
the modernist philosophers themselves emphasise, as
does M. Bergson, whom some of them follow, and say
the Catholic church itself ought to follow in order to be
saved—for prophets are constitutionally without a sense
of humour. These philosophers maintain that intelligence is merely a convenient method of picking one's
way through the world of matter, that it is a falsification
of life, and wholly unfit to grasp the roots of it. We
may well be of another opinion, if we think the roots
of life are not in consciousness but in nature, which

intelligence alone can reveal; but we must agree that in
life itself intelligence is a superficial growth, and easily
blighted, and that the experience of the vanity of the
world, of sin, of salvation, of miracles, of strange
revelations, and of mystic loves is a far deeper, more
primitive, and therefore probably more lasting human
possession than is that of clear historical or scientific
ideas.

Now religious experience, as I have said, may take other
forms than the Christian, and within Christianity it may
take other forms than the Catholic; but the Catholic form
is as good as any intrinsically for the devotee himself, and
it has immense advantages over its probable rivals in
charm, in comprehensiveness, in maturity, in internal
rationality, in external adaptability; so much so that a
strong anti-clerical government, like the French, cannot
safely leave the church to be overwhelmed by the forces
of science, good sense, ridicule, frivolity, and avarice
(all strong forces in France), but must use violence as well
to do it. In the English church, too, it is not those who
accept the deluge, the resurrection, and the sacraments
only as symbols that are the vital party, but those who
accept them literally; for only these have anything to
say to the poor, or to the rich, that can refresh them.
In a frank supernaturalism, in a tight clericalism, not in
a pleasant secularisation, lies the sole hope of the church.
Its sole dignity also lies there. It will not convert the
world; it never did and it never could. It will remain
a voice crying in the wilderness; but it will believe what
it cries, and there will be some to listen to it in the future,
as there have been many in the past. As to modernism,

it is suicide. It is the last of those concessions to the spirit of the world which half-believers and double-minded prophets have always been found making; but it is a mortal concession. It concedes everything; for it concedes that everything in Christianity, as Christians hold it, is an illusion.

III

THE PHILOSOPHY OF M. HENRI BERGSON

THE most representative and remarkable of living philosophers is M. Henri Bergson. Both the form and the substance of his works attract universal attention. His ideas are pleasing and bold, and at least in form wonderfully original; he is persuasive without argument and mystical without conventionality; he moves in the atmosphere of science and free thought, yet seems to transcend them and to be secretly religious. An undercurrent of zeal and even of prophecy seems to animate his subtle analyses and his surprising fancies. He is eloquent, and to a public rather sick of the half-education it has received and eager for some inspiriting novelty he seems more eloquent than he is. He uses the French language (and little else is French about him) in the manner of the more recent artists in words, retaining the precision of phrase and the measured judgments which are traditional in French literature, yet managing to envelop everything in a penumbra of emotional suggestion. Each expression of an idea is complete in itself; yet these expressions are often varied and constantly metaphorical, so that we are led to feel that much in that idea has remained unexpressed and is indeed inexpressible.

Studied and insinuating as M. Bergson is in his style, he is no less elaborate in his learning. In the history of philosophy, in mathematics and physics, and especially in natural history he has taken great pains to survey the ground and to assimilate the views and spirit of the most recent scholars. He might be called outright an expert in all these subjects, were it not for a certain externality and want of radical sympathy in his way of conceiving them. A genuine historian of philosophy, for instance, would love to rehearse the views of great thinkers, would feel their eternal plausibility, and in interpreting them would think of himself as little as they ever thought of him. But M. Bergson evidently regards Plato or Kant as persons who did or did not prepare the way for some Bergsonian insight. The theory of evolution, taken enthusiastically, is apt to exercise an evil influence on the moral estimation of things. First the evolutionist asserts that later things grow out of earlier, which is true of things in their causes and basis, but not in their values; as modern Greece proceeds out of ancient Greece materially but does not exactly crown it. The evolutionist, however, proceeds to assume that later things are necessarily better than what they have grown out of: and this is false altogether. This fallacy reinforces very unfortunately that inevitable esteem which people have for their own opinions, and which must always vitiate the history of philosophy when it is a philosopher that writes it. A false subordination comes to be established among systems, as if they moved in single file and all had the last, the author's system, for their secret goal. In Hegel, for instance, this conceit is conspicuous, in spite of his mastery in the dramatic presentation of points of view, for his way of reconstructing history was, on the surface, very sympathetic. He too, like M. Bergson, proceeded from learning to intuition, and feigned at every turn to identify himself with what he was describing, especially if this was a philosophical attitude or temper. Yet in reality his historical judgments were forced and brutal: Greece was but a stepping-stone to Prussia, Plato and Spinoza found their higher synthesis in himself, and (though he may not say so frankly) Jesus Christ and St. Francis realised their better selves in Luther. Actual spiritual life, the thoughts, affections, and pleasures of individuals, passed with Hegel for so much moonshine; the true spirit was " objective," it was simply the movement of those circumstances in which actual spirit arose. He was accordingly contemptuous of everything intrinsically good, and his idealism consisted in forcing the natural world into a formula of evolution and then worshipping it as the embodiment of the living God. But under the guise of optimism and belief in a cosmic reason this is mere idolatry of success—a malign superstition, by which all moral independence is crushed out and conscience enslaved to chronology; and it is no marvel if, somewhat to relieve this subjection, history in turn was expurgated, marshalled, and distorted, that it might pass muster for the work of the Holy Ghost.

In truth the value of spiritual life is intrinsic and centred at every point. It is never wholly recoverable. To recover it at all, an historian must have a certain detachment and ingenuousness; knowing the dignity and simplicity of his own mind, he must courteously attribute the same dignity and simplicity to others, unless their avowed attitude prevents; this is to be an intelligent critic and to write history like a gentleman. The truth, which all philosophers alike are seeking, is eternal. It lies as near to one age as to another; the means of discovery alone change, and not always for the better. The course of evolution is no test of what is true or good; else nothing could be good intrinsically nor true simply and ultimately; on the contrary, it is the approach to truth and excellence anywhere, like the approach of tree tops to the sky, that tests the value of evolution, and determines whether it is moving upward or downward or in a circle.

M. Bergson accordingly misses fire when, for instance, in order utterly to damn a view which he has been criticising, and which may be open to objection on other grounds, he cries that those who hold it " *retardent sur Kant;* " as if a clock were the compass of the mind, and he who was one minute late was one point off the course. Kant was a hard honest thinker, more sinned against than sinning, from whom a great many people in the nineteenth century have taken their point of departure, departing as far as they chose; but if a straight line of progress could be traced at all through the labyrinth of philosophy, Kant would not lie in that line. His thought is essentially excentric and sophisticated, being largely based on two inherited blunders, which a truly progressive philosophy would have to begin by avoiding, thus leaving Kant on one side, and weathering his philosophy, as one might Scylla or Charybdis. The one blunder was that of the English malicious psychology which had maintained since the time of Locke that the ideas in the mind are the only objects of knowledge, instead of being the knowledge of objects. The other blunder was that of Protestantism that, in groping after that moral freedom which is so ineradicable a need of a pure spirit, thought to find it in a revision of revelation, tradition, and prejudice, so as to be able to cling to these a little longer. How should a system so local, so accidental, and so unstable as Kant's be prescribed as a sort of catechism for all humanity? The tree of knowledge has many branches, and all its fruits are not condemned to hang for ever from that one gnarled and contorted bough. M. Bergson himself " lags behind " Kant on those points on which his better insight requires it, as, for instance, on the reality of time; but with regard to his own philosophy I am afraid he thinks that all previous systems empty into it, which is hardly true, and that all future systems must flow out of it, which is hardly necessary.

The embarrassment that qualifies M. Bergson's attainments in mathematics and physics has another and more personal source. He understands, but he trembles. Non-human immensities frighten him, as they did Pascal. He suffers from cosmic agoraphobia. We might think empty space an innocent harmless thing, a mere opportunity to move, which ought to be highly prized by all devotees of motion. But M. Bergson is instinctively a mystic, and his philosophy deliberately discredits the existence of anything except in immediacy, that is, as an experience of the heart. What he dreads in space is that the heart should be possessed by it, and transformed into it. He dreads that the imagination should be fascinated by the homogeneous and static, hypnotised by geometry, and actually lost in *Auseinandersein*. This would be a real death and petrifaction of consciousness, frozen into contemplation of a monotonous infinite void. What is warm and desirable is rather the sense of variety and succession, as if all visions radiated from the occupied focus or hearth of the self. The more concentration at this habitable point, with the more mental perspectives opening backwards and forwards through time, in a word, the more personal and historical the apparition, the better it would be. Things must be reduced again to what they seem; it is vain and terrible to take them for what we find they are. M. Bergson is at bottom an apologist for very old human prejudices, an apologist for animal illusion. His whole labour is a plea for some vague but comfortable faith which he dreads to have stolen from him by the progress of art and knowledge. There is a certain trepidation, a certain suppressed instinct to snap at and sting the hated oppressor, as if some desperate small being were at bay before a horrible monster. M. Bergson is afraid of space, of mathematics, of necessity, and of eternity; he is afraid of the intellect and the possible discoveries of science; he is afraid of nothingness and death. These fears may prevent him from being a philosopher in the old and noble sense of the word; but they sharpen his sense for many a psychological problem, and make him the spokesman of many an inarticulate soul. Animal timidity and animal illusion are deep in the heart of all of us. Practice may compel us to bow to the conventions of the intellect, as to those of polite society; but secretly,

in our moments of immersion in ourselves, we may find
them a great nuisance, even a vain nightmare. Could
we only listen undisturbed to the beat of protoplasm in
our hearts, would not that oracle solve all the riddles of
the universe, or at least avoid them?

To protect this inner conviction, however, it is necessary for the mystic to sally forth and attack the enemy
on his own ground. If he refuted physics and mathematics simply out of his own faith, he might be accused
of ignorance of the subject. He will therefore study it
conscientiously, yet with a certain irritation and haste
to be done with it, somewhat as a Jesuit might study
Protestant theology. Such a student, however, is apt
to lose his pains; for in retracing a free inquiry in his
servile spirit, he remains deeply ignorant, not indeed of
its form, but of its nature and value. Why, for instance,
has M. Bergson such a horror of mechanical physics?
He seems to think it a black art, dealing in unholy
abstractions, and rather dangerous to salvation, and he
keeps his metaphysical exorcisms and antidotes always
at hand, to render it innocuous, at least to his own soul.
But physical science never solicited of anybody that he
should be wholly absorbed in the contemplation of atoms,
and worship them; that we must worship and lose
ourselves in reality, whatever reality may be, is a mystic
aberration, which physical science does nothing to foster.
Nor does any critical physicist suppose that what he
describes is the whole of the object; he merely notes the
occasions on which its sensible qualities appear, and cal-
culates events. Because the calculable side of nature
is his province, he does not deny that events have other

aspects—the psychic and the moral, for instance—no less real in their way, in terms of which calculation would indeed be impossible. If he chances to call the calculable elements of nature her substance, as it is proper to do, that name is given without passion; he may perfectly well proclaim with Goethe that it is in the accidents, in the *farbiger Abglanz*, that we have our life. And if it be for his freedom that the mystic trembles, I imagine any man of science would be content with M. Bergson's assertion that true freedom is the *sense* of freedom, and that in any intelligible statement of the situation, even the most indeterministic, this freedom disappears; for it is an immediate experience, not any scheme of relation between events.

The horror of mechanical physics arises, then, from attributing to that science pretensions and extensions which it does not have; it arises from the habits of theology and metaphysics being imported inopportunely into science. Similarly when M. Bergson mentions mathematics, he seems to be thinking of the supposed authority it exercises—one of Kant's confusions—over the empirical world, and trying to limit and subordinate that authority, lest movement should somehow be removed from nature, and vagueness from human thought. But nature and human thought are what they are; they have enough affinity to mathematics, as it happens, to suggest that study to our minds, and to give those who go deep into it a great, though partial, mastery over things. Nevertheless a true mathematician is satisfied with the hypothetical and ideal cogency of his science, and puts its dignity in that. Moreover,

M. Bergson has the too pragmatic notion that the use
of mathematics is to keep our accounts straight in this
business world; whereas its inherent use is emancipating
and Platonic, in that it shows us the possibility of other
worlds, less contingent and perturbed than this one.   If
he allows himself any excursus from his beloved immediacy, it is only in the interests of practice; he little
knows the pleasures of a liberal mind, ranging over the
congenial realm of internal accuracy and ideal truth,
where it can possess itself of what treasures it likes in
perfect security and freedom.   An artist in his work-
manship, M. Bergson is not an artist in his allegiance;
he has no respect for what is merely ideal.

For this very reason, perhaps, he is more at home in
natural history than in the exact sciences. He has the
gift of observation, and can suggest vividly the actual
appearance of natural processes, in contrast to the
verbal paraphrase of these processes which is sometimes
taken to explain them.   He is content to stop at habit
without formulating laws; he refuses to assume that the
large obvious cycles of change in things can be reduced
to mechanism, that is, to minute included cycles repeated
ad libitum. He may sometimes defend this refusal by
sophistical arguments, as when he says that mechanism
would require the last stage of the universe to be simul-
taneous with the first, forgetting that the unit of
mechanism is not a mathematical equation but some
observed typical event. The refusal itself, however,
would be honest scepticism enough were it made with
no *arrière pensée*, but simply in view of the immense
complexity of the facts and the extreme simplicity of

the mechanical hypothesis. In such a situation, to halt
at appearances might seem the mark of a true naturalist
and a true empiricist not misled by speculative haste
and the human passion for system and simplification.
At the first reading, M. Bergson's *Evolution Créatrice*
may well dazzle the professional naturalist and seem to
him an illuminating confession of the nature and limits
of his science; yet a second reading, I have good
authority for saying, may as easily reverse that impression. M. Bergson never reviews his facts in order
to understand them, but only if possible to discredit
others who may have fancied they understood. He
raises difficulties, he marks the problems that confront
the naturalist, and the inadequacy of explanations that
may have been suggested. Such criticism would be a
valuable beginning if it were followed by the suggestion
of some new solution; but the suggestion only is that
no solution is possible, that the phenomena of life are
simply miraculous, and that it is in the tendency or
vocation of the animal, not in its body or its past, that
we must see the ground of what goes on before us.

With such a philosophy of science, it is evident that
all progress in the understanding of nature would cease,
as it ceased after Aristotle. The attempt would again
be abandoned to reduce gross and obvious cycles of
change, such as generation, growth, and death, to
minute latent cycles, so that natural history should offer
a picturesque approach to universal physics. If for the
magic power of types, invoked by Aristotle, we substituted with M. Bergson the magic power of the *élan
vital*, that is, of evolution in general, we should be

referring events not to finer, more familiar, more pervasive processes, but to one all-embracing process, unique and always incomplete. Our understanding would end in something far vaguer and looser than what our observation began with. Aristotle at least could refer particulars to their specific types, as medicine and social science are still glad enough to do, to help them in guessing and in making a learned show before the public. But if divination and eloquence—for science is out of the question—were to invoke nothing but a fluid tendency to grow, we should be left with a flat history of phenomena and no means of prediction or even classification. All knowledge would be reduced to gossip, infinitely diffuse, perhaps enlisting our dramatic feelings, but yielding no intellectual mastery of experience, no practical competence, and no moral lesson. The world would be a serial novel, to be continued for ever, and all men mere novel-readers.

Nothing is more familiar to philosophers nowadays than that criticism of knowledge by which we are thrown back upon the appearances from which science starts, upon what is known to children and savages, whilst all that which long experience and reason may infer from those appearances is set down as so much hypothesis; and indeed it is through hypothesis that latent being, if such there be, comes before the mind at all. Now such criticism of knowledge might have been straightforward and ingenuous. It might have simply disclosed the fact, very salutary to meditate upon, that the whole frame of nature, with the minds that animate it, is disclosed to us by intelligence; that if we were not intelligent our sensations would exist for us without meaning anything, as they exist for idiots. The criticism of knowledge, however, has usually been taken maliciously, in the sense that it is the idiots only that are not deceived; for any interpretation of sensation is a mental figment, and while experience may have any extent it will it cannot possibly, they say, have expressive value; it cannot reveal anything going on beneath. Intelligence and science are accordingly declared to have no penetration, no power to disclose what is latent, for nothing latent exists; they can at best furnish symbols for past or future sensations and the order in which they arise ; they can be seven-league boots for striding over the surface of sentience.

This negative dogmatism as to knowledge was rendered harmless and futile by the English philosophers, in that they maintained at the same time that everything happens exactly *as if* the intellect were a true instrument of discovery, and *as if* a material world underlay our experience and furnished all its occasions. Hume, Mill, and Huxley were scientific at heart, and full of the intelligence they dissected; they seemed to cry to nature: Though thou dost not exist, yet will I trust in thee. Their idealism was a theoretical scruple rather than a passionate superstition. Not so M. Bergson; he is not so simple as to invoke the malicious criticism of knowledge in order to go on thinking rationalistically. Reason and science make him deeply uncomfortable. His point accordingly is not merely that mechanism is a hypothesis, but that it is a wrong hypothesis. Events do not come as if mechanism brought them about; they come, at least in the organic world, as if a magic destiny, and inscrutable ungovernable effort, were driving them on.

Thus M. Bergson introduces metaphysics into natural history; he invokes, in what is supposed to be science, the agency of a power, called the *élan vital*, on a level with the " Will " of Schopenhauer or the " Unknowable Force " of Herbert Spencer. But there is a scientific vitalism also, which it is well to distinguish from the metaphysical sort. The point at issue between vitalism and mechanism in biology is whether the living processes in nature can be resolved into a combination of the material. The material processes will always remain vital, if we take this word in a descriptive and poetic sense; for they will contain a movement having a certain idiosyncrasy and taking a certain time, like the fall of an apple. The movement of nature is never dialectical; the first part of any event does not logically imply the last part of it. Physics is descriptive, historical, reporting after the fact what are found to be the habits of matter. But if these habits are constant and calculable we call the vitality of them mechanical. Thus the larger processes of nature, no matter how vital they may be and whatever consciousness may accompany them, will always be mechanical if they can be calculated and predicted, being a combination of the more minute and widespread processes which they contain. The only question therefore is: Do processes such as nutrition and reproduction arise by a combination of such events as the fall of apples? Or are they irreducible events, and units of mechanism by themselves? That is the dilemma as it appears in science. Both possibilities will always remain open, because however far mechanical analysis may go, many phenomena, as human apprehension presents them, will always remain irreducible to any common denominator with the rest; and on the other hand, wherever the actual reduction of the habits of animals to those of matter may have stopped, we can never know that a further reduction is impossible.

The balance of reasonable presumption, however, is not even. The most inclusive movements known to us in nature, the astronomical, are calculable, and so are the most minute and pervasive processes, the chemical. These are also, if evolution is to be accepted, the earliest processes upon which all others have supervened and out of which, as it were, they have grown. Apart from miraculous intervention, therefore, the assumption seems to be inevitable that the intermediate processes are calculable too, and compounded out of the others. The appearance to the contrary presented in animal and social life is easily explicable on psychological grounds. We read inevitably in terms of our passions those things which affect them or are analogous to what involves passion in ourselves; and when the mechanism of them is hidden from us, as is that of our bodies, we suppose that these passions which we find on the surface in ourselves, or read into other creatures, are the substantial and only forces that carry on our part of the world. Penetrating this illusion, dispassionate observers in all ages have received the general impression that nature is one and mechanical. This was, and still remains, a general impression only; but I suspect no one who walks the earth with his eyes open would be concerned to resist it, were it not for certain fond human conceits which such a view would rebuke and, if accepted, would tend to obliterate. The psychological illusion that our ideas and purposes are original facts and forces (instead of expressions in consciousness of facts and forces which are material) and the practical and optical illusion that everything wheels about us in this world—these are the primitive persuasions which the enemies of naturalism have always been concerned to protect.

One might indeed be a vitalist in biology, out of pure caution and conscientiousness, without sharing those prejudices; and many a speculative philosopher has been free from them who has been a vitalist in metaphysics. Schopenhauer, for instance, observed that the cannon-ball which, if self-conscious, would think it moved freely, would be quite right in thinking so. The " Will " was as evident to him in mechanism as in animal life. M. Bergson, in the more hidden reaches of his thought, seems to be a universal vitalist; apparently an *élan vital* must have existed once to deposit in inorganic matter the energy stored there, and to set mechanism going. But he relies on biology alone to prove the present existence of an independent effort to live; this is needed to do what mechanism, as he thinks, could never do; it is not needed to do, as in Schopenhauer, what mechanism does. M. Bergson thus introduces his metaphysical force as a peculiar requirement of biology; he breaks the continuity of nature; he loses the poetic justification of a metaphysical vitalism; he asks us to believe that life is not a natural expression of material being, but an alien and ghostly madness descending into it—I say a ghostly madness, for why should disembodied life wish that the body should live? This vitalism is not a kind of biology more prudent and literal than the mechanical kind (as a scientific vitalism would be), but far less legitimately speculative. Nor is it a frank and thorough mythology, such as the total spectacle of the universe might suggest to an imaginative genius. It is rather a popular animism, insisting on a sympathetic interpretation of nature where human sympathy is quick and easy, and turning this sympathy into a revelation of the absolute, but leaving the rest of nature cold, because to sympathise with its movement there is harder for anxious, self-centred mortals, and requires a disinterested mind. M. Bergson would have us believe that mankind is what nature has set her heart on and the best she can do, for whose sake she has been long making very special efforts. We are fortunate that at least her darling is all mankind and not merely Israel.

In spite, then, of M. Bergson's learning as a naturalist and his eye for the facts—things Aristotle also possessed —he is like Aristotle profoundly out of sympathy with nature. Aristotle was alienated from nature and any penetrating study of it by the fact that he was a disciple of Socrates, and therefore essentially a moralist and a logician. M. Bergson is alienated from nature by something quite different; he is the adept of a very modern, very subtle, and very arbitrary art, that of literary psychology. In this art the imagination is invited to conceive things as if they were all centres of passion and sensation. Literary psychology is not a science; it is practised by novelists and poets; yet if it is to be brilliantly executed it demands a minute and extended observation of life. Unless your psychological novelist had crammed his memory with pictures of the ways and aspects of men he would have no starting-point for his psychological fictions; he would not be able to render them circumstantial and convincing. Just so M. Bergson's achievements in psychological fiction, to be so brilliantly executed as they are, required all his learning. The history of philosophy, mathematics, and physics, and above all natural history, had to supply him first with suggestions; and if he is not really a master in any of those fields, that is not to be wondered at. His heart is elsewhere. To write a universal biological romance, such as he has sketched for us in his system, he would ideally have required all scientific knowledge, but only as Homer required the knowledge of seamanship, general-ship, statecraft, augury, and charioteering, in order to turn the aspects of them into poetry, and not with that technical solidity which Plato unjustly blames him for not possessing. Just so M. Bergson's proper achieve-ment begins where his science ends, and his philosophy lies entirely beyond the horizon of possible discoveries or empirical probabilities. In essence, it is myth or fable; but in the texture and degree of its fabulousness it differs notably from the performances of previous metaphysicians. Primitive poets, even ancient philo-sophers, were not psychologists; their fables were com-pacted out of elements found in practical life, and they reckoned in the units in which language and passion reckon — wooing, feasting, fighting, vice, virtue, happi-ness, justice. Above all, they talked about persons or about ideals; this man, this woman, this typical thought or sentiment was what fixed their attention and seemed to them the ultimate thing. Not so M. Bergson: he is a microscopic psychologist, and even in man what he studies by preference is not some integrated passion or idea, but something far more recondite; the minute texture of sensation, memory, or impulse. Sharp analysis is required to distinguish or arrest these elements, yet these are the predestined elements of his fable; and so his anthropomorphism is far less obvious than that of most poets and theologians, though no less real.

This peculiarity in the terms of the myth carries with it a notable extension in its propriety. The social and moral phenomena of human life cannot be used in interpreting life elsewhere without a certain conscious humour. This makes the charm of avowed writers of fable; their playful travesty and dislocation of things human, which would be puerile if they meant to be naturalists, render them piquant moralists; for they are not really interpreting animals, but under the mask of animals maliciously painting men. Such fables are morally interesting and plausible just because they are psychologically false. If Æsop could have reported what lions and lambs, ants and donkeys, really feel and think, his poems would have been perfect riddles to the public; and they would have had no human value except that of illustrating, to the truly speculative philosopher, the irresponsible variety of animal consciousness and its incommensurable types. Now M. Bergson's psychological fictions, being drawn from what is rudimentary in man, have a better chance of being literally true beyond man. Indeed what he asks us to do, and wishes to do himself, is simply to absorb so completely the aspect and habit of things that the soul of them may take possession of us: that we may know by intuition the *élan vital* which the world expresses, just as Paolo, in Dante, knew by intuition the *élan vital* that the smile of Francesca expressed.

The correctness of such an intuition, however, rests on a circumstance which M. Bergson does not notice, because his psychology is literary and not scientific. It rests on the possibility of imitation. When the organism observed and that of the observer have a similar structure and can imitate one another, the idea produced in the observer by intent contemplation is like the experience present to the person contemplated. But where this contagion of attitude, and therefore of feeling, is impossible, our intuition of our neighbours' souls remains subjective and has no value as a revelation. Psychological novelists, when they describe people such as they themselves are or might have been, may describe them truly; but beyond that limit their personages are merely plausible, that is, such as might be conceived by an equally ignorant reader in the presence of the same external indications. So, for instance, the judgment which a superficial traveller passes on foreign manners or religions is plausible to him and to his compatriots just because it represents the feeling that such manifestations awaken in strangers and does not attempt to convey the very different feeling really involved for the natives; had the latter been discovered and expressed the traveller's book would have found little understanding and no sale in his own country. This plausibility to the ignorant is present in all spontaneous myth. Nothing more need be demanded of irresponsible fiction, which makes no pretensions to be a human document, but is merely a human entertainment.

Now, a human psychology, even of the finest grain, when it is applied to the interpretation of the soul of matter, or of the soul of the whole universe, obviously yields a view of the irresponsible and subjective sort; for it is not based on any close similarity between the observed and the observer: man and the ether, man and cosmic evolution, cannot mimic one another, to discover mutually how they feel. But just because merely human, such an interpretation may remain always plausible to man; and it would be an admirable entertainment if there were no danger that it should be taken seriously. The idea Paul has of Peter, Spinoza observes, expresses the nature of Peter less than it betrays that of Paul; and so an idea framed by a man of the consciousness of things in general reveals the mind of that man rather than the mind of the universe; but the mind of the man too may be worth knowing, and the illusive hope of discovering everything may lead him truly to disclose himself. Such a disclosure of the lower depths of man by himself is M. Bergson's psychology; and the psychological romance, purporting to describe the inward nature of the universe, which he has built out of that introspection, is his metaphysics.

Many a point in this metaphysics may seem strange, fantastic, and obscure; and so it really is, when dislocated and projected metaphysically; but not one will

be found to be arbitrary; not one but is based on attentive introspection and perception of the immediate.
Take, for example, what is M. Bergson's starting-point,
his somewhat dazzling doctrine that to be is to last, or
rather to feel oneself endure. This is a hypostasis of
" true " (*i.e.* immediately felt) duration. In a sensuous
day-dream past feelings survive in the present, images
of the long ago are shuffled together with present sensations, the roving imagination leaves a bright wake behind
it like a comet, and pushes a rising wave before it, like
the bow of a ship; all is fluidity, continuity without
identity, novelty without surprise. Hence, too, the
doctrine of freedom: the images that appear in such a
day-dream are often congruous in character with those
that preceded, and mere prolongations of them; but
this prolongation itself modifies them, and what
develops is in no way deducible or predictable out of
what exists. This situation is perfectly explicable
scientifically. The movement of consciousness will be
self-congruous and sustained when it rests on continuous processes in the same tissues, and yet quite unpredictable from within, because the direct sensuous
report of bodily processes (in nausea, for instance, or in
hunger) contains no picture of their actual mechanism.
Even wholly new features, due to little crises in bodily
life, may appear in a dream to flow out of what already
exists, yet freely develop it; because in dreams comparison, the attempt to be consistent, is wholly in
abeyance, and also because the new feature will come
imbedded in others which are not new, but have
dramatic relevance in the story. So immediate con-

sciousness yields the two factors of Bergsonian freedom, continuity and indetermination.

Again, take the somewhat disconcerting assertion that movement exists when there is nothing that moves, and no space that it moves through. In vision, perhaps, it is not easy to imagine a consciousness of motion without some presentation of a field, and of a distinguishable something in it; but if we descend to somatic feelings (and the more we descend, with M. Bergson, the closer we are to reality), in shooting pains or the sense of intestinal movements, the feeling of a change and of a motion is certainly given in the absence of all idea of a *mobile* or of distinct points (or even of a separate field) through which it moves; consciousness begins with the sense of change, and the terms of the felt process are only qualitative limits, bred out of the felt process itself. Even a more paradoxical tenet of our philosopher's finds its justification here. He says that the units of motion are indivisible, that they are acts; so that to solve the riddle about Achilles and the tortoise we need no mathematics of the infinitesimal, but only to ask Achilles how he accomplishes the feat. Achilles would reply that in so many strides he would do it; and we may be surprised to learn that these strides are indivisible, so that, apparently, Achilles could not have stumbled in the middle of one, and taken only half of it. Of course, in nature, in what non-Bergsonians call reality, he could: but not in his immediate feeling, for if he had stumbled, the real stride, that which he was aware of taking, would have been complete at the stumbling-point. It is certain that consciousness comes in stretches, in breaths: all its data are æsthetic wholes, like visions or snatches of melody; and we should never be aware of anything were we not aware of something all at once.

When a man has taught himself—and it is a difficult art—to revert in this way to rudimentary consciousness and to watch himself live, he will be able, if he likes, to add a plausible chapter to speculative psychology. He has unearthed in himself the animal sensibility which has thickened, budded, and crystallised into his present somewhat intellectual image of the world. He has touched again the vegetative stupor, the multiple disconnected landscapes, the " blooming buzzing confusion " which his reason has partly set in order. May he not have in all this a key to the consciousness of other creatures? Animal psychology, and sympathy with the general life of nature, are vitiated both for naturalists and for poets by the human terms they must use, terms which presuppose distinctions which non-human beings probably have not made. These distinctions correct the illusions of immediate appearance in ways which only a long and special experience has imposed upon us, and they should not be imported into other souls. We are old men trying to sing the loves of children; we are wingless bipeds trying to understand the gods. But the data of the immediate are hardly human; it is probable that at that level all sentience is much alike. From that common ground our imagination can perhaps start safely, and follow such hints as observation furnishes, until we learn to live and feel as other living things do, or as nature may live and feel as a whole. Instinct, for instance, need not be, as our human prejudice suggests, a rudimentary intelligence; it may be a parallel sort of sensibility, an imageless awareness of the presence and character of other things, with a superhuman ability to change oneself so as to meet them. Do we not feel something of this sort ourselves in love, in art, in religion? M. Bergson is a most delicate and charming poet on this theme, and a plausible psychologist; his method of accumulating and varying his metaphors, and leaving our intuition to itself under that artful stimulus, is the only judicious and persuasive method he could have employed, and his knack at it is wonderful. We recover, as we read, the innocence of the mind. It seems no longer impossible that we might, like the wise men in the story-books, learn the language of birds; we share for the moment the siestas of plants; and we catch the quick consciousness of the waves of light, vibrating at inconceivable rates, each throb forgotten as the next follows upon it; and we may be tempted to play on Shakespeare and say:

> "Like as the waves make towards the pebbled shore,
> So do *their spirits* hasten to their end."

Some reader of M. Bergson might say to himself: All this is ingenious introspection and divination; grant that it is true, and how does that lead to a new theory of the universe? You have been studying surface appearances and the texture of primitive consciousness; that is a part of the internal rumble of this great engine of the world. How should it loosen or dissolve that engine, as your philosophy evidently professes that it must? That nature exists we perceive whenever we resume our intellectual and practical life,

interrupted for a moment by this interesting reversion
to the immediate. The consciousness which in introspection we treat as an object is, in operation, a cognitive
activity: it demonstrates the world. You would never
yourself have conceived the minds of ethereal vibrations,
or of birds, or of ants, or of men suspending their intelligence, if you had known of no men, ants, birds, or ether.
It is the material objects that suggest to you their souls,
and teach you how to conceive them. How then should
the souls be substituted for the bodies, and abolish them?

Poor guileless reader! If philosophers were straightforward men of science, adding each his mite to the
general store of knowledge, they would all substantially
agree, and while they might make interesting discoveries, they would not herald each his new transformation of the whole universe. But philosophers are
either revolutionists or apologists, and some of them, like
M. Bergson, are revolutionists in the interests of apolo-
getics. Their art is to create some surprising inversion
of things, some system of the universe contrary to
common apprehension, or to defend some such inverted
system, propounded by poets long ago, and perhaps
consecrated by religion. It would not require a great
man to say calmly: Men, birds, even ether-waves, if you
will, feel after this and this fashion. The greatness and
the excitement begin when he says: Your common sense,
your practical intellect, your boasted science have
entirely deceived you; see what the real truth is
instead! So M. Bergson is bent on telling us that the
immediate, as he describes it, is the sole reality; all else
is unreal, artificial, and a more or less convenient symbol

in discourse—discourse itself being taken, of course, for a movement in immediate sensibility, which is what it is existentially, but never for an excursion into an independent logical realm, which is what it is spiritually and in intent. So we must revise all our psychological observations, and turn them into metaphysical dogmas. It would be nothing to say simply: *For immediate feeling* the past is contained in the present, movement is prior to that which moves, spaces are many, disconnected, and incommensurable, events are indivisible wholes, perception is in its object and identical with it, the future is unpredictable, the complex is bred out of the simple, and evolution is creative, its course being obedient to a general tendency or groping impulse, not to any exact law. No, we must say instead: *In the universe at large* the whole past is preserved bodily in the present; duration is real and space is only imagined; all is motion, and there is nothing substantial that moves; times are incommensurable; men, birds, and waves are nothing but the images of them (our perceptions, like their spirits, being some compendium of these images); chance intervenes in the flux, but evolution is due to an absolute Effort which exists *in vacuo* and is simplicity itself; and this Effort, without having an idea of what it pursues, nevertheless produces it out of nothing.

The accuracy or the hollowness of M. Bergson's doctrine, according as we take it for literary psychology or for natural philosophy, will appear clearly in the following instance. "Any one," he writes,[1] "who has

---

[1] "Introduction à la Métaphysique." *Revue de Métaphysique et de Morale*, Janvier, 1903.

ever practised literary composition knows very well that, after he has devoted long study to the subject, collected all the documents, and taken all his notes, one thing more is needful before he can actually embark on the work of composition; namely, an effort, often a very painful one, to plant himself all at once in the very heart of the subject, and to fetch from as profound a depth as possible the momentum by which he need simply let himself be borne along in the sequel. This momentum, as soon as it is acquired, carries the mind forward along a path where it recovers all the facts it had gathered together, and a thousand other details besides. The momentum develops and breaks up of itself into particulars that might be retailed *ad infinitum*. The more he advances the more he finds; he will never have exhausted the subject; and nevertheless if he turns round suddenly to face the momentum he feels at his back and see what it is, it eludes him; for it is not a thing but a direction of movement, and though capable of being extended indefinitely, it is simplicity itself."

This is evidently well observed: heighten the tone a little, and you might have a poem on those joyful pangs of gestation and parturition which are not denied to a male animal. It is a description of the *sensation* of literary composition, of the *immediate experience* of a writer as words and images rise into his mind. He cannot summon his memories explicitly, for he would first have to remember them to do so; his consciousness of inspiration, of literary creation, is nothing but a consciousness of pregnancy and of a certain " direction of movement," as if he were being wafted in a balloon; and just in its

moments of highest tension his mind is filled with mere
expectancy and mere excitement, without images, plans,
or motives; and what guides it is inwardly, as M. Bergson
says, simplicity itself. Yet excellent as such a description is psychologically, it is a literary confession rather
than a piece of science; for scientific psychology is a
part of natural history, and when in nature we come
upon such a notable phenomenon as this, that some men
write and write eloquently, we should at once study the
antecedents and the conditions under which this occurs;
we should try, by experiment if possible, to see what
variations in the result follow upon variations in the
situation. At once we should begin to perceive how
casual and superficial are those data of introspection
which M. Bergson's account reproduces. Does that
painful effort, for instance, occur always? Is it the
moral source, as he seems to suggest, of the good and
miraculous fruits that follow? Not at all: such an
effort is required only when the writer is overworked,
or driven to express himself under pressure; in the
spontaneous talker or singer, in the orator surpassing
himself and overflowing with eloquence, there is no
effort at all; only facility, and joyous undirected abundance. We should further ask whether *all* the facts
previously gathered are recovered, and all correctly, and
what relation the " thousand other details " have to them;
and we should find that everything was controlled and
supplied by the sensuous endowment of the literary man,
his moral complexion, and his general circumstances.
And we should perceive at the same time that the
momentum which to introspection was so mysterious

was in fact the discharge of many automatisms long imprinted on the system, a system (as growth and disease show) that has its internal vegetation and crises of maturity, to which facility and error in the recovery of the past, and creation also, are closely attached.   Thus we should utterly refuse to say that this momentum was capable of being extended indefinitely or was simplicity itself.   It may be a good piece of literary psychology to say that simplicity precedes complexity, for it precedes complexity in consciousness.   Consciousness dwindles and flares up most irresponsibly, so long as its own flow alone is regarded, and it continually arises out of nothing, which indeed is simplicity itself.   But it does not arise without real conditions outside, which cannot be discovered by introspection, nor divined by that literary psychology which proceeds by imagining what introspection might yield in others.

There is a deeper mystification still in this passage, where a writer is said to " plant himself in the very heart of the subject." The general tenor of M. Bergson's philosophy warrants us in taking this quite literally to mean that the field from which inspiration draws its materials is not the man's present memory nor even his past experience, but the subject itself which that experience and this memory regard: in other words, what we write about and our latent knowledge are the same thing. When Shakespeare was composing his *Antony and Cleopatra*, for instance, he planted himself in the very heart of Rome and of Egypt, and in the very heart of the Queen of Egypt herself; what he had gathered from Plutarch and from elsewhere was, according to M.

Bergson's view, a sort of glimpse of the remote reality itself, as if by telepathy he had been made to witness some part of it; or rather as if the scope of his consciousness had been suddenly extended in one direction, so as to embrace and contain bodily a bit of that outlying experience.   Thus when the poet sifts his facts and sets his imagination to work at unifying and completing them, what he does is to pierce to Egypt, Rome, and the inner consciousness of Cleopatra, to fetch *thence* the profound momentum which is to guide him in composition; and it is there, not in the adventitious later parts of his own mind, that he should find the thousand other details which he may add to the picture.

Here again, in an exaggerated form, we have a transcript of the immediate, a piece of really wonderful introspection, spoiled by being projected into a theory of nature, which it spoils in its turn.   Doubtless Shakespeare, in the heat of dramatic vision, lived his characters, transported himself to their environment, and felt the passion of each, as we do in a dream, dictating their unpremeditated words.   But all this is in imagination; it is true only within the framework of our dream.   In reality, of course, Shakespeare never pierced to Rome nor to Egypt; his elaborations of his data are drawn from his own feelings and circumstances, not from those of Cleopatra.   This transporting oneself into the heart of a subject is a loose metaphor: the best one can do is to transplant the subject into one's own heart and draw *from oneself* impulses as profound as possible with which to vivify tradition and make it over in one's own image. Yet I fear that to speak so is rationalism, and would be found to involve, to the horror of our philosopher, that life is cognitive and spiritual, but dependent, discontinuous, and unsubstantial. What he conceives instead is that consciousness is a stuff out of which things are made, and has all the attributes, even the most material, of its several objects; and that there is no possibility of knowing, save by becoming what one is trying to know. So perception, for him, lies where its object does, and is some part of it; memory is the past experience itself, somehow shining through into the present; and Shakespeare's Cleopatra, I should infer, would have to be some part of Cleopatra herself—in those moments when she spoke English.

It is hard to be a just critic of mysticism because mysticism can never do itself justice in words. To conceive of an external actual Cleopatra and an external actual mind of Shakespeare is to betray the cause of pure immediacy; and I suspect that if M. Bergson heard of such criticisms as I am making, he would brush them aside as utterly blind and scholastic. As the mystics have always said that God was not far from them, but dwelt in their hearts, meaning this pretty literally: so this mystical philosophy of the immediate, which talks sometimes so scientifically of things and with such intimacy of knowledge, feels that these things are not far from it, but dwell literally in its heart. The revelation and the sentiment of them, if it be thorough, is just what the things are. The total aspects to be discerned in a body *are* that body; and the movement of those aspects, when you enact it, *is* the spirit of that body, and at the same time a part of your own spirit. To suppose that a man's consciousness (either one's own or other people's) is a separate fact over and above the shuffling of the things he feels, or that these things are anything over and above the feeling of them which exists more or less everywhere in diffusion—that, for the mystic, is to be once for all hopelessly intellectual, dualistic, and diabolical. If you cannot shed the husk of those dead categories—space, matter, mind, truth, person—life is shut out of your heart. And the mystic, who always speaks out of experience, is certainly right in this, that a certain sort of life is shut out by reason, the sort that reason calls dreaming or madness; but he forgets that reason too is a kind of life, and that of all the kinds— mystical, passionate, practical, æsthetic, intellectual— with their various degrees of light and heat, the life of reason is that which some people may prefer. I confess I am one of these, and I am not inclined, even if I were able, to reproduce M. Bergson's sentiments as he feels them. He is his own perfect expositor. All a critic can aim at is to understand these sentiments as existing facts, and to give them the place that belongs to them in the moral world. To understand, in most cases, is intimacy enough.

Herbert Spencer says somewhere that the yolk of an egg is homogeneous, the highly heterogeneous bird being differentiated in it by the law of evolution. I cannot think what assured Spencer of this homogeneity in the egg, except the fact that perhaps it all tasted alike, which might seem good proof to a pure empiricist. Leibnitz, on the contrary, maintained that the organisa- tion of nature was infinitely deep, every part consisting of an endless number of discrete elements. Here we may observe the difference between good philosophy and bad. The idea of Leibnitz is speculative and far outruns the evidence, but it is speculative in a well-advised, penetrating, humble, and noble fashion; while the idea of Spencer is foolishly dogmatic, it is a piece of ignorant self-sufficiency, like that insular empiricism that would deny that Chinamen were real until it had actually seen them. Nature is richer than experience and wider than divination; and it is far rasher and more arrogant to declare that any part of nature is simple than to suggest the sort of complexity that perhaps it might have. M. Bergson, however, is on the side of Spencer. After studiously examining the egg on every side — for he would do more than taste it—and considering the source and destiny of it, he would summon his intuition to penetrate to the very heart of it, to its spirit, and then he would declare that this spirit was a vital momentum without parts and without ideas, and was simplicity itself. He would add that it was the free and original creator of the bird, because it is of the essence of spirit to bestow more than it possesses and to build better than it knows. Undoubtedly actual spirit is simple and does not know how it builds; but for that very reason actual spirit does not really create or build anything, but merely watches, now with sympathetic, now with shocked attention, what is being created and built for it. Doubtless new things are always arising, new islands, new persons, new philosophies; but that the real cause of them should be simpler than they, that their Creator, if I may use this language, should be ignorant and give more than he has, who can stomach that?

Let us grant, however, since the thing is not abstractly inconceivable, that eggs really have no structure. To what, then, shall we attribute the formation of birds? Will it follow that evolution, or differentiation, or the law of the passage from the homogeneous to the heterogeneous, or the dialectic of the concept of pure being, or the impulse towards life, or the vocation of spirit is what actually hatches them? Alas, these words are but pedantic and rhetorical cloaks for our ignorance, and to project them behind the facts and regard them as presiding from thence over the course of nature is a piece of the most deplorable scholasticism. If eggs are really without structure, the true causes of the formation of birds are the last conditions, whatever they may be, that introduce that phenomenon and determine its character—the type of the parents, the act of fertilisation, the temperature, or whatever else observation might find regularly to precede and qualify that new birth in nature. These facts, if they were the ultimate and deepest facts in the case, would be the ultimate and only possible terms in which to explain it. They would constitute the mechanism of reproduction; and if nature were no finer than that in its structure, science could not go deeper than that in its discoveries. And although it is frivolous to suppose that nature ends in this way at the limits of our casual apprehension, and has no hidden roots, yet philosophically that would be as good a stopping place as any other. Ultimately we should have to be satisfied with some factual conjunction and method in events. If atoms and their collisions, by any chance, were the ultimate and inmost facts discoverable, they would supply the explanation of everything, in the only sense in which anything existent can be explained at all. If somebody then came to us enthusiastically and added that the Will of the atoms so to be and move was the true cause, or the Will of God that they should move so, he would not be reputed, I suppose, to have thrown a bright light on the subject.

Yet this is what M. Bergson does in his whole defence of metaphysical vitalism, and especially in the instance of the evolution of eyes by two different methods, which is his palmary argument. Since in some molluscs and in vertebrates organs that coincide in being organs of vision are reached by distinct paths, it cannot have been the propulsion of mechanism in each case, he says, that guided the developments, which, being divergent, would never have led to coincident results, but the double development must have been guided by a common *tendency towards vision*. Suppose (what some young man in a laboratory may by this time have shown to be false) that M. Bergson's observations have sounded the facts to the bottom; it would then be of the ultimate nature of things that, given light and the other conditions, the two methods of development will end in eyes; just as, for a peasant, it is of the ultimate nature of things that puddles can be formed in two quite opposite ways, by rain falling from heaven and by springs issuing from the earth; but as the peasant would not have reached a profound insight into nature if he had proclaimed the presence in her of a *tendency to puddles*, to be formed in inexplicably different ways; so the philosopher attains to no profound insight when he proclaims in her a *tendency to vision.* If those words express more than ignorance, they express the love of it. Even if the vitalists were right in despairing of further scientific discoveries, they would be wrong in offering their verbiage as a substitute. Nature may possibly have only a very loose hazy constitution, to be watched and understood as sailors watch and understand the weather; but Neptune and Æolus are not thereby proved to be the authors of storms. Yet M. Bergson thinks if life could only be safely shown to arise unaccountably, that would prove the invisible efficacy of a mighty tendency to life. But would the ultimate contexture and miracle of things be made less arbitrary, and less a matter of brute fact, by the presence behind them of an actual and arbitrary effort that such should be their nature? If this word " effort " is not a mere figure of rhetoric, a name for a movement in things of which the end happens to interest us more than the beginning, if it is meant to be an effort actually and consciously existing, then we must proceed to ask: Why did this effort exist? Why did it choose that particular end to strive for? How did it reach the conception of that end, which had never been realised before, and which no existent nature demanded for its fulfilment? How did the effort, once made specific, select the particular matter it was to transform? Why did this matter respond to the disembodied effort that it should change its habits? Not one of these questions is easier to answer than the question why nature is living or animals have eyes. Yet without seeking to solve the only real problem, namely, how nature is actually constituted, this introduction of metaphysical powers raises all the others, artificially and without occasion. This side of M. Bergson's philosophy illustrates the worst and most familiar vices of metaphysics. It marvels at some appearance, not to investigate it, but to give it an unctuous name. Then it turns this name into a power, that by its operation creates the appearance. This is simply verbal mythology or the hypostasis of words, and there would be some excuse for a rude person who should call it rubbish.

The metaphysical abuse of psychology is as extraordinary in modern Europe as that of fancy ever was in India or of rhetoric in Greece. We find, for instance, Mr. Bradley murmuring, as a matter almost too obvious to mention, that the existence of anything not sentience is unmeaning to him; or, if I may put this evident principle in other words, that nothing is able to exist unless something else is able to discover it. Yet even if discovered the poor candidate for existence would be foiled, for it would turn out to be nothing but a modification of the mind falsely said to discover it. Existence and discovery are conceptions which the malicious criticism of knowledge (which is the psychology of knowledge abused) pretends to have discarded and outgrown altogether; the conception of immediacy has taken their place. This malicious criticism of knowledge is based on the silent assumption that knowledge is impossible. Whenever you mention anything, it baffles you by talking instead about your idea of what you mention; and if ever you describe the origin of anything it substitutes, as a counter-theory, its theory of the origin of your description. This, however, would not be a counter-theory at all if the criticism of knowledge had not been corrupted into a negative dogma, maintaining that ideas of things are the only things possible and that therefore only ideas and not things can have an origin. Nothing could better illustrate how deep this cognitive impotence has got into people's bones than the manner in which, in the latest schools of philosophy, it is being disavowed; for unblushing idealism is distinctly out of fashion. M. Bergson tells us he has solved a difficulty that seemed hopeless by avoiding a fallacy common to idealism and realism. The difficulty was that if you started with self-existent matter you could never arrive at mind, and if you started with self-existent mind you could never arrive at matter. The fallacy was that both schools innocently supposed there was an existing world to discover, and each thought it possible that its view should describe that world as it really was. What now is M. Bergson's solution? That no articulated world, either material or psychical, exists at all, but only a tendency or enduring effort to evolve images of both sorts; or rather to evolve images which in their finer texture and vibration are images of matter, but which grouped and foreshortened in various ways are images of minds. The idea of nature and the idea of consciousness are two apperceptions or syntheses of the same stuff of experience. The two worlds thus become substantially identical, continuous, and superposable; each can merge insensibly into the other. " To perceive all the influences of all the points of all bodies would be to sink to the condition of a material object." [1]   To

<hr>

[1] *Matière et Mémoire*, p. 38.

perceive some of these influences, by having created organs that shut out the others, is to be a mind.

This solution is obtained by substituting, as usual, the ideas of things for the things themselves and cheating the honest man who was talking about objects by answering him as if he were talking about himself. Certainly, if we could limit ourselves to feeling life flow and the whole world vibrate, we should not raise the question debated between realists and idealists; but not to raise a question is one thing and to have solved it is another. What has really been done is to offer us a history, *on the assumption of idealism,* of the idea of mind and the idea of matter. This history may be correct enough psychologically, and such as a student of the life of reason might possibly come to; but it is a mere evasion of the original question concerning the relation of this mental evolution to the world it occurs in. In truth, an enveloping world is assumed by these hereditary idealists not to exist; they rule it out *a priori,* and the life of reason is supposed by them to constitute the whole universe. To be sure, they say they transcend idealism no less than realism, because they mark the point where, by contrast or selection from other objects, the mind has come to be distinguished: but the subterfuge is vain, because by " mind " they mean simply the idea of mind, and they give no name, except perhaps experience, to the mind that forms that idea. Matter and mind, for these transcendentalists posing as realists, merge and flow so easily together only because both are images or groups of images in an original mind presupposed but never honestly posited. It is in this forgotten mind, also, as the professed idealists urge, that the relations of proximity and simultaneity between various lives can alone subsist, if to subsist is to be experienced.

There is, however, one point of real difference, at least initially, between the idealism of M. Bergson and that of his predecessors. The universal mind, for M. Bergson, is in process of actual transformation. It is not an omniscient God but a cosmic sensibility. In this sensibility matter, with all its vibrations felt in detail, forms one moving panorama together with all minds, which are patterns visible at will from various points of view in that same woof of matter; and so the great experiment crawls and shoots on, the dream of a giant without a body, mindful of the past, uncertain of the future, shuffling his images, and threading his painful way through a labyrinth of cross-purposes.

Such at least is the notion which the reader gathers from the prevailing character of M. Bergson's words; but I am not sure that it would be his ultimate conclusion. Perhaps it is to be out of sympathy with his spirit to speak of an ultimate conclusion at all; nothing comes to a conclusion and nothing is ultimate. Many dilemmas, however, are inevitable, and if the master does not make a choice himself, his pupils will divide and trace the alternative consequences for themselves in each direction. If they care most for a real fluidity, as William James did, they will stick to something like what I have just described; but if they care most for immediacy, as we may suspect that M. Bergson does, they will transform that view into something far more orthodox. For a real fluidity and an absolute immediacy are not com-

patible. To believe in real change you must put some
trust in representation, and if you posit a real past and
a real future you posit independent objects. In absolute
immediacy, on the contrary, instead of change taken
realistically, you can have only a feeling of change. The
flux becomes an idea in the absolute, like the image of
a moving spiral, always flowing outwards or inwards,
but with its centre and its circumference always immovable. Duration, we must remember, is simply the
sense of lasting; no time is real that is not lived through.
Therefore various lives cannot be dated in a common
time, but have no temporal relations to one another.
Thus, if we insist on immediacy, the vaunted novelty of
the future and the inestimable freedom of life threaten
to become (like all else) the given *feeling* of novelty or
freedom, in passing from a given image of the past to a
given image of the future—all these terms being contained in the present; and we have reverted to the
familiar conception of absolute immutability in absolute
life. M. Bergson has studied Plotinus and Spinoza; I
suspect he has not studied them in vain.

Nor is this the only point at which this philosophy,
when we live a while with it, suddenly drops its mask of
novelty and shows us a familiar face. It would seem,
for instance, that beneath the drama of creative evolution
there was a deeper nature of things. For apparently
creative evolution (apart from the obstacle of matter,
which may be explained away idealistically) has to submit
to the following conditions: first, to create in sequence,
not all at once; second, to create some particular
sequence only, not all possible sequences side by side;

and third, to continue the one sequence chosen, since if
the additions of every new moment were irrelevant to the
past, no sequence, no vital persistence or progress would
be secured, and all effort would be wasted.   These are
compulsions; but it may also, I suppose, be thought a
duty on the part of the vital impulse to be true to its initial
direction and not to halt, as it well might, like the self-
reversing Will of Schopenhauer, on perceiving the result
of its spontaneous efforts.   Necessity would thus appear
behind liberty and duty before it.   This summons to
life to go on, and these conditions imposed upon it, might
then very plausibly be attributed to a Deity existing
beyond the world, as is done in religious tradition; and
such a doctrine, if M. Bergson should happen to be holding it in reserve, would perhaps help to explain some
obscurities in his system, such, for instance, as the power
of potentiality to actualise itself, of equipoise to become
suddenly emphasis on one particular part, and of spirit
to pursue an end chosen before it is conceived, and when
there is no nature to predetermine it.

It has been said that M. Bergson's system precludes
ethics: I cannot think that observation just.   Apart
from the moral inspiration which appears throughout
his philosophy, which is indeed a passionate attempt to
exalt (or debase) values into powers, it offers, I should
say, two starting-points for ethics.   In the first place,
the *élan vital* ought not to falter, although it can do so:
therefore to persevere, labour, experiment, propagate,
must be duties, and the opposite must be sins.   In the
second place, freedom, in adding uncaused increments to
life, ought to do so in continuation of the whole past,

though it might do so frivolously: therefore it is a duty
to be studious, consecutive, loyal; you may move in
any direction but you must carry the whole past with
you. I will not say this suggests a sound system of
ethics, because it would be extracted from dogmas which
are physical and incidentally incredible; nor would it
represent a mature and disillusioned morality, because
it would look to the future and not to the eternal; nevertheless it would be deeply ethical, expressing the feelings
that have always inspired Hebraic morality.

A good way of testing the calibre of a philosophy is
to ask what it thinks of death. Philosophy, said Plato,
is a meditation on death, or rather, if we would do justice
to his thought, an aspiration to live disembodied; and
Schopenhauer said that the spectacle of death was the
first provocation to philosophy. M. Bergson has not
yet treated of this subject; but we may perhaps perceive for ourselves the place that it might occupy in his
system.[1] Life, according to him, is the original and
absolute force. In the beginning, however, it was only
a potentiality or tendency. To become specific lives,
life had to emphasise and bring exclusively to consciousness, here and there, special possibilities of living; and
where these special lives have their chosen boundary

---

[1] M. Bergson has shown at considerable length that the idea of non-
existence is more complex, psychologically, than the idea of existence,
and posterior to it. He evidently thinks this disposes of the reality
of non-existence also: for it is the reality that he wishes to exorcise
by his words. If, however, non-existence and the idea of non-existence
were identical, it would have been impossible for me not to exist before
I was born: my non-existence then would be more complex than my
existence now, and posterior to it. The initiated would not recoil
from this consequence, but it might open the eyes of some catechumens.
It is a good test of the malicious theory of knowledge.

(if this way of putting it is not too Fichtean) they posit or create a material environment. Matter is the view each life takes of what for it are rejected or abandoned possibilities of living. This might show how the absolute will to live, if it was to be carried out, would have to begin by evoking a sense of dead or material things about it; it would not show how death could ever overtake the will itself. If matter were merely the periphery which life has to draw round itself, in order to be a definite life, matter could never abolish any life; as the ring of a circus or the sand of the arena can never abolish the show for which they have been prepared. Life would then be fed and defined by matter, as an artist is served by the matter he needs to carry on his art.

Yet in actual life there is undeniably such a thing as danger and failure. M. Bergson even thinks that the facing of increased dangers is one proof that vital force is an absolute thing; for if life were an equilibrium, it would not displace itself and run new risks of death, by making itself more complex and ticklish, as it does in the higher organisms and the finer arts.[1] Yet if life is the only substance, how is such a risk of death possible at all? I suppose the special life that arises about a given nucleus of feeling, by emphasising some of the

[1] This argument against mechanism is a good instance of the difficulties which mythological habits of mind import unnecessarily into science. An equilibrium would not displace itself! But an equilibrium is a natural result, not a magical entity. It is continually displaced, as its constituents are modified by internal movements or external agencies; and while many a time the equilibrium is thereby destroyed altogether, sometimes it is replaced by a more elaborate and perilous equilibrium; as glaciers carry many rocks down, but leave some, here and there, piled in the most unlikely pinnacles and pagodas.

relations which that feeling has in the world, might be abolished if a greater emphasis were laid on another set of its relations, starting from some other nucleus. We must remember that these selections, according to M. Bergson, are not apperceptions merely. They are creative efforts. The future constitution of the flux will vary in response to them. Each mind sucks the world, so far as it can, into its own vortex. A cross apperception will then amount to a contrary force. Two souls will not be able to dominate the same matter in peace and friendship. Being forces, they will pull that matter in different ways. Each soul will tend to devour and to direct exclusively the movement influenced by the other soul. The one that succeeds in ruling that movement will live on; the other, I suppose, will die, although M. Bergson may not like that painful word. He says the lower organisms store energy for the higher organisms to use; but when a sheep appropriates the energy stored up in grass, or a man that stored up in mutton, it looks as if the grass and the sheep had perished. Their *élan vital* is no longer theirs, for in this rough world to live is to kill. Nothing arises in nature, Lucretius says, save helped by the death of some other thing. Of course, this is no defeat for the *élan vital* in general; for according to our philosopher the whole universe from the beginning has been making for just that supreme sort of consciousness which man, who eats the mutton, now possesses. The sheep and the grass were only things by the way and scaffolding for our precious humanity. But would it not be better if some being should arise nobler than man, not requiring abstract intellect nor artificial weapons, but endowed with instinct and intuition and, let us say, the power of killing by radiating electricity? And might not men then turn out to have been mere explosives, in which energy was stored for convenient digestion by that superior creature? A shocking thought, no doubt, like the thought of death, and more distressing to our vital feelings than is the pleasing assimilation of grass and mutton in our bellies. Yet I can see no ground, except a desire to flatter oneself, for not crediting the *élan vital* with some such digestive intention. M. Bergson's system would hardly be more speculative if it entertained this possibility, and it would seem more honest.

The vital impulse is certainly immortal; for if we take it in the naturalistic exoteric sense, for a force discovered in biology, it is an independent agent coming down into matter, organising it against its will, and stirring it like the angel the pool of Bethesda. Though the ripples die down, the angel is not affected. He has merely flown away. And if we take the vital impulse mystically and esoterically, as the *only* primal force, creating matter in order to play with it, the immortality of life is even more obvious; for there is then nothing else in being that could possibly abolish it. But when we come to immortality for the individual, all grows obscure and ambiguous. The original tendency of life was certainly cosmic and not distinguished into persons: we are told it was like a wireless message sent at the creation which is being read off at last by the humanity of to-day. In the naturalistic view, the diversity of persons would seem to be due to the different material conditions under which one and the same spiritual purpose must fight its way towards realisation in different times and places. It is quite conceivable, however, that in the mystical view the very sense of the original message should comport this variety of interpretations, and that the purpose should always have been to produce diverse individuals.

The first view, as usual, is the one which M. Bergson has prevailingly in mind, and communicates most plausibly; while he holds to it he is still talking about the natural world, and so we still know what he is talking about. On this view, however, personal immortality would be impossible; it would be, if it were aimed at, a self-contradiction in the aim of life; for the diversity of persons would be due to impediments only, and souls would differ simply in so far as they mutilated the message which they were all alike trying to repeat. They would necessarily, when the spirit was victorious, be reabsorbed and identified in the universal spirit. This view also seems most consonant with M. Bergson's theory of primitive reality, as a flux of fused images, or a mind lost in matter; to this view, too, is attributable his hostility to intelligence, in that it arrests the flux, divides the fused images, and thereby murders and devitalises reality. Of course the destiny of spirit would not be to revert to that diffused materiality; for the original mind lost in matter had a very short memory; it was a sort of cosmic trepidation only, whereas the ultimate mind would remember all that, in its efforts after freedom, it had ever superadded to that trepidation or made it turn into. Even the abstract views of things taken by the practical intellect would, I fear, have to burden the universal memory to the end. We should be remembered, even if we could no longer exist.

On the other more profound view, however, might not personal immortality be secured? Suppose the original message said: Translate me into a thousand tongues! In fulfilling its duty, the universe would then continue to divide its dream into phantom individuals; as it had to insulate its parts in the beginning in order to dominate and transform them freely, so it would always continue to insulate them, so as not to lose its cross-vistas and its mobility. There is no reason, then, why individuals should not live for ever. But a condition seems to be involved which may well make belief stagger. It would be impossible for the universe to divide its images into particular minds unless it preserved the images of their particular bodies also. Particular minds arise, according to this philosophy, in the interests of practice: which means, biologically, to secure a better adjustment of the body to its environment, so that it may survive. Mystically, too, the fundamental force is a half-conscious purpose that practice, or freedom, should come to be; or rather, that an apparition or experience of practice and freedom should arise; for in this philosophy appearance is all. To secure this desirable apparition of practice special tasks are set to various nuclei in felt space (such, for instance, as the task to *see*), and the image of a body (in this case that of an eye) is gradually formed, in order to execute that task; for evidently the Absolute can see only if it looks, and to look it must first choose a point of view and an optical method. This point of view and this method posit the individual; they fix him in time and space, and determine the quality and range of his passive experience: they are his body. If the Absolute, then, wishes to retain the individual not merely as one of its memories but as one of its organs of practical life, it must begin by retaining the image of his body. His body must continue to figure in that landscape of nature which the absolute life, as it pulses, keeps always composing and recomposing. Otherwise a personal mind, a sketch of things made from the point of view and in the interests of that body, cannot be preserved.

M. Bergson, accordingly, should either tell us that our bodies are going to rise again, or he should not tell us, or give us to understand, that our minds are going to endure. I suppose he cannot venture to preach the resurrection of the body to this weak-kneed generation; he is too modern and plausible for that. Yet he is too amiable to deny to our dilated nostrils some voluptuous whiffs of immortality. He asks if we are not " led to suppose " that consciousness passes through matter to be tempered like steel, to constitute distinct personalities, and prepare them for a higher existence. Other animal minds are but human minds arrested; men at last (what men, I wonder?) are " capable of remembering all and willing all and controlling their past and their future," so that " we shall have no repugnance in admitting that in man, though perhaps in man alone, consciousness pursues its path beyond this earthly life." Elsewhere he says, in a phrase already much quoted and perhaps destined to be famous, that in man the spirit can "spurn every kind of resistance and break through many an obstacle, perhaps even death." Here the tenor has ended on the inevitable high note, and the gallery is delighted. But was that the note set down for him in the music? And has he not sung it in falsetto?

The immediate knows nothing about death; it takes intelligence to conceive it; and that perhaps is why M. Bergson says so little about it, and that little so far from serious. But he talks a great deal about life, he feels he has penetrated deeply into its nature; and yet death, together with birth, is the natural analysis of what life is. What is this creative purpose, that must wait for sun and rain to set it in motion? What is this life, that in any individual can be suddenly extinguished by a bullet? What is this *élan vital*, that a little fall in temperature would banish altogether from the universe? The study of death may be out of fashion, but it is never out of season. The omission of this, which is almost the omission of wisdom from philosophy, warns us that in M. Bergson's thought we have something occasional and partial, the work of an astute apologist, a party man, driven to desperate speculation by a timid attachment to prejudice. Like other terrified idealisms, the system of M. Bergson has neither good sense, nor rigour, nor candour, nor solidity. It is a brilliant attempt to confuse the lessons of experience by refining upon its texture, an attempt to make us halt, for the love of primitive illusions, in the path of discipline and reason. It is likely to prove a successful attempt, because it flatters the weaknesses of the moment, expresses them with emotion, and covers them with a feint at scientific speculation. It is not, however, a powerful system, like that of Hegel, capable of bewildering and obsessing many who have no natural love for shams. M. Bergson will hardly bewilder; his style is too clear, the field where his just observations lie—the immediate—is too well defined, and the mythology which results from projecting the terms of the immediate into the absolute, and turning them into powers, is too obviously verbal. He will not long impose on any save those who enjoy being imposed upon; but for a long time he may increase their number. His doctrine is indeed alluring. Instead of telling us, as a stern and contrite philosophy would, that the truth is remote, difficult, and almost undiscoverable by human efforts, that the universe is vast and unfathomable, yet that the knowledge of its ways is precious to our better selves, if we would not live befooled, this philosophy rather tells us that nothing is truer or more precious than our rudimentary consciousness, with its vague instincts and premonitions, that everything ideal is fictitious, and that the universe, at heart, is as palpitating and irrational as ourselves. Why then strain the inquiry? Why seek to dominate passion by understanding it? Rather live on; work, it matters little at what, and grow, it matters nothing in what direction. Exert your instinctive powers of vegetation and emotion; let your philosophy itself be a frank expression of this flux, the roar of the ocean in your little sea-shell, a momentary posture of your living soul, not a stark adoration of things reputed eternal.

So the intellectual faithlessness and the material

servility of the age are flattered together and taught to justify themselves theoretically. They cry joyfully, *non peccavi*, which is the modern formula for confession. M. Bergson's philosophy itself is a confession of a certain mystical rebellion and atavism in the contemporary mind. It will remain a beautiful monument to the passing moment, a capital film for the cinematograph of history, full of psychological truth and of a kind of restrained sentimental piety. His thought has all the charm that can go without strength and all the competence that can go without mastery. This is not an age of mastery; it is confused with too much business; it has no brave simplicity. The mind has forgotten its proper function, which is to crown life by quickening it into intelligence, and thinks if it could only prove that it accelerated life, that might perhaps justify its existence; like a philosopher at sea who, to make himself useful, should blow into the sail.

IV

THE PHILOSOPHY OF MR. BERTRAND RUSSELL

I. A NEW SCHOLASTICISM

IN its chase after idols this age has not wholly forgotten the gods, and reason and faith in reason are not left without advocates. Some years ago, at Trinity College, Cambridge, Mr. G. E. Moore began to produce a very deep impression amongst the younger spirits by his powerful and luminous dialectic. Like Socrates, he used all the sharp arts of a disputant in the interests of common sense and of an almost archaic dogmatism. Those who heard him felt how superior his position was, both in rigour and in force, to the prevailing inversions and idealisms. The abuse of psychology, rampant for two hundred years, seemed at last to be detected and challenged; and the impressionistic rhetoric that philosophy was saturated with began to be squeezed out by clear questions, and by a disconcerting demand for literal sincerity. German idealism, when we study it as a product of its own age and country, is a most engaging phenomenon; it is full of afflatus, sweep, and deep searchings of heart; but it is essentially romantic and egotistical, and all in it that is not soliloquy is mere system-making and sophistry. Therefore when it is taught by unromantic people *ex cathedra*, in stentorian tones, and represented as the rational foundation of science and religion, with neither of which it has any honest sympathy, it becomes positively odious—one of the worst impostures and blights to which a youthful imagination could be subjected. It is chiefly against the incubus of this celestial monster that Mr. Moore dared to lift up his eyes; and many a less courageous or less clear-sighted person was thankful to him for it. But a man with such a mission requires a certain narrowness and concentration of mind; he has to be intolerant and to pound a good deal on the same notes. We need not wonder if Mr. Moore has written rather meagrely, and with a certain vehemence and want of imagination.

All this, however, was more than made up for by the powerful ally who soon came to his aid. Mr. Bertrand Russell began by adopting Mr. Moore's metaphysics, but he has given as much as he has received. Apart from his well-known mathematical attainments, he possesses by inheritance the political and historical mind, and an intrepid determination to pierce convention and look to ultimate things. He has written abundantly and, where the subject permits, with a singular lucidity, candour, and charm. Especially his *Philosophical Essays* and his little book on *The Problems of Philosophy* can be read with pleasure by any intelligent person, and give a tolerably rounded picture of the tenets of the school. Yet it must be remembered that Mr. Russell, like Mr. Moore, is still young and his thoughts have not assumed their ultimate form. Moreover, he lives in an atmosphere of academic disputation which makes one technical point after another acquire a preponderating influence in his thoughts.

His book on *The Problems of Philosophy* is admirable in style, temper, and insight, but it hardly deserves its title; it treats principally, in a somewhat personal and partial way, of the relation of knowledge to its objects, and it might rather have been called " The problems which Moore and I have been agitating lately." Indeed, his philosophy is so little settled as yet that every new article and every fresh conversation revokes some of his former opinions, and places the crux of philosophical controversy at a new point. We are soon made aware that exact thinking and true thinking are not synonymous, but that one exact thought, in the same mind, may be the exact opposite of the next. This inconstancy, which after all does not go very deep, is a sign of sincerity and pure love of truth; it marks the freshness, the vivacity, the self-forgetfulness, the logical ardour belonging to this delightful reformer. It may seem a paradox, but at bottom it is not, that the vitalists should be oppressed, womanish, and mystical, and only the intellectualists keen, argumentative, fearless, and full of life. I mention this casualness and inconstancy in Mr. Russell's utterances not to deride them, but to show the reader how impossible it is, at this juncture, to give a comprehensive account of his philosophy, much less a final judgment upon it.

The principles most fundamental and dominant in his thought are perhaps the following: That the objects the mind deals with, whether material or ideal, are what and where the mind says they are, and independent of it; that some general principles and ideas have to be assumed to be valid not merely for thought but for things; that relations may subsist, arise, and disappear between things without at all affecting these things internally; and that the nature of everything is just what it is, and not to be confused either with its origin or with any opinion about it. These principles, joined with an obvious predilection for Plato and Leibnitz among philosophers, lead to the following doctrines, among others: that the mind or soul is an entity separate from its thoughts and pre-existent; that a material world exists in space and time; that its substantial elements may be infinite in number, having position and quality, but no extension, so that each mind or soul might well be one of them; that both the existent and the ideal worlds may be infinite, while the ideal world contains an infinity of things not realised in the actual world; and that this ideal world is knowable by a separate mental consideration, a consideration which is, however, empirical in spirit, since the ideal world of ethics, logic, and mathematics has a special and surprising constitution, which we do not make but must attentively discover.

The reader will perceive, perhaps, that if the function of philosophy is really, as the saying goes, to give us assurance of God, freedom, and immortality, Mr. Russell's philosophy is a dire failure. In fact, its author sometimes gives vent to a rather emphatic pessimism about this world; he has a keen sense for the manifold absurdities of existence. But the sense for absurdities is not without its delights, and Mr. Russell's satirical wit is more constant and better grounded than his despair. I should be inclined to say of his philosophy what he himself has said of that of Leibnitz, that it is at its best in those subjects which are most remote from human life. It needs to be very largely supplemented and much ripened and humanised before it can be called satisfactory or wise; but time may bring these fulfilments, and meantime I cannot help thinking it auspicious in the highest degree that, in a time of such impressionistic haste and plebeian looseness of thought, scholastic rigour should suddenly raise its head again, aspiring to seriousness, solidity, and perfection of doctrine: and this not in the interests of religious orthodoxy, but precisely in the most emancipated and unflinchingly radical quarter. It is refreshing and reassuring, after the confused, melodramatic ways of philosophising to which the idealists and the pragmatists have accustomed us, to breathe again the crisp air of scholastic common sense. It is good for us to be held down, as the Platonic Socrates would have held us, to saying what we really believe, and sticking to what we say. We seem to regain our intellectual birthright when we are allowed to declare our genuine intent, even in philosophy, instead of begging some kind psychologist to investigate our " meaning " for us, or even waiting for the flux of events to endow us with what " meaning " it will. It is also instructive to have the ethical attitude purified of all that is not ethical and turned explicitly into what, in its moral capacity, it essentially is: a groundless pronouncement upon the better and the worse.

Here a certain one-sidedness begins to make itself felt in Mr. Russell's views. The ethical attitude doubtless has no *ethical* ground, but that fact does not prevent it from having a *natural* ground; and the observer of the animate creation need not have much difficulty in seeing what that natural ground is. Mr. Russell, however, refuses to look also in that direction. He insists, rightly enough, that good is predicated categorically by the conscience; he will not remember that all life is not moral bias merely, and that, in the very act of recognising excellence and pursuing it, we may glance back over our shoulder and perceive how our moral bias is conditioned, and what basis it has in the physical order of things. This backward look, when the hand is on the plough, may indeed confuse our ethical self-expression, both in theory and in practice; and I am the last to deny the need of insisting, in ethics, on ethical judgments in all their purity and dogmatic sincerity. Such insistence, if we had heard more of it in our youth, might have saved many of us from chronic entanglements; and there is nothing, next to Plato, which ought to be more recommended to the young philosopher than the teachings of Messrs. Russell and Moore, if he wishes to be a moralist and a logician, and not merely to seem one. Yet this salutary doctrine, though correct, is inadequate. It is a monocular philosophy, seeing outlines clear, but missing the solid bulk and perspective of things. We need binocular vision to quicken the whole mind and yield a full image of reality. Ethics should be controlled by a physics that perceives the material ground and the relative status of whatever is moral. Otherwise ethics itself tends to grow narrow, strident, and fanatical; as may be observed in asceticism and puritanism, or, for the matter of that, in Mr. Moore's uncivilised leaning towards the doctrine of retributive punishment, or in

Mr. Russell's intolerance of selfishness and patriotism, and in his refusal to entertain any pious reverence for the nature of things. The quality of wisdom, like that of mercy, is not strained. To choose, to love and hate, to have a moral life, is inevitable and legitimate in the part; but it is the function of the part as part, and we must keep it in its place if we wish to view the whole in its true proportions. Even to express justly the aim of our own life we need to retain a constant sympathy with what is animal and fundamental in it, else we shall give a false place, and too loud an emphasis, to our definitions of the ideal. However, it would be much worse not to reach the ideal at all, or to confuse it for want of courage and sincerity in uttering our true mind; and it is in uttering our true mind that Mr. Russell can help us, even if our true mind should not always coincide with his.

In the following pages I do not attempt to cover all Mr. Russell's doctrine (the deeper mathematical parts of it being beyond my comprehension), and the reader will find some speculations of my own interspersed in what I report of his. I merely traverse after him three subjects that seem of imaginative interest, to indicate the inspiration and the imprudences, as I think them, of this young philosophy.

II. THE STUDY OF ESSENCE

" The solution of the difficulties which formerly surrounded the mathematical infinite is probably," says Mr. Russell, " the greatest achievement of which our own age has to boast. . . . It was assumed as self-evident, until Cantor and Dedekind established the opposite, that if, from any collection of things, some were taken away, the number of things left must always be less than the original number of things. This assumption, as a matter of fact, holds only of finite collections; and the rejection of it, where the infinite is concerned, has been shown to remove all the difficulties that hitherto baffled human reason in this matter." And he adds in another place: " To reconcile us, by the exhibition of its awful beauty, to the reign of Fate . . . is the task of tragedy. But mathematics takes us still further from what is human, into the region of absolute necessity, to which not only the actual world, but every possible world, must conform; and even here it builds a habitation, or rather finds a habitation eternally standing, where our ideals are fully satisfied and our best hopes are not thwarted. It is only when we thoroughly understand the entire independence of ourselves, which belongs to this world that reason finds, that we can adequately realise the profound importance of its beauty."

Mathematics seems to have a value for Mr. Russell akin to that of religion. It affords a sanctuary to which to flee from the world, a heaven suffused with a serene radiance and full of a peculiar sweetness and consolation. " Real life," he writes, " is to most men a long second-best, a perpetual compromise between the ideal and the possible; but the world of pure reason knows no compromise, no practical limitations, no barrier to the creative activity embodying in splendid edifices the passionate aspiration after the perfect from which all great work springs. Remote from human passions, remote even from the pitiful laws of nature, the generations have gradually created an ordered cosmos where pure thought can dwell as in its natural home, and where one, at least, of our nobler impulses can escape from the dreary exile of the actual world." This study is one of "those elements in human life which merit a place in heaven." "The true spirit of delight, the exaltation, the sense of being more than man, which is the touchstone of the highest excellence, is to be found in mathematics as surely as in poetry."

This enthusiastic language might have, I should think, an opposite effect upon some readers to that which Mr. Russell desires. It might make them suspect that the claim to know an absolute ideal necessity, so satisfying to one of our passionate impulses, might be prompted by the same conceit, and subject to the same illusion, as the claim to know absolute truth in religion. Beauty, when attributed to necessary relations between logical entities, casts a net of subjectivity over them; and at this net the omnivorous empiricist might be tempted to haul, until he fancied he had landed the whole miraculous draught of fishes. The fish, however, would have slipped through the meshes; and it would be only his own vital emotion, projected for a moment into the mathematical world, that he would be able to draw back and hug to his bosom. Eternal truth is as disconsolate as it is consoling, and as dreary as it is interesting: these moral values are, in fact, values which the activity of contemplating that sort of truth has for different minds; and it is no congruous homage offered to ideal necessity, but merely a private endearment, to call it beautiful or good. The case is not such as if we were dealing with existence. Existence is arbitrary; it is a questionable thing needing justification; and we, at least, cannot justify it otherwise than by taking note of some affinity which it may show to human aspirations. Therefore our private endearments, when we call some existing thing good or beautiful, are not impertinent; they assign to this chance thing its only assignable excuse for being, namely, the service it may chance to render to the spirit. But ideal necessity or, what is the same thing, essential possibility has its excuse for being in itself, since it is not contingent or questionable at all. The affinity which the human mind may develop to certain provinces of essence is adventitious to those essences, and hardly to be mentioned in their presence. It is something the mind has acquired, and may lose. It is an incident in the life of reason, and no inherent characteristic of eternal necessity.

The realm of essence contains the infinite multitude of Leibnitz's possible worlds, many of these worlds being very small and simple, and consisting merely of what might be presented in some isolated moment of feeling. If any such feeling, however, or its object, never in fact occurs, the essence that it would have presented if it had occurred remains possible merely; so that nothing can ever exist in nature or for consciousness which has not a prior and independent locus in the realm of essence. When a man lights upon a thought or is interested in tracing a relation, he does not introduce those objects into the realm of essence, but merely selects them from the plenitude of what lies there eternally. The ground of this selection lies, of course, in his human nature and circumstances; and the satisfaction he may find in so exercising his mind will be a consequence of his mental disposition and of the animal instincts beneath. Two and two would still make four if I were incapable of counting, or if I found it extremely painful to do so, or if I thought it naïve and pre-Kantian of these numbers not to combine in a more vital fashion, and make five. So also, if I happen to enjoy counting, or to find the constancy of numbers sublime, and the reversibility of the processes connecting them consoling, in contrast to the irrevocable flux of living things, all this is due to my idiosyncrasy. It is no part of the essence of numbers to be congenial to me; but it has perhaps become a part of my genius to have affinity to them.

And how, may I ask, has it become a part of my genius? Simply because nature, of which I am a part, and to which all my ideas must refer if they are to be relevant to my destiny, happens to have mathematical form. Nature had to have some form or other, if it was to exist at all; and whatever form it had happened to take would have had its prior place in the realm of essence, and its essential and logical relations there. That particular part of the realm of essence which nature chances to exemplify or to suggest is the part that may be revealed to me, and that is the predestined focus of all my admirations. Essence as such has no power to reveal itself, or to take on existence; and the human mind has no power or interest to trace all essence. Even the few essences which it has come to know, it cannot undertake to examine exhaustively; for there are many features nestling in them, and many relations radiating from them, which no one needs or cares to attend to. The implications which logicians and mathematicians actually observe in the terms they use are a small selection from all those that really obtain, even in their chosen field; so that, for instance, as Mr. Russell was telling us, it was only the other day that Cantor and Dedekind observed that although time continually eats up the days and years, the possible future always remains as long as it was before. This happens to be a fact interesting to mankind. Apart from the mathematical puzzles it may help to solve, it opens before existence a vista of perpetual youth, and the vital stress in us leaps up in recognition of its inmost ambition. Many other things are doubtless implied in infinity which, if we noticed them, would leave us quite cold; and still others, no doubt, are inapprehensible with our sort and degree of intellect. There is of course nothing in essence which an intellect postulated *ad hoc* would not be able to apprehend; but the kind of intellect we know of and possess is an expression of vital adjustments, and is tethered to nature.

That a few eternal essences, then, with a few of their necessary relations to one another, do actually appear to us, and do fascinate our attention and excite our wonder, is nothing paradoxical. This is merely what was bound to happen, if we became aware of anything at all; for the essence embodied in anything is eternal and has necessary relations to some other essences. The air of presumption which there might seem to be in proclaiming that mathematics reveals what has to be true always and everywhere, vanishes when we remember that everything that is true of any essence is true of it always and everywhere. The most trivial truths of logic are as necessary and eternal as the most important; so that it is less of an achievement than it sounds when we say we have grasped a truth that is eternal and necessary.

This fact will be more clearly recognised, perhaps, if we remember that the cogency of our ideal knowledge follows upon our intent in fixing its object. It hangs on a virtual definition, and explicates it. We cannot oblige anybody or anything to reproduce the idea which we have chosen; but that idea will remain the idea it is whether forgotten or remembered, exemplified or not exemplified in things. To penetrate to the foundation of being is possible for us only because the foundation of being is distinguishable quality; were there no set of differing characteristics, one or more of which an existing thing might appropriate, existence would be altogether impossible. The realm of essence is merely the system or chaos of these fundamental possibilities, the catalogue of all exemplifiable natures; so that any experience whatsoever must tap the realm of essence, and throw the light of attention on one of its constituent forms. This is, if you will, a trivial achievement; what would be really a surprising feat, and hardly to be credited, would be that the human mind should grasp the *constitution of nature ;* that is, should discover which is the particular essence, or the particular system of essences, which actual existence illustrates. In the matter of physics, truly, we are reduced to skimming the surface, since we have to start from our casual experiences, which form the most superficial stratum of nature, and the most unstable. Yet these casual experiences, while they leave us so much in the dark as to their natural basis and environment, necessarily reveal each its ideal object, its specific essence; and we need only arrest our attention upon it, and define it to ourselves, for an eternal possibility, and some of its intrinsic characters, to have been revealed to our thought.

Whatever, then, a man's mental and moral habit might be, it would perforce have affinity to some essence or other; his life would revolve about some congenial ideal object; he would find some sorts of form, some types of relation, more visible, beautiful, and satisfying than others. Mr. Russell happens to have a mathematical genius, and to find comfort in laying up his treasures in the mathematical heaven. It would be highly desirable that this temperament should be more common; but even if it were universal it would not reduce mathematical essence to a product of human attention, nor raise the " beauty " of mathematics to part of its essence. I do not mean to suggest that Mr. Russell attempts to do the latter; he speaks explicitly of the *value* of mathematical study, a point in ethics and not directly in logic; yet his moral philosophy is itself so much assimilated to logic that the distinction between the two becomes somewhat dubious; and as Mr. Russell will never succeed in convincing us that moral values are independent of life, he may, quite against his will, lead us to question the independence of essence, with that blind gregarious drift of all ideas, in this direction or in that, which is characteristic of human philosophising.

III. THE CRITIQUE OF PRAGMATISM

The time has not yet come when a just and synthetic account of what is called pragmatism can be expected of any man. The movement is still in a nebulous state, a state from which, perhaps, it is never destined to issue. The various tendencies that compose it may soon cease to appear together; each may detach itself and be lost in the earlier system with which it has most affinity. A good critic has enumerated " Thirteen Pragmatisms; " and besides such distinguishable tenets, there are in pragmatism echoes of various popular moral forces, like democracy, impressionism, love of the concrete, respect for success, trust in will and action, and the habit of relying on the future, rather than on the past, to justify one's methods and opinions. Most of these things are characteristically American; and Mr. Russell touches on some of them with more wit than sympathy. Thus he writes: " The influence of democracy in promoting pragmatism is visible in almost every page of William James's writing. There is an impatience of authority, an unwillingness to condemn widespread prejudices, a tendency to decide philosophical questions by putting them to a vote, which contrast curiously with the usual dictatorial tone of philosophic writings. . . . A thing which simply *is* true, whether you like it or not, is to him as hateful as a Russian autocracy; he feels that he is escaping from a prison, made not by stone walls but by ' hard facts,' when he has humanised truth, and made it, like the police force in a democracy, the servant of the people instead of their master. The democratic temper pervades even the religion of the pragmatists; they have the religion they have chosen, and the traditional reverence is changed into satisfaction with their own handiwork. ' The prince of darkness,' James says, ' may be a gentleman, as we are told he is, but whatever the God of earth and heaven is, he can surely be no gentleman.' He is rather, we should say, conceived by pragmatists as an elected president, to whom we give a respect which is really a tribute to the wisdom of our own choice. A government in which we have no voice is repugnant to the democratic temper. William James carries up to heaven the revolt of his New England ancestors: the Power to which we can yield respect must be a George Washington rather than a George III."

A point of fundamental importance, about which pragmatists have been far from clear, and perhaps not in agreement with one another, is the sense in which their psychology is to be taken. " The facts that fill the imaginations of pragmatists," Mr. Russell writes, " are psychical facts; where others might think of the starry heavens, pragmatists think of the perception of the starry heavens; where others think of God, pragmatists think of the belief in God, and so on. In discussing the sciences, they never think, like scientific specialists, about the facts upon which scientific theories are based; they think about the theories themselves. Thus their initial question and their habitual imaginative background are both psychological." This is so true that unless we make the substitution into psychic terms instinctively, the whole pragmatic view of things will seem paradoxical, if not actually unthinkable. For instance, pragmatists might protest against the accusation that "they never think about the facts upon which scientific theories are based," for they lay a great emphasis on facts. Facts are the cash which the credit of theories hangs upon. Yet this protest, though sincere, would be inconclusive, and in the end it would illustrate Mr. Russell's observation, rather than refute it. For we should presently learn that these facts can be made by thinking, that our faith in them may contribute to their reality, and may modify their nature; in other words, these facts are our immediate apprehensions of fact, which it is indeed conceivable that our temperaments, expectations, and opinions should modify. Thus the pragmatist's reliance on facts does not carry him beyond the psychic sphere; his facts are only his personal experiences. Personal experiences may well be the basis for no less personal myths; but the effort of intelligence and of science is rather to find the basis of the personal experiences themselves; and this non-psychic basis of experience is what common sense calls the facts, and what practice is concerned with. Yet these are not the *pragmata* of the pragmatist, for it is only the despicable intellectualist that can arrive at them; and the bed-rock of facts that the pragmatist builds upon is avowedly drifting sand. Hence the odd expressions, new to literature and even to grammar, which bubble up continually in pragmatist writings. "For illustration take the former fact that the earth is flat," says one, quite innocently; and another observes that "two centuries later, nominalism was evidently true, because it alone would legitimise the local independence of cities." Lest we should suppose that the historical sequence of these " truths " or illusions is, at least, fixed and irreversible, we are soon informed that the past is always changing, too; that is (if I may rationalise this mystical dictum), that history is always being rewritten, and that the growing present adds new relations to the past, which lead us to conceive or to describe it in some new fashion. Even if the ultimate inference is not drawn, and we are not told that this changing idea of the past is the only past that exists—the real past being unattainable and therefore, for personal idealism, non-existent—it is abundantly clear that the effort to distinguish fact from theory cannot be successful, so long as the psychological way of thinking prevails; for a theory, psychologically considered, is a bare fact in the experience of the theorist, and the other facts of his experience are so many other momentary views, so many scant theories, to be immediately superseded by other " truths in the plural." Sensations and ideas are really distinguishable only by reference to what is assumed to lie without; of which external reality experience is always an effect (and in that capacity is called sensation) and often at the same time an apprehension (and in that capacity is called idea).

It is a crucial question, then, in the interpretation of pragmatism, whether the psychological point of view, undoubtedly prevalent in that school, is the only or the ultimate point of view which it admits. The habit of studying ideas rather than their objects might be simply a matter of emphasis or predilection. It might merely indicate a special interest in the life of reason, and be an effort, legitimate under any system of philosophy, to recount the stages by which human thought, developing in the bosom of nature, may have reached its present degree of articulation. I myself, for instance, like to look at things from this angle: not that I have ever doubted the reality of the natural world, or been able to take very seriously any philosophy that denied it, but precisely because, when we take the natural world for granted, it becomes a possible and enlightening inquiry to ask how the human animal has come to discover his real environment, in so far as he has done so, and what dreams have intervened or supervened in the course of his rational awakening. On the other hand, a psychological point of view might be equivalent to the idealistic doctrine that the articulation of human thought constitutes the only structure of the universe, and its whole history. According to this view, pragmatism would seem to be a revised version of the transcendental logic, leaving logic still transcendental, that is, still concerned with the evolution of the categories. The revision would consist chiefly in this, that empirical verification, utility, and survival would take the place of dialectical irony as the force governing the evolution. It would still remain possible for other methods of approach than this transcendental pragmatism, for instinct, perhaps, or for revelation, to bring us into contact with things-in-themselves. A junction might thus be effected with the system of M. Bergson, which would lead to this curious result: that pragmatic logic would be the method of intelligence, because intelligence is merely a method, useful in practice, for the symbolic and improper representation of reality; while another non-pragmatic method—sympathy and dream—would alone be able to put us in possession of direct knowledge and genuine truth. So that, after all, the pragmatic " truth " of working ideas would turn out to be what it has seemed hitherto to mankind, namely, no real truth, but rather a convenient sort of fiction, which ceases to deceive when once its merely pragmatic value is discounted by criticism.

I remember once putting a question on this subject to Professor James; and his answer was one which I am glad to be able to record. In relation to his having said that " as far as the past facts go, there is no difference . . . be the atoms or be the God their cause," [1] I asked whether, if God had been the cause, apart from the value of the idea of him in our calculations, his existence would not have made a difference to *him*, as he would be presumably self-conscious. " Of course," said Professor James, " but I wasn't considering that side of the matter; I was thinking of our idea." The choice of the subjective point of view, then, was deliberate here, and frankly arbitrary; it was not intended to exclude the possibility or legitimacy of the objective attitude. And the original reason for deliberately ignoring, in this way, the realistic way of thinking, even while admitting that it represents the real state of affairs, would have been, I suppose, that what could be verified was always some further effect of the real objects, and never those real objects themselves; so that for interpreting and predicting our personal experience only the hypothesis of objects was pertinent, while the objects themselves, except as so represented, were

[1] *Pragmatism*, p. 101.

useless and unattainable.   The case, if I may adapt a
comparison of Mr. Russell's, was as if we possessed a
catalogue of the library at Alexandria, all the books being
lost for ever; it would be only in the catalogue that we
could practically verify their existence or character,
though doubtless, by some idle flight of imagination, we
might continue to think of the books, as well as of those
titles in the catalogue which alone could appear to us
in experience.   Pragmatism, approached from this side,
would then seem to express an acute critical conscience,
a sort of will not to believe; not to believe, I mean, more
than is absolutely necessary for solipsistic practice.

Such economical faith, enabling one to dissolve the
hard materialistic world into a work of mind, which mind
might outflank, was traditional in the radical Emersonian
circles in which pragmatism sprang up.   It is one of the
approaches to the movement; yet we may safely regard
the ancestral transcendentalism of the pragmatists as
something which they have turned their back upon, and
mean to disown.   It is destined to play no part in the
ultimate result of pragmatism.   This ultimate result
promises to be, on the contrary, a direct materialistic sort
of realism.   This alone is congruous with the scientific
affinities of the school and its young-American temper.
Nor is the transformation very hard to effect.   The world
of solipsistic practice, if you remove the romantic self
that was supposed to evoke it, becomes at once the
sensible world; and the problem is only to find a place
in the mosaic of objects of sensation for those cognitive
and moral functions which the soul was once supposed to
exercise in the presence of an independent reality.   But

this problem is precisely the one that pragmatists boast they have already solved; for they have declared that consciousness does not exist, and that objects of sensation (which at first were called feelings, experiences, or " truths ") know or mean one another when they lead to one another, when they are poles, so to speak, in the same vital circuit. The spiritual act which was supposed to take things for its object is to be turned into " objective spirit," that is, into dynamic relations between things. The philosopher will deny that he has any other sort of mind himself, lest he should be shut up in it again, like a sceptical and disconsolate child; while if there threatens to be any covert or superfluous reality in the self-consciousness of God, nothing will be easier than to deny that God is self-conscious; for indeed, if there is no consciousness on earth, why should we imagine that there is any in heaven? The psychologism with which the pragmatists started seems to be passing in this way, in the very effort to formulate it pragmatically, into something which, whatever it may be, is certainly not psychologism. But the bewildered public may well ask whether it is pragmatism either.

There is another crucial point in pragmatism which the defenders of the system are apt to pass over lightly, but which Mr. Russell regards (justly, I think) as of decisive importance. Is, namely, the pragmatic account of truth intended to cover all knowledge, or one kind of knowledge only? Apparently the most authoritative pragmatists admit that it covers one kind only; for there are two sorts of self-evidence in which, they say, it is not concerned: first, the dialectical relation between essences;

and second, the known occurrence or experience of facts.
There are obvious reasons why these two kinds of cog-
nitions, so interesting to Mr. Russell, are not felt by
pragmatists to constitute exceptions worth considering.
Dialectical relations, they will say, are verbal only; that
is, they define ideal objects, and certainty in these cases
does not coerce existence, or touch contingent fact at all.
On the other hand, such apprehension as seizes on some
matter of fact, as, for instance, " I feel pain," or " I
expected to feel this pain, and it is now verifying my
expectation," though often true propositions, are not
theoretical truths; they are not, it is supposed, questionable beliefs but rather immediate observations. Yet
many of these apprehensions of fact (or all, perhaps, if
we examine them scrupulously) involve the veracity of
memory, surely a highly questionable sort of truth; and,
moreover, verification, the pragmatic test of truth, would
be obviously impossible to apply, if the prophecy supposed
to be verified were not assumed to be truly remembered.
How shall we know that our expectation is fulfilled, if
we do not know directly that we had such an expectation?
But if we know our past experience directly—not merely
knew it when present, but know now what it was, and
how it has led down to the present—this amounts to
enough knowledge to make up a tolerable system of the
universe, without invoking pragmatic verification or
" truth " at all. I have never been able to discover
whether, by that perception of fact which is not " truth "
but fact itself, pragmatists meant each human apprehension taken singly, or the whole series of these apprehensions. In the latter case, as in the philosophy of

M. Bergson, all past reality might constantly lie open to retentive intuition, a form of knowledge soaring quite over the head of any pragmatic method or pragmatic " truth." It looks, indeed, as if the history of at least personal experience were commonly taken for granted by pragmatists, as a basis on which to rear their method. Their readiness to make so capital an assumption is a part of their heritage from romantic idealism. To the romantic idealist science and theology are tales which ought to be reduced to an empirical equivalent in his personal experience; but the tale of his personal experience itself is a sacred figment, the one precious conviction of the romantic heart, which it would be heartless to question. Yet here is a kind of assumed truth which cannot be reduced to its pragmatic meaning, because it must be true literally in order that the pragmatic meaning of other beliefs may be conceived or tested at all.

Now, if it be admitted that the pragmatic theory of truth does not touch our knowledge either of matters of fact or of the necessary implications of ideas, the question arises: What sort of knowledge remains for pragmatic theory to apply to? Simply, Mr. Russell answers, those "working hypotheses" to which "prudent people give only a low degree of belief." For "we hold different beliefs with very different degrees of conviction. Some—such as the belief that I am sitting in a chair, or that $2+2=4$—can be doubted by few except those who have had a long training in philosophy. Such beliefs are held so firmly that non-philosophers who deny them are put into lunatic asylums. Other beliefs, such as the facts of history, are held rather less firmly. . . . Beliefs about the future, as that the sun will rise to-morrow and that the trains will run approximately as in Bradshaw, may be held with almost as great conviction as beliefs about the past. Scientific laws are generally believed less firmly. . . . Philosophical beliefs, finally, will, with most people, take a still lower place, since the opposite beliefs of others can hardly fail to induce doubt. Belief, therefore, is a matter of degree. To speak of belief, disbelief, doubt, and suspense of judgment as the only possibilities is as if, from the writing on the thermometer, we were to suppose that blood heat, summer heat, temperate, and freezing were the only temperatures." Beliefs which require to be confirmed by future experience, or which actually refer to it, are evidently only presumptions; it is merely the truth of presumptions that empirical logic applies to, and only so long as they remain presumptions. Presumptions may be held with very different degrees of assurance, and yet be acted upon, in the absence of any strong counter-suggestion; as the confidence of lovers or of religious enthusiasts may be at blood heat at one moment and freezing at the next, without a change in anything save in the will to believe. The truth of such presumptions, whatever may be the ground of them, depends in fact on whether they are to lead (or, rather, whether the general course of events is to lead) to the further things presumed; for these things are what presumptions refer to explicitly.

It sometimes happens, however, that presumptions (being based on voluminous blind instinct rather than on distinct repeated observations) are expressed in consciousness by some symbol or myth, as when a man says he believes in his luck; the presumption really regards particular future chances and throws of the dice, but the emotional and verbal mist in which the presumption is wrapped, veils the pragmatic burden of it; and a metaphysical entity arises, called luck, in which a man may think he believes rather than in a particular career that may be awaiting him. Now since this entity, luck, is a mere word, confidence in it, to be justified at all, must be transferred to the concrete facts it stands for. Faith in one's luck must be pragmatic, but simply because faith in such an entity is not needful nor philosophical at all. The case is the same with working hypotheses, when that is all they are; for on this point there is some confusion. Whether an idea is a working hypothesis merely or an anticipation of matters open to eventual inspection may not always be clear. Thus the atomic theory, in the sense in which most philosophers entertain it to-day, seems to be a working hypothesis only; for they do not seriously believe that there are atoms, but in their ignorance of the precise composition of matter, they find it convenient to speak of it as if it were composed of indestructible particles. But for Democritus and for many modern men of science the atomic theory is not a working hypothesis merely; they do not regard it as a provisional makeshift; they regard it as a probable, if not a certain, anticipation of what inspection would discover to be the fact, could inspection be carried so far; in other words, they believe the atomic theory is true. If they are right, the validity of this theory would not be that of pragmatic " truth " but of pragmatic " fact "; for it would be a view, such as memory or intuition or sensation might give us, of experienced objects in their experienced relations; it would be the communication to us, in a momentary dream, of what would be the experience of a universal observer. It would be knowledge of reality in M. Bergson's sense. Pragmatic " truth," on the contrary, is the relative and provisional justification of fiction; and pragmatism is not a theory of truth at all, but a theory of theory, when theory is instrumental.

For theory too has more than one signification. It may mean such a symbolic or foreshortened view, such a working hypothesis, as true and full knowledge might supersede; or it may mean this true and full knowledge itself, a synthetic survey of objects of experience in their experimental character. Algebra and language are theoretical in the first sense, as when a man believes in his luck; historical and scientific imagination are theoretical in the second sense, when they gather objects of experience together without distorting them. But it is only to the first sort of theory that pragmatism can be reasonably applied; to apply it also to the second would be to retire into that extreme subjectivism which the leading pragmatists have so hotly disclaimed. We find, accordingly, that it is only when a theory is avowedly unreal, and does not ask to be believed, that the value of it is pragmatic; since in that case belief passes consciously from the symbols used to the eventual facts in which the symbolism terminates, and for which it stands.

It may seem strange that a definition of truth should have been based on the consideration of those ideas exclusively for which truth is not claimed by any critical person, such ideas, namely, as religious myths or the graphic and verbal machinery of science. Yet the fact is patent, and if we considered the matter historically it might not prove inexplicable. Theology has long applied the name truth pre-eminently to fiction. When the conviction first dawned upon pragmatists that there was no absolute or eternal truth, what they evidently were thinking of was that it is folly, in this changing world, to pledge oneself to any final and inflexible creed. The pursuit of truth, since nothing better was possible, was to be accepted instead of the possession of it. But it is characteristic of Protestantism that, when it gives up anything, it transfers to what remains the unction, and often the name, proper to what it has abandoned. So, if truth was no longer to be claimed or even hoped for, the value and the name of truth could be instinctively transferred to what was to take its place—spontaneous, honest, variable conviction. And the sanctions of this conviction were to be looked for, not in the objective reality, since it was an idle illusion to fancy we could get at that, but in the growth of this conviction itself, and in the prosperous adventure of the whole soul, so courageous in its self-trust, and so modest in its dogmas.

Science, too, has often been identified, not with the knowledge men of science possess, but with the language they use. If science meant knowledge, the science of Darwin, for instance, would lie in his observations of plants and animals, and in his thoughts about the probable ancestors of the human race—all knowledge of actual or possible facts. It would not be knowledge of selection or of spontaneous variation, terms which are mere verbal bridges over the gaps in that knowledge, and

mark the *lacunæ* and unsolved problems of the science.
Yet it is just such terms that seem to clothe " Science "
in its pontifical garb; the cowl is taken for the monk; and
when a penetrating critic, like M. Henri Poincaré, turned
his subtle irony upon them, the public cried that he had
announced the " bankruptcy of science," whereas it is
merely the language of science that he had reduced to its
pragmatic value—to convenience and economy in the
registering of facts—and had by no means questioned that
positive and cumulative knowledge of facts which science
is attaining.   It is an incident in the same general confusion that a critical epistemology, like pragmatism,
analysing these figments of scientific or theological theory,
should innocently suppose that it was analysing truth;
while the only view to which it really attributes truth is
its view of the system of facts open to possible experience,
a system which those figments presuppose and which
they may help us in part to divine, where it is accidentally
hidden from human inspection.

IV. HYPOSTATIC ETHICS

If Mr. Russell, in his essay on " The Elements of Ethics,"
had wished to propitiate the unregenerate naturalist,
before trying to convert him, he could not have chosen a
more skilful procedure; for he begins by telling us
that " what is called good conduct is conduct which is
a means to other things which are good on their own
account; and hence . . . the study of what is good or
bad on its own account must be included in ethics."

Two consequences are involved in this: first, that ethics is concerned with the economy of all values, and not with " moral " goods only, or with duty; and second, that values may and do inhere in a great variety of things and relations, all of which it is the part of wisdom to respect, and if possible to establish. In this matter, according to our author, the general philosopher is prone to one error and the professed moralist to another. " The philosopher, bent on the construction of a system, is inclined to simplify the facts unduly . . . and to twist them into a form in which they can all be deduced from one or two general principles. The moralist, on the other hand, being primarily concerned with conduct, tends to become absorbed in means, to value the actions men ought to perform more than the ends which such actions serve. . . . Hence most of what they value in this world would have to be omitted by many moralists from any imagined heaven, because there such things as self-denial and effort and courage and pity could find no place. . . . Kant has the bad eminence of combining both errors in the highest possible degree, since he holds that there is nothing good except the virtuous will—a view which simplifies the good as much as any philosopher could wish, and mistakes means for ends as completely as any moralist could enjoin."

Those of us who are what Mr. Russell would call ethical sceptics will be delighted at this way of clearing the ground; it opens before us the prospect of a moral philosophy that should estimate the various values of things known and of things imaginable, showing what combinations of goods are possible in any one rational system, and (if fancy could stretch so far) what different rational systems would be possible in places and times remote enough from one another not to come into physical conflict. Such ethics, since it would express in reflection the dumb but actual interests of men, might have both influence and authority over them; two things which an alien and dogmatic ethics necessarily lacks. The joy of the ethical sceptic in Mr. Russell is destined, however, to be short-lived. Before proceeding to the expression of concrete ideals, he thinks it necessary to ask a preliminary and quite abstract question, to which his essay is chiefly devoted; namely, what is the right definition of the predicate " good," which we hope to apply in the sequel to such a variety of things? And he answers at once: The predicate " good " is indefinable. This answer he shows to be unavoidable, and so evidently unavoidable that we might perhaps have been absolved from asking the question; for, as he says, the so-called definitions of " good "—that it is pleasure, the desired, and so forth— are not definitions of the predicate " good," but designations of the things to which this predicate is applied by different persons. Pleasure, and its rivals, are not synonyms for the abstract quality " good," but names for classes of concrete facts that are supposed to possess that quality. From this correct, if somewhat trifling, observation, however, Mr. Russell, like Mr. Moore before him, evokes a portentous dogma. Not being able to define good, he hypostasises it. " Good and bad," he says, " are qualities which belong to objects independently of our opinions, just as much as round and square do; and when two people differ as to whether a thing is good, only one of them can be right, though it may be very hard to know which is right." "We cannot maintain that for me a thing ought to exist on its own account, while for you it ought not; that would merely mean that one of us is mistaken, since in fact everything either ought to exist, or ought not." Thus we are asked to believe that good attaches to things for no reason or cause, and according to no principles of distribution; that it must be found there by a sort of receptive exploration in each separate case; in other words, that it is an absolute, not a relative thing, a primary and not a secondary quality.

That the quality " good " is indefinable is one assertion, and obvious; but that the presence of this quality is unconditioned is another, and astonishing. My logic, I am well aware, is not very accurate or subtle; and I wish Mr. Russell had not left it to me to discover the connection between these two propositions. Green is an indefinable predicate, and the specific quality of it can be given only in intuition; but it is a quality that things acquire under certain conditions, so much so that the same bit of grass, at the same moment, may have it from one point of view and not from another. Right and left are indefinable; the difference could not be explained without being invoked in the explanation; yet everything that is to the right is not to the right on no condition, but obviously on the condition that some one is looking in a certain direction; and if some one else at the same time is looking in the opposite direction, what is truly to the right will be truly to the left also. If Mr. Russell thinks this is a contradiction, I understand why the universe does

not please him. The contradiction would be real, undoubtedly, if we suggested that the *idea* of good was at
any time or in any relation the *idea* of evil, or the *intuition*
of right that of left, or the *quality* of green that of yellow;
these disembodied essences are fixed by the intent that
selects them, and in that ideal realm they can never have
any relations except the dialectical ones implied in their
nature, and these relations they must always retain.
But the contradiction disappears when, instead of considering the qualities in themselves, we consider the
things of which those qualities are aspects; for the
qualities of things are not compacted by implication, but
are conjoined irrationally by nature, as she will; and the
same thing may be, and is, at once yellow and green, to
the left and to the right, good and evil, many and one,
large and small; and whatever verbal paradox there may
be in this way of speaking (for from the point of view of
nature it is natural enough) had been thoroughly explained and talked out by the time of Plato, who com-
plained that people should still raise a difficulty so trite
and exploded.[1] Indeed, while square is always square,

[1] Plato, *Philebus*, 14, D. The dialectical element in this dialogue is
evidently the basis of Mr. Russell's, as of Mr. Moore's, ethics; but
they have not adopted the other elements in it, I mean the political
and the theological. As to the political element, Plato everywhere
conceives the good as the eligible in life, and refers it to human nature
and to the pursuit of happiness—that happiness which Mr. Russell,
in a rash moment, says is but a name which some people prefer to give
to pleasure. Thus in the *Philebus* (11, D) the good looked for is
declared to be " some state and disposition of the soul which has the
property of making all men happy "; and later (66, D) the conclusion
is that insight is better than pleasure " as an element in human life."
As to the theological element, Plato, in hypostasising the good, does
not hypostasise it as good, but as cause or power, which is, it seems
to me, the sole category that justifies hypostasis, and logically involves

and round round, a thing that is round may actually be square also, if we allow it to have a little body, and to be a cylinder.

But perhaps what suggests this hypostasis of good is rather the fact that what others find good, or what we ourselves have found good in moods with which we retain no sympathy, is sometimes pronounced by us to be bad; and far from inferring from this diversity of experience that the present good, like the others, corresponds to a particular attitude or interest of ours, and is dependent upon it, Mr. Russell and Mr. Moore infer instead that the presence of the good must be independent of all interests, attitudes, and opinions.   They imagine that the truth of a proposition attributing a certain relative quality to an object contradicts the truth of another proposition, attributing to the same object an opposite relative quality. Thus if a man here and another man at the antipodes call opposite directions up, " only one of them can be right, though it may be very hard to know which is right."

To protect the belated innocence of this state of mind, Mr. Russell, so far as I can see, has only one argument, and one analogy.   The argument is that " if this were

it; for if things have a ground at all, that ground must exist before them and beyond them.   Hence the whole Platonic and Christian scheme, in making the good independent of private will and opinion, by no means makes it independent of the direction of nature in general and of human nature in particular; for all things have been created with an innate predisposition towards the creative good, and are capable of finding happiness in nothing else.   Obligation, in this system, remains internal and vital.   Plato attributes a single vital direction and a single moral source to the cosmos.   This is what determines and narrows the scope of the true good; for the true good is that relevant to nature.   Plato would not have been a dogmatic moralist, had he not been a theist.

not the case, we could not reason with a man as to what is right." "We do in fact hold that when one man approves of a certain act, while another disapproves, one of them is mistaken, which would not be the case with a mere emotion. If one man likes oysters and another dislikes them, we do not say that either of them is mistaken." In other words, we are to maintain our prejudices, however absurd, lest it should become unnecessary to quarrel about them! Truly the debating society has its idols, no less than the cave and the theatre. The analogy that comes to buttress somewhat this singular argument is the analogy between ethical propriety and physical or logical truth. An ethical proposition may be correct or incorrect, in a sense justifying argument, when it touches what is good as a means, that is, when it is not intrinsically ethical, but deals with causes and effects, or with matters of fact or necessity. But to speak of the truth of an ultimate good would be a false collocation of terms; an ultimate good is chosen, found, or aimed at; it is not opined. The ultimate intuitions on which ethics rests are not debatable, for they are not opinions we hazard but preferences we feel; and it can be neither correct nor incorrect to feel them. We may assert these preferences fiercely or with sweet reasonableness, and we may be more or less incapable of sympathising with the different preferences of others; about oysters we may be tolerant, like Mr. Russell, and about character intolerant; but that is already a great advance in enlightenment, since the majority of mankind have regarded as hateful in the highest degree any one who indulged in pork, or beans, or frogs' legs, or who had a weakness for anything called " unnatural "; for it is the things that offend their animal instincts that intense natures have always found to be, intrinsically and *par excellence*, abominations.

I am not sure whether Mr. Russell thinks he has disposed of this view where he discusses the proposition that the good is the desired and refutes it on the ground that " it is commonly admitted that there are bad desires; and when people speak of bad desires, they seem to mean desires for what is bad." Most people undoubtedly call desires bad when they are generically contrary to their own desires, and call objects that disgust them bad, even when other people covet them. This human weakness is not, however, a very high authority for a logician to appeal to, being too like the attitude of the German lady who said that Englishmen called a certain object *bread*, and Frenchmen called it *pain*, but that it really was *Brod*. Scholastic philosophy is inclined to this way of asserting itself; and Mr. Russell, though he candidly admits that there are ultimate differences of opinion about good and evil, would gladly minimise these differences, and thinks he triumphs when he feels that the prejudices of his readers will agree with his own; as if the constitutional unanimity of all human animals, supposing it existed, could tend to show that the good they agreed to recognise was independent of their constitution.

In a somewhat worthier sense, however, we may admit that there are desires for what is bad, since desire and will, in the proper psychological sense of these words, are incidental phases of consciousness, expressing but not constituting those natural relations that make one thing good for another. At the same time the words desire and will are often used, in a mythical or transcendental sense, for those material dispositions and instincts by which vital and moral units are constituted. It is in reference to such constitutional interests that things are " really " good or bad; interests which may not be fairly represented by any incidental conscious desire. No doubt any desire, however capricious, represents some momentary and partial interest, which lends to its objects a certain real and inalienable value; yet when we consider, as we do in human society, the interests of men, whom reflection and settled purposes have raised more or less to the ideal dignity of individuals then passing fancies and passions may indeed have bad objects, and be bad themselves, in that they thwart the more comprehensive interests of the soul that entertains them. Food and poison are such only relatively, and in view of particular bodies, and the same material thing may be food and poison at once; the child, and even the doctor, may easily mistake one for the other. For the human system whiskey is truly more intoxicating than coffee, and the contrary opinion would be an error; but what a strange way of vindicating this real, though relative, distinction, to insist that whiskey is more intoxicating in itself, without reference to any animal; that it is pervaded, as it were, by an inherent intoxication, and stands dead drunk in its bottle! Yet just in this way Mr. Russell and Mr. Moore conceive things to be dead good and dead bad. It is such a view, rather than the naturalistic one, that renders reasoning and self-criticism impossible in morals; for wrong desires, and false opinions as to value, are conceivable only because a point of reference or criterion is available to prove them such. If no point of reference and no criterion were admitted to be relevant, nothing but physical stress could give to one assertion of value greater force than to another. The shouting moralist no doubt has his place, but not in philosophy.

That good is not an intrinsic or primary quality, but relative and adventitious, is clearly betrayed by Mr. Russell's own way of arguing, whenever he approaches some concrete ethical question. For instance, to show that the good is not pleasure, he can avowedly do nothing but appeal " to ethical judgments with which almost every one would agree." He repeats, in effect, Plato's argument about the life of the oyster, having pleasure with no knowledge. Imagine such mindless pleasure, as intense and prolonged as you please, and would you choose it? Is it your good? Here the British reader, like the blushing Greek youth, is expected to answer instinctively, No! It is an *argumentum ad hominem* (and there can be no other kind of argument in ethics); but the man who gives the required answer does so not because the answer is self-evident, which it is not, but because he is the required sort of man. He is shocked at the idea of resembling an oyster. Yet changeless pleasure, without memory or reflection, without the wearisome intermixture of arbitrary images, is just what the mystic, the voluptuary, and perhaps the oyster find to be good. Ideas, in their origin, are probably signals of alarm; and the distress which they marked in the beginning always clings to them in some measure, and causes many a soul, far more profound than that of the young Protarchus or of the British reader, to long for them to cease altogether. Such a radical hedonism is indeed inhuman; it undermines all conventional ambitions, and is not a possible foundation for political or artistic life. But that is all we can say against it. Our humanity cannot annul the incommensurable sorts of good that may be pursued in the world, though it cannot itself pursue them. The impossibility which people labour under of being satisfied with pure pleasure as a goal is due to their want of imagination, or rather to their being dominated by an imagination which is exclusively human.

The author's estrangement from reality reappears in his treatment of egoism, and most of all in his " Free Man's Religion." Egoism, he thinks, is untenable because " if I am right in thinking that my good is the only good, then every one else is mistaken unless he admits that my good, not his, is the only good." " Most people . . . would admit that it is better two people's desires should be satisfied than only one person's. . . . Then what is good is not good *for me* or *for you*, but is simply good." " It is, indeed, so evident that it is better to secure a greater good for A than a lesser good for B, that it is hard to find any still more evident principle by which to prove this. And if A happens to be some one else, and B to be myself, that cannot affect the question, since it is irrelevant to the general question who A and B may be." To the question, as the logician states it after transforming men into letters, it is certainly irrelevant; but it is not irrelevant to the case as it arises in nature. If two goods are somehow rightly pronounced to be equally good, no circumstance can render one better than the other. And if the locus in which the good is to arise is somehow pronounced to be indifferent, it will certainly be indifferent whether that good arises in me or in you. But how shall these two pronouncements be made? In practice, values cannot be compared save as represented or enacted in the private imagination of somebody: for we could not conceive that an alien good *was* a good (as Mr. Russell cannot conceive that the life of an ecstatic oyster is a good) unless we could sympathise with it in some way in our own persons; and on the warmth which we felt in so representing the alien good would hang our conviction that it was truly valuable, and had worth in comparison with our own good. The voice of reason, bidding us prefer the greater good, no matter who is to enjoy it, is also nothing but the force of sympathy, bringing a remote existence before us vividly *sub specie boni*. Capacity for such sympathy measures the capacity to recognise duty and therefore, in a moral sense, to have it. Doubtless it is conceivable that all wills should become co-operative, and that nature should be ruled magically by an exact and universal sympathy; but this situation must be actually attained in part, before it can be conceived or judged to be an authoritative ideal. The tigers cannot regard it as such, for it would suppress the tragic good called ferocity, which makes, in their eyes, the chief glory of the universe. Therefore the inertia of nature, the ferocity of beasts, the optimism of mystics, and the selfishness of men and nations must all be accepted as conditions for the peculiar goods, essentially incommensurable, which they can generate severally. It is misplaced vehemence to call them intrinsically detestable, because they do not (as they cannot) generate or recognise the goods we prize.

In the real world, persons are not abstract egos, like *A* and *B*, so that to benefit one is clearly as good as to benefit another. Indeed, abstract egos could not be benefited, for they could not be modified at all, even if somehow they could be distinguished. It would be the qualities or objects distributed among them that would carry, wherever they went, each its inalienable cargo of value, like ships sailing from sea to sea. But it is quite vain and artificial to imagine different goods charged with such absolute and comparable weights; and actual egoism is not the thin and refutable thing that Mr. Russell makes of it. What it really holds is that a given man, oneself, and those akin to him, are qualitatively better than other beings; that the things they prize are intrinsically better than the things prized by others; and that therefore there is no injustice in treating these chosen interests as supreme. The injustice, it is felt, would lie rather in not treating things so unequal unequally. This feeling may, in many cases, amuse the impartial observer, or make him indignant; yet it may, in every case, according to Mr. Russell, be absolutely just. The refutation he gives of egoism would not dissuade any fanatic from exterminating all his enemies with a good conscience; it would merely encourage him to assert that what he was ruthlessly establishing was the absolute good. Doubtless such conscientious tyrants would be wretched themselves, and compelled to make sacrifices which would cost them dear; but that would only extend, as it were, the pernicious egoism of that part of their being which they had allowed to usurp a universal empire. The twang of intolerance and of self-mutilation is not absent from the ethics of Mr. Russell and Mr. Moore, even as it stands; and one trembles to think what it may become in the mouths of their disciples. Intolerance itself is a form of egoism, and to condemn egoism intolerantly is to share it.

I cannot help thinking that a consciousness of the relativity of values, if it became prevalent, would tend to render people more truly social than would a belief that things have intrinsic and unchangeable values, no matter what the attitude of any one to them may be. If we said that goods, including the right distribution of goods, are relative to specific natures, moral warfare would continue, but not with poisoned arrows. Our private sense of justice itself would be acknowledged to have but a relative authority, and while we could not have a higher duty than to follow it, we should seek to meet those whose aims were incompatible with it as we meet things physically inconvenient, without insulting them as if they were morally vile or logically contemptible. Real unselfishness consists in sharing the interests of others. Beyond the pale of actual unanimity the only possible unselfishness is chivalry—a recognition of the inward right and justification of our enemies fighting against us. This chivalry has long been practised in the battle-field without abolishing the causes of war; and it might conceivably be extended to all the conflicts of men with one another, and of the warring elements within each breast. Policy, hypnotisation, and even surgery

may be practised without exorcisms or anathemas.
When a man has decided on a course of action, it is a
vain indulgence in expletives to declare that he is sure
that course is absolutely right. His moral dogma
expresses its natural origin all the more clearly the more
hotly it is proclaimed; and ethical absolutism, being a
mental grimace of passion, refutes what it says by what
it is. Sweeter and more profound, to my sense, is the
philosophy of Homer, whose every line seems to breathe
the conviction that what is beautiful or precious has not
thereby any right to existence; nothing has such a right;
nor is it given us to condemn absolutely any force—god
or man—that destroys what is beautiful or precious, for
it has doubtless something beautiful or precious of its
own to achieve.

The consequences of a hypostasis of the good are no
less interesting than its causes. If the good were independent of nature, it might still be conceived as relevant
to nature, by being its creator or mover; but Mr. Russell
is not a theist after the manner of Socrates; his good is
not a power. Nor would representing it to be such long
help his case; for an ideal hypostasised into a cause
achieves only a mythical independence. The least
criticism discloses that it is natural laws, zoological
species, and human ideals, that have been projected into
the empyrean; and it is no marvel that the good should
attract the world where the good, by definition, is whatever the world is aiming at. The hypostasis accomplished
by Mr. Russell is more serious, and therefore more
paradoxical. If I understand it, it may be expressed as
follows: In the realm of eternal essences, before anything

exists, there are certain essences that have this remarkable property, that they ought to exist, or at least that, if anything exists, it ought to conform to them. What exists, however, is deaf to this moral emphasis in the eternal; nature exists for no reason; and, indeed, why should she have subordinated her own arbitrariness to a good that is no less arbitrary? This good, however, is somehow good notwithstanding; so that there is an abysmal wrong in its not being obeyed. The world is, in principle, totally depraved; but as the good is not a power, there is no one to redeem the world. The saints are those who, imitating the impotent dogmatism on high, and despising their sinful natural propensities, keep asserting that certain things are in themselves good and others bad, and declaring to be detestable any other saint who dogmatises differently. In this system the Calvinistic God has lost his creative and punitive functions, but continues to decree groundlessly what is good and what evil, and to love the one and hate the other with an infinite love or hatred. Meanwhile the reprobate need not fear hell in the next world, but the elect are sure to find it here.

What shall we say of this strangely unreal and strangely personal religion? Is it a ghost of Calvinism, returned with none of its old force but with its old aspect of rigidity? Perhaps: but then, in losing its force, in abandoning its myths, and threats, and rhetoric, this religion has lost its deceptive sanctimony and hypocrisy; and in retaining its rigidity it has kept what made it noble and pathetic; for it is a clear dramatic expression of that human spirit—in this case a most pure and heroic spirit—which it strives so hard to dethrone. After all, the hypostasis of the good is only an unfortunate incident in a great accomplishment, which is the discernment of the good. I have dwelt chiefly on this incident, because in academic circles it is the abuses incidental to true philosophy that create controversy and form schools. Artificial systems, even when they prevail, after a while fatigue their adherents, without ever having convinced or refuted their opponents, and they fade out of existence not by being refuted in their turn, but simply by a tacit agreement to ignore their claims: so that the true insight they were based on is too often buried under them. The hypostasis of philosophical terms is an abuse incidental to the forthright, unchecked use of the intellect; it substitutes for things the limits and distinctions that divide them. So physics is corrupted by logic; but the logic that corrupts physics is perhaps correct, and when it is moral dialectic, it is more important than physics itself. Mr. Russell's ethics *is* ethics. When we mortals have once assumed the moral attitude, it is certain that an indefinable value accrues to some things as opposed to others, that these things are many, that combinations of them have values not belonging to their parts, and that these valuable things are far more specific than abstract pleasure, and far more diffused than one's personal life. What a pity if this pure morality, in detaching itself impetuously from the earth, whose bright satellite it might be, should fly into the abyss at a tangent, and leave us as much in the dark as before!

V

SHELLEY: OR THE POETIC VALUE OF REVOLUTIONARY PRINCIPLES

IT is possible to advocate anarchy in criticism as in politics, and there is perhaps nothing coercive to urge against a man who maintains that any work of art is good enough, intrinsically and incommensurably, if it pleased anybody at any time for any reason. In practice, however, the ideal of anarchy is unstable. Irrefutable by argument, it is readily overcome by nature. It melts away before the dogmatic operation of the anarchist's own will, as soon as he allows himself the least creative endeavour. In spite of the infinite variety of what is merely possible, human nature and will have a somewhat definite constitution, and only what is harmonious with their actual constitution can long maintain itself in the moral world. Hence it is a safe principle in the criticism of art that technical proficiency, and brilliancy of fancy or execution, cannot avail to establish a great reputation. They may dazzle for a moment, but they cannot absolve an artist from the need of having an important subject-matter and a sane humanity.

If this principle is accepted, however, it might seem that certain artists, and perhaps the greatest, might not fare well at our hands. How would Shelley, for instance, stand such a test? Every one knows the judgment passed on Shelley by Matthew Arnold, a critic who evidently relied on this principle, even if he preferred to speak only in the name of his personal tact and literary experience. Shelley, Matthew Arnold said, was " a beautiful and ineffectual angel, beating his wings in a luminous void in vain." In consequence he declared that Shelley was not a classic, especially as his private circle had had an unsavoury morality, to be expressed only by the French word *sale*, and as moreover Shelley himself occasionally showed a distressing want of the sense of humour, which could only be called *bête*. These strictures, if a bit incoherent, are separately remarkably just. They unmask essential weaknesses not only in Shelley, but in all revolutionary people. The life of reason is a heritage and exists only through tradition. Half of it is an art, an adjustment to an alien reality, which only a long experience can teach: and even the other half, the inward inspiration and ideal of reason, must be also a common inheritance in the race, if people are to work together or so much as to understand one another. Now the misfortune of revolutionists is that they are disinherited, and their folly is that they wish to be disinherited even more than they are. Hence, in the midst of their passionate and even heroic idealisms, there is commonly a strange poverty in their minds, many an ugly turn in their lives, and an ostentatious vileness in their manners. They wish to be the leaders of mankind, but they are wretched representatives of humanity. In the concert of nature it is hard to keep in tune with oneself if one is out of tune with everything.

We should not then be yielding to any private bias, but simply noting the conditions under which art may exist and may be appreciated, if we accepted the classical principle of criticism and asserted that substance, sanity, and even a sort of pervasive wisdom are requisite for supreme works of art. On the other hand—who can honestly doubt it?—the rebels and individualists are the men of direct insight and vital hope. The poetry of Shelley in particular is typically poetical. It is poetry divinely inspired; and Shelley himself is perhaps no more ineffectual or more lacking in humour than an angel properly should be. Nor is his greatness all a matter of æsthetic abstraction and wild music. It is a fact of capital importance in the development of human genius that the great revolution in Christendom against Christianity, a revolution that began with the Renaissance and is not yet completed, should have found angels to herald it, no less than that other revolution did which began at Bethlehem; and that among these new angels there should have been one so winsome, pure, and rapturous as Shelley. How shall we reconcile these conflicting impressions? Shall we force ourselves to call the genius of Shelley second rate because it was revolutionary, and shall we attribute all enthusiasm for him to literary affectation or political prejudice? Or shall we rather abandon the orthodox principle that an important subject-matter and a sane spirit are essential to great works? Or shall we look for a different issue out of our perplexity, by asking if the analysis and comprehension are not perhaps at fault which declare that these things are not present in Shelley's poetry? This last is the direction in which I conceive the truth to lie. A little consideration will show us that Shelley really has a great subject-matter—what ought to be; and that he has a real humanity—though it is humanity in the seed, humanity in its internal principle, rather than in those deformed expressions of it which can flourish in the world.

Shelley seems hardly to have been brought up; he grew up in the nursery among his young sisters, at school among the rude boys, without any affectionate guidance, without imbibing any religious or social tradition. If he received any formal training or correction, he instantly rejected it inwardly, set it down as unjust and absurd, and turned instead to sailing paper boats, to reading romances or to writing them, or to watching with delight the magic of chemical experiments. Thus the mind of Shelley was thoroughly disinherited; but not, like the minds of most revolutionists, by accident and through the niggardliness of fortune, for few revolutionists would be such if they were heirs to a baronetcy. Shelley's mind disinherited itself out of allegiance to itself, because it was too sensitive and too highly endowed for the world into which it had descended. It rejected ordinary education, because it was incapable of assimilating it. Education is suitable to those few animals whose faculties are not completely innate, animals that, like most men, may be perfected by experience because they are born with various imperfect alternative instincts rooted equally in their system. But most animals, and a few men, are not of this sort. They cannot be educated, because they are born complete. Full of predeterminate intuitions, they are without intelligence, which is the power of seeing things as they are. Endowed with a specific, unshakable faith, they are impervious to experience: and as they burst the womb they bring ready-made with them their final and only possible system of philosophy.

Shelley was one of these spokesmen of the *a priori*, one of these nurslings of the womb, like a bee or a butterfly; a dogmatic, inspired, perfect, and incorrigible creature. He was innocent and cruel, swift and wayward, illuminated and blind. Being a finished child of nature, not a joint product, like most of us, of nature, history, and society, he abounded miraculously in his own clear sense, but was obtuse to the droll, miscellaneous lessons of fortune. The cannonade of hard, inexplicable facts that knocks into most of us what little wisdom we have left Shelley dazed and sore, perhaps, but uninstructed. When the storm was over, he began chirping again his own natural note. If the world continued to confine and obsess him, he hated the world, and gasped for freedom. Being incapable of understanding reality, he revelled in creating world after world in idea. For his nature was not merely pre-determined and obdurate, it was also sensitive, vehement, and fertile. With the soul of a bird, he had the senses of a man-child; the instinct of the butterfly was united in him with the instinct of the brooding fowl and of the pelican. This winged spirit had a heart. It darted swiftly on its appointed course, neither expecting nor understanding opposition; but when it met opposition it did not merely flutter and collapse; it was inwardly outraged, it protested proudly against fate, it cried aloud for liberty and justice.

The consequence was that Shelley, having a nature preformed but at the same time tender, passionate, and moral, was exposed to early and continual suffering. When the world violated the ideal which lay so clear before his eyes, that violation filled him with horror. If to the irrepressible gushing of life from within we add the suffering and horror that continually checked it, we shall have in hand, I think, the chief elements of his genius.

Love of the ideal, passionate apprehension of what ought to be, has for its necessary counterpart condemnation of the actual, wherever the actual does not conform to that ideal. The spontaneous soul, the soul of the child, is naturally revolutionary; and when the revolution fails, the soul of the youth becomes naturally pessimistic. All moral life and moral judgment have this deeply romantic character; they venture to assert a private ideal in the face of an intractable and omnipotent world. Some moralists begin by feeling the attraction of untasted and ideal perfection. These, like Plato, excel in elevation, and they are apt to despise rather than to reform the world. Other moralists begin by a revolt against the actual, at some point where they find the actual particularly galling. These excel in sincerity; their purblind conscience is urgent, and they are reformers in intent and sometimes even in action. But the ideals they frame are fragmentary and shallow, often mere provisional vague watchwords, like liberty, equality, and fraternity; they possess no positive visions or plans for moral life as a whole, like Plato's *Republic*. The utopian or visionary moralists are often rather dazed by this wicked world; being well-intentioned but impotent, they often take comfort in fancying that the ideal they pine for is already actually embodied on earth, or is about to be embodied on earth in a decade or two, or at least is embodied eternally in a sphere immediately above the earth, to which we shall presently climb, and be happy for ever.

Lovers of the ideal who thus hastily believe in its reality are called idealists, and Shelley was an idealist in almost every sense of that hard-used word. He early became an idealist after Berkeley's fashion, in that he discredited the existence of matter and embraced a psychological or (as it was called) intellectual system of the universe. In his drama *Hellas* he puts this view with evident approval into the mouth of Ahasuerus:

> " This whole
> Of suns and worlds and men and beasts and flowers,
> With all the silent or tempestuous workings
> By which they have been, are, or cease to be,
> Is but a vision;—all that it inherits
> Are motes of a sick eye, bubbles and dreams.
> Thought is its cradle and its grave; nor less
> The future and the past are idle shadows
> Of thought's eternal flight—they have no being:
> Nought is but that which feels itself to be."

But Shelley was even more deeply and constantly an idealist after the manner of Plato; for he regarded the good as a magnet (inexplicably not working for the moment) that draws all life and motion after it; and he looked on the types and ideals of things as on eternal realities that subsist, beautiful and untarnished, when the glimmerings that reveal them to our senses have died away. From the infinite potentialities of beauty in the abstract, articulate mind draws certain bright forms—

the Platonic ideas—"the gathered rays which are reality," as Shelley called them: and it is the light of these ideals cast on objects of sense that lends to these objects some degree of reality and value, making out of them "lovely apparitions, dim at first, then radiant . . . the progeny immortal of painting, sculpture, and rapt poesy."

The only kind of idealism that Shelley had nothing to do with is the kind that prevails in some universities, that Hegelian idealism which teaches that perfect good is a vicious abstraction, and maintains that all the evil that has been, is, and ever shall be is indispensable to make the universe as good as it possibly could be. In this form, idealism is simply contempt for all ideals, and a hearty adoration of things as they are; and as such it appeals mightily to the powers that be, in church and in state; but in that capacity it would have been as hateful to Shelley as the powers that be always were, and as the philosophy was that flattered them. For his moral feeling was based on suffering and horror at what is actual, no less than on love of a visioned good. His conscience was, to a most unusual degree, at once elevated and sincere. It was inspired in equal measure by prophecy and by indignation. He was carried away in turn by enthusiasm for what his ethereal and fertile fancy pictured as possible, and by detestation of the reality forced upon him instead. Hence that extraordinary moral fervour which is the soul of his poetry. His imagination is no playful undirected kaleidoscope; the images, often so tenuous and metaphysical, that crowd upon him, are all sparks thrown off at white heat,

embodiments of a fervent, definite, unswerving inspiration. If we think that the *Cloud* or the *West Wind* or
the *Witch of the Atlas* are mere fireworks, poetic dust, a
sort of *bataille des fleurs* in which we are pelted by a
shower of images—we have not understood the passion
that overflows in them, as any long-nursed passion may,
in any of us, suddenly overflow in an unwonted profusion
of words. This is a point at which Francis Thompson's
understanding of Shelley, generally so perfect, seems to
me to go astray. The universe, Thompson tells us, was
Shelley's box of toys. " He gets between the feet of the
horses of the sun. He stands in the lap of patient
Nature, and twines her loosened tresses after a hundred
wilful fashions, to see how she will look nicest in his
song." This last is not, I think, Shelley's motive; it is
not the truth about the spring of his genius. He undoubtedly shatters the world to bits, but only to build it
nearer to the heart's desire, only to make out of its
coloured fragments some more Elysian home for love,
or some more dazzling symbol for that infinite beauty
which is the need—the profound, aching, imperative
need—of the human soul. This recreative impulse of
the poet's is not wilful, as Thompson calls it: it is moral.
Like the *Sensitive Plant*

> " It loves even like Love,—its deep heart is full;
> It desires what it has not, the beautiful."

The question for Shelley is not at all what will look
nicest in his song; that is the preoccupation of mincing
rhymesters, whose well is soon dry. Shelley's abundance
has a more generous source; it springs from his passion for
picturing what would be best, not in the picture, but in

the world. Hence, when he feels he has pictured or divined it, he can exclaim:

> " The joy, the triumph, the delight, the madness,
> The boundless, overflowing, bursting gladness,
> The vaporous exultation, not to be confined!
> Ha! Ha! the animation of delight,
> Which wraps me like an atmosphere of light,
> And bears me as a cloud is borne by its own wind! "

To match this gift of bodying forth the ideal Shelley had his vehement sense of wrong; and as he seized upon and recast all images of beauty, to make them more perfectly beautiful, so, to vent his infinite horror of evil, he seized on all the worst images of crime or torture that he could find, and recast them so as to reach the quintessence of distilled badness. His pictures of war, famine, lust, and cruelty are, or seem, forced, although perhaps, as in the *Cenci*, he might urge that he had historical warrant for his descriptions, far better historical warrant, no doubt, than the beauty and happiness actually to be found in the world could give him for his *Skylark*, his *Epipsychidion*, or his *Prometheus*. But to exaggerate good is to vivify, to enhance our sense of moral coherence and beautiful naturalness; it is to render things more graceful, intelligible, and congenial to the spirit which they ought to serve. To aggravate evil, on the contrary, is to darken counsel—already dark enough—and the want of truth to nature in this pessimistic sort of exaggeration is not compensated for by any advantage. The violence and, to my feeling, the wantonness of these invectives—for they are invectives in intention and in effect—may have seemed justified to Shelley by his political purpose. He was thirsting to destroy kings, priests, soldiers, parents, and heads of colleges—to destroy them, I mean, in their official capacity; and the exhibition of their vileness in all its diabolical purity might serve to remove scruples in the half-hearted. We, whom the nineteenth century has left so tender to historical rights and historical beauties, may wonder that a poet, an impassioned lover of the beautiful, could have been such a leveller, and such a vandal in his theoretical destructiveness. But here the legacy of the eighteenth century was speaking in Shelley, as that of the nineteenth is speaking in us: and moreover, in his own person, the very fertility of imagination could be a cause of blindness to the past and its contingent sanctities. Shelley was not left standing aghast, like a Philistine, before the threatened destruction of all traditional order. He had, and knew he had, the seeds of a far lovelier order in his own soul; there he found the plan or memory of a perfect commonwealth of nature ready to rise at once on the ruins of this sad world, and to make regret for it impossible.

So much for what I take to be the double foundation of Shelley's genius, a vivid love of ideal good on the one hand, and on the other, what is complementary to that vivid love, much suffering and horror at the touch of actual evils. On this double foundation he based an opinion which had the greatest influence on his poetry, not merely on the subject-matter of it, but also on the exuberance and urgency of emotion which suffuses it. This opinion was that all that caused suffering and horror in the world could be readily destroyed: it was the belief in perfectibility.

An animal that has rigid instincts and an *a priori* mind is probably very imperfectly adapted to the world he comes into: his organs cannot be moulded by experience and use; unless they are fitted by some miraculous pre-established harmony, or by natural selection, to things as they are, they will never be reconciled with them, and an eternal war will ensue between what the animal needs, loves, and can understand and what the outer reality offers. So long as such a creature lives— and his life will be difficult and short—events will continually disconcert and puzzle him; everything will seem to him unaccountable, inexplicable, unnatural. He will not be able to conceive the real order and connection of things sympathetically, by assimilating his habits of thought to their habits of evolution. His faculties being innate and unadaptable will not allow him to correct his presumptions and axioms; he will never be able to make nature the standard of naturalness. What contradicts his private impulses will seem to him to contradict reason, beauty, and necessity. In this paradoxical situation he will probably take refuge in the conviction that what he finds to exist is an illusion, or at least not a fair sample of reality. Being so perverse, absurd, and repugnant, the given state of things must be, he will say, only accidental and temporary. He will be sure that his own *a priori* imagination is the mirror of all the eternal proprieties, and that as his mind can move only in one predetermined way, things cannot be prevented from moving in that same way save by some strange violence done to their nature. It would be easy, therefore, to set everything right again: nay, everything must be on the point of righting itself spontaneously. Wrong, of its very essence, must be in unstable equilibrium. The conflict between what such a man feels ought to exist and what he finds actually existing must, he will feel sure, end by a speedy revolution in things, and by the removal of all scandals; that it should end by the speedy removal of his own person, or by such a revolution in his demands as might reconcile him to existence, will never occur to him; or, if the thought occurs to him, it will seem too horrible to be true.

Such a creature cannot adapt himself to things by education, and consequently he cannot adapt things to himself by industry. His choice lies absolutely between victory and martyrdom. But at the very moment of martyrdom, martyrs, as is well known, usually feel assured of victory. The *a priori* spirit will therefore be always a prophet of victory, so long as it subsists at all. The vision of a better world at hand absorbed the Israelites in exile, St. John the Baptist in the desert, and Christ on the cross. The martyred spirit always says to the world it leaves, " This day thou shalt be with me in paradise."

In just this way, Shelley believed in perfectibility. In his latest poems—in *Hellas*, in *Adonais*—he was perhaps a little inclined to remove the scene of perfectibility to a metaphysical region, as the Christian church soon removed it to the other world. Indeed, an earth really made perfect is hardly distinguishable from a posthumous heaven: so profoundly must everything in it be changed, and so angel-like must every one in it become. Shelley's earthly paradise, as described in

Prometheus and in *Epipsychidion,* is too festival-like, too much of a mere culmination, not to be fugitive: it cries aloud to be translated into a changeless and metaphysical heaven, which to Shelley's mind could be nothing but the realm of Platonic ideas, where " life, like a dome of many-coloured glass," no longer " stains the white radiance of eternity." But the age had been an age of revolution and, in spite of disappointments, retained its faith in revolution; and the young Shelley was not satisfied with a paradise removed to the intangible realms of poetry or of religion; he hoped, like the old Hebrews, for a paradise on earth. His notion was that eloquence could change the heart of man, and that love, kindled there by the force of reason and of example, would transform society. He believed, Mrs. Shelley tells us, " that mankind had only to will that there should be no evil, and there would be none." And she adds: " That man could be so perfectionised as to be able to expel evil from his own nature, and from the greater part of creation, was the cardinal point of his system." This cosmic extension of the conversion of men reminds one of the cosmic extension of the Fall conceived by St. Augustine; and in the *Prometheus* Shelley has allowed his fancy, half in symbol, half in glorious physical hyperbole, to carry the warm contagion of love into the very bowels of the earth, and even the moon, by reflection, to catch the light of love, and be alive again.

Shelley, we may safely say, did not understand the real constitution of nature. It was hidden from him by a cloud, all woven of shifting rainbows and bright tears. Only his emotional haste made it possible for him to entertain such opinions as he did entertain; or rather, it was inevitable that the mechanism of nature, as it is in its depths, should remain in his pictures only the shadowiest of backgrounds. His poetry is accordingly a part of the poetry of illusion; the poetry of truth, if we have the courage to hope for such a thing, is reserved for far different and yet unborn poets. But it is only fair to Shelley to remember that the moral being of mankind is as yet in its childhood; all poets play with images not understood; they touch on emotions sharply, at random, as in a dream; they suffer each successive vision, each poignant sentiment, to evaporate into nothing, or to leave behind only a heart vaguely softened and fatigued, a gentle languor, or a tearful hope. Every modern school of poets, once out of fashion, proves itself to have been sadly romantic and sentimental. None has done better than to spangle a confused sensuous pageant with some sparks of truth, or to give it some symbolic relation to moral experience. And this Shelley has done as well as anybody: all other poets also have been poets of illusion. The distinction of Shelley is that his illusions are so wonderfully fine, subtle, and palpitating; that they betray passions and mental habits so singularly generous and pure. And why? Because he did not believe in the necessity of what is vulgar, and did not pay that demoralising respect to it, under the title of fact or of custom, which it exacts from most of us. The past seemed to him no valid precedent, the present no final instance. As he believed in the imminence of an overturn that should make all things new, he was not checked by any divided allegiance, by any sense that he was straying into the vapid or fanciful, when he created what he justly calls " Beautiful idealisms of moral excellence."

That is what his poems are fundamentally—the *Skylark*, and the *Witch of the Atlas*, and the *Sensitive Plant* no less than the grander pieces. He infused into his gossamer world the strength of his heroic conscience. He felt that what his imagination pictured was a true symbol of what human experience should and might pass into. Otherwise he would have been aware of playing with idle images; his poetry would have been mere millinery and his politics mere business; he would have been a worldling in art and in morals. The clear fire, the sustained breath, the fervent accent of his poetry are due to his faith in his philosophy. As Mrs. Shelley expressed it, he " had no care for any of his poems that did not emanate from the depths of his mind, and develop some high and abstruse truth." Had his poetry not dealt with what was supreme in his own eyes, and dearest to his heart, it could never have been the exquisite and entrancing poetry that it is. It would not have had an adequate subject-matter, as, in spite of Matthew Arnold, I think it had; for nothing can be empty that contains such a soul. An angel cannot be ineffectual if the standard of efficiency is moral; he is what all other things bring about, when they are effectual. And a void that is alive with the beating of luminous wings, and of a luminous heart, is quite sufficiently peopled. Shelley's mind was angelic not merely in its purity and fervour, but also in its moral authority, in its prophetic strain. What was conscience in his generation was life in him.

The mind of man is not merely a sensorium. His intelligence is not merely an instrument for adaptation. There is a germ within, a nucleus of force and organisation, which can be unfolded, under favourable circumstances, into a perfection inwardly determined. Man's constitution is a fountain from which to draw an infinity of gushing music, not representing anything external, yet not unmeaning on that account, since it represents the capacities and passions latent in him from the beginning. These potentialities, however, are no oracles of truth. Being innate they are arbitrary; being *a priori* they are subjective; but they are good principles for fiction, for poetry, for morals, for religion. They are principles for the true expression of man, but not for the true description of the universe. When they are taken for the latter, fiction becomes deception, poetry illusion, morals fanaticism, and religion bad science. The orgy of delusion into which we are then plunged comes from supposing the *a priori* to be capable of controlling the actual, and the innate to be a standard for the true. That rich and definite endowment which might have made the distinction of the poet, then makes the narrowness of the philosopher. So Shelley, with a sort of tyranny of which he does not suspect the possible cruelty, would impose his ideal of love and equality upon all creatures; he would make enthusiasts of clowns and doves of vultures. In him, as in many people, too intense a need of loving excludes the capacity for intelligent sympathy. His feeling cannot accommodate itself to the inequalities of human nature: his good will is a geyser, and will not consent to grow cool, and to water the flat and vulgar

reaches of life. Shelley is blind to the excellences of
what he despises, as he is blind to the impossibility of
realising what he wants. His sympathies are narrow
as his politics are visionary, so that there is a certain
moral incompetence in his moral intensity. Yet his
abstraction from half of life, or from nine-tenths of it,
was perhaps necessary if silence and space were to be won
in his mind for its own upwelling, ecstatic harmonies.
The world we have always with us, but such spirits we
have not always. And the spirit has fire enough within
to make a second stellar universe.

An instance of Shelley's moral incompetence in moral
intensity is to be found in his view of selfishness and evil.
From the point of view of pure spirit, selfishness is quite
absurd. As a contemporary of ours has put it: " It is
so evident that it is better to secure a greater good for A
than a lesser good for B that it is hard to find any still
more evident principle by which to prove this. And if
A happens to be some one else, and B to be myself, that
cannot affect the question." It is very foolish not to
love your neighbour as yourself, since his good is no less
good than yours. Convince people of this—and who can
resist such perfect logic?—and *presto* all property in
things has disappeared, all jealousy in love, and all
rivalry in honour. How happy and secure every one
will suddenly be, and how much richer than in our mean,
blind, competitive society! The single word love—and
we have just seen that love is a logical necessity—offers
an easy and final solution to all moral and political
problems. Shelley cannot imagine why this solution is
not accepted, and why logic does not produce love. He

can only wonder and grieve that it does not; and since selfishness and ill-will seem to him quite gratuitous, his ire is aroused; he thinks them unnatural and monstrous. He could not in the least understand evil, even when he did it himself; all villainy seemed to him wanton, all lust frigid, all hatred insane. All was an abomination alike that was not the lovely spirit of love.

Now this is a very unintelligent view of evil; and if Shelley had had time to read Spinoza—an author with whom he would have found himself largely in sympathy —he might have learned that nothing is evil in itself, and that what is evil in things is not due to any accident in creation, nor to groundless malice in man. Evil is an inevitable aspect which things put on when they are struggling to preserve themselves in the same habitat, in which there is not room or matter enough for them to prosper equally side by side. Under these circumstances the partial success of any creature—say, the cancer-microbe—is an evil from the point of view of those other creatures—say, men—to whom that success is a defeat. Shelley sometimes half perceived this inevitable tragedy. So he says of the fair lady in the *Sensitive Plant :*

> " All killing insects and gnawing worms,
> And things of obscene and unlovely forms,
> She bore in a basket of Indian woof,
> Into the rough woods far aloof—
> In a basket of grasses and wild flowers full,
> The freshest her gentle hands could pull
> For the poor banished insects, whose intent,
> Although they did ill, was innocent.''

Now it is all very well to ask cancer-microbes to be reasonable, and go feed on oak-leaves, if the oak-leaves do not object; oak-leaves might be poison for them, and in any case cancer-microbes cannot listen to reason; they must go on propagating where they are, unless they are quickly and utterly exterminated. And fundamentally men are subject to the same fatality exactly; they cannot listen to reason unless they are reasonable; and it is unreasonable to expect that, being animals, they should be reasonable exclusively. Imagination is indeed at work in them, and makes them capable of sacrificing themselves for any idea that appeals to them, for their children, perhaps, or for their religion. But they are not more capable of sacrificing themselves to what does not interest them than the cancer-microbes are of sacrificing themselves to men.

When Shelley marvels at the perversity of the world, he shows his ignorance of the world. The illusion he suffers from is constitutional, and such as larks and sensitive plants are possibly subject to in their way: what he is marvelling at is really that anything should exist at all not a creature of his own moral disposition. Consequently the more he misunderstands the world and bids it change its nature, the more he expresses his own nature: so that all is not vanity in his illusion, nor night in his blindness. The poet sees most clearly what his ideal is; he suffers no illusion in the expression of his own soul. His political utopias, his belief in the power of love, and his cryingly subjective and inconstant way of judging people are one side of the picture; the other is his lyrical power, wealth, and ecstasy. If he had understood universal nature, he would not have so glorified in his own. And his own nature was worth glorifying; it was, I think, the purest, tenderest, richest, most rational nature ever poured forth in verse. I have not read in any language such a full expression of the unadulterated instincts of the mind. The world of Shelley is that which the vital monad within many of us— I will not say within all, for who shall set bounds to the variations of human nature?—the world which the vital monad within many of us, I say, would gladly live in if it could have its way.

Matthew Arnold said that Shelley was not quite sane; and certainly he was not quite sane, if we place sanity in justness of external perception, adaptation to matter, and docility to the facts; but his lack of sanity was not due to any internal corruption; it was not even an internal eccentricity. He was like a child, like a Platonic soul just fallen from the Empyrean; and the child may be dazed, credulous, and fanciful; but he is not mad. On the contrary, his earnest playfulness, the constant distraction of his attention from observation to day-dreams, is the sign of an inward order and fecundity appropriate to his age. If children did not see visions, good men would have nothing to work for. It is the soul of observant persons, like Matthew Arnold, that is apt not to be quite sane and whole inwardly, but some-what warped by familiarity with the perversities of real things, and forced to misrepresent its true ideal, like a tree bent by too prevalent a wind. Half the fertility of such a soul is lost, and the other half is denaturalised. No doubt, in its sturdy deformity, the practical mind is an instructive and not unpleasing object, an excellent, if somewhat pathetic, expression of the climate in which

it is condemned to grow, and of its dogged clinging to an
ingrate soil; but it is a wretched expression of its innate
possibilities. Shelley, on the contrary, is like a palm-
tree in the desert or a star in the sky; he is perfect in the
midst of the void. His obtuseness to things dynamic—
to the material order—leaves his whole mind free to
develop things æsthetic after their own kind; his
abstraction permits purity, his playfulness makes room
for creative freedom, his ethereal quality is only humanity
having its way.

We perhaps do ourselves an injustice when we think
that the heart of us is sordid; what is sordid is rather the
situation that cramps or stifles the heart. In itself our
generative principle is surely no less fertile and generous
than the generative principle of crystals or flowers. As
it can produce a more complex body, it is capable of producing a more complex mind; and the beauty and life of
this mind, like that of the body, is all predetermined in
the seed. Circumstances may suffer the organism to
develop, or prevent it from doing so; they cannot
change its plan without making it ugly and deformed.
What Shelley's mind draws from the outside, its fund
of images, is like what the germ of the body draws from
the outside, its food—a mass of mere materials to transform and reorganise. With these images Shelley con-
structs a world determined by his native genius, as the
seed organises out of its food a predetermined system of
nerves and muscles. Shelley's poetry shows us the
perfect but naked body of human happiness. What
clothes circumstances may compel most of us to add
may be a necessary concession to climate, to custom, or

to shame; they can hardly add a new vitality or any beauty comparable to that which they hide.

When the soul, as in Shelley's case, is all goodness, and when the world seems all illegitimacy and obstruction, we need not wonder that *freedom* should be regarded as a panacea. Even if freedom had not been the idol of Shelley's times, he would have made an idol of it for himself. " I never could discern in him," says his friend Hogg, " any more than two principles. The first was a strong, irrepressible love of liberty. . . . The second was an equally ardent love of toleration . . . and . . . an intense abhorrence of persecution." We all fancy nowadays that we believe in liberty and abhor persecution; but the liberty we approve of is usually only a variation in social compulsions, to make them less galling to our latest sentiments than the old compulsions would be if we retained them. Liberty of the press and liberty to vote do not greatly help us in living after our own mind, which is, I suppose, the only positive sort of liberty. From the point of view of a poet, there can be little essential freedom so long as he is forbidden to live with the people he likes, and compelled to live with the people he does not like. This, to Shelley, seemed the most galling of tyrannies; and free love was, to his feeling, the essence and test of freedom. Love must be spontaneous to be a spiritual bond in the beginning and it must remain spontaneous if it is to remain spiritual. To be bound by one's past is as great a tyranny to pure spirit as to be bound by the sin of Adam, or by the laws of Artaxerxes; and those of us who do not believe in the possibility of free love ought to declare frankly that we do not, at bottom, believe in the possibility of freedom.

> " I never was attached to that great sect
> Whose doctrine is that each one should select,
> Out of the crowd, a mistress or a friend
> And all the rest, though fair and wise, commend
> To cold oblivion; though it is the code
> Of modern morals, and the beaten road
> Which those poor slaves with weary footsteps tread
> Who travel to their home among the dead
> By the broad highway of the world, and so
> With one chained friend, perhaps a jealous foe,
> The dreariest and the longest journey go.
> True love in this differs from gold and clay,
> That to divide is not to take away.
> Love is like understanding that grows bright
> Gazing on many truths. . . . Narrow
> The heart that loves, the brain that contemplates,
> The life that wears, the spirit that creates
> One object and one form, and builds thereby
> A sepulchre for its eternity! "

The difficulties in reducing this charming theory of love to practice are well exemplified in Shelley's own life. He ran away with his first wife not because she inspired any uncontrollable passion, but because she declared she was a victim of domestic oppression and threw herself upon him for protection. Nevertheless, when he discovered that his best friend was making love to her, in spite of his free-love principles, he was very seriously annoyed. When he presently abandoned her, feeling a spiritual affinity in another direction, she drowned herself in the Serpentine: and his second wife needed all her natural sweetness and all her inherited philosophy to reconcile her to the waves of Platonic enthusiasm for other ladies which periodically swept the too sensitive heart of her husband. Free love would not, then, secure freedom from complications; it would not remove the present occasion for jealousy, reproaches, tragedies, and the dragging of a lengthening chain. Freedom of spirit cannot be translated into freedom of action; you may amend laws, and customs, and social entanglements, but you will still have them; for this world is a lumbering mechanism and not, like love, a plastic dream. Wisdom is very old and therefore often ironical, and it has long taught that it is well for those who would live in the spirit to keep as clear as possible of the world: and that marriage, especially a free-love marriage, is a snare for poets. Let them endure to love freely, hopelessly, and infinitely, after the manner of Plato and Dante, and even of Goethe, when Goethe really loved: that exquisite sacrifice will improve their verse, and it will not kill them. Let them follow in the traces of Shelley when he wrote in his youth: " I have been most of the night pacing a church-yard. I must now engage in scenes of strong interest. . . . I expect to gratify some of this insatiable feeling in poetry. . . . I slept with a loaded pistol and some poison last night, but did not die." Happy man if he had been able to add, " And did not marry! "

Last among the elements of Shelley's thought I may perhaps mention his atheism. Shelley called himself an atheist in his youth; his biographers and critics usually say that he was, or that he became, a pantheist. He was an atheist in the sense that he denied the orthodox conception of a deity who is a voluntary creator, a legislator, and a judge; but his aversion to Christianity was not founded on any sympathetic or imaginative knowledge of it; and a man who preferred the *Paradiso* of

Dante to almost any other poem, and preferred it to the popular *Inferno* itself, could evidently be attracted by Christian ideas and sentiment the moment they were presented to him as expressions of moral truth rather than as gratuitous dogmas.   A pantheist he was in the sense that he felt how fluid and vital this whole world is; but he seems to have had no tendency to conceive any conscious plan or logical necessity connecting the different parts of the whole; so that rather than a pantheist he might be called a panpsychist; especially as he did not subordinate morally the individual to the cosmos.   He did not surrender the authority of moral ideals in the face of physical necessity, which is properly the essence of pantheism.   He did the exact opposite; so much so that the chief characteristic of his philosophy is its Promethean spirit.   He maintained that the basis of moral authority was internal, diffused among all individuals; that it was the natural love of the beautiful and the good wherever it might spring, and however fate might oppose it.

> "To suffer . . .
> To forgive . . .
> To defy Power . . .
> To love and bear; to hope, till hope creates
> From its own wreck the thing it contemplates;
> Neither to change, nor falter, nor repent;
> This . . . is to be
> Good, great and joyous, beautiful and free."

Shelley was also removed from any ordinary atheism by his truly speculative sense for eternity.   He was a thorough Platonist.   All metaphysics perhaps is poetry, but Platonic metaphysics is good poetry, and to this class Shelley's belongs.   For instance:

> " The pure spirit shall flow
> Back to the burning fountain whence it came,
> A portion of the eternal, which must glow
> Through time and change, unquenchably the same.
> Peace, peace! he is not dead, he doth not sleep!
> He hath awakened from the dream of life.
> 'Tis we who, lost in stormy visions, keep
> With phantoms an unprofitable strife.
>
> " He is made one with Nature.   There is heard
> His voice in all her music, from the moan
> Of thunder, to the song of night's sweet bird.
>
> " He is a portion of the loveliness
> Which once he made more lovely.
>
> " The splendours of the firmament of time
> May be eclipsed, but are extinguished not:
> Like stars to their appointed height they climb,
> And death is a low mist which cannot blot
> The brightness it may veil.   When lofty thought
> Lifts a young heart above its mortal lair,
> . . . the dead live there."

Atheism or pantheism of this stamp cannot be taxed with being gross or materialistic; the trouble is rather that it is too hazy in its sublimity.   The poet has not perceived the natural relation between facts and ideals so clearly or correctly as he has felt the moral relation between them.   But his allegiance to the intuition which defies, for the sake of felt excellence, every form of idolatry or cowardice wearing the mask of religion— this allegiance is itself the purest religion; and it is capable of inspiring the sweetest and most absolute poetry.   In daring to lay bare the truths of fate, the poet creates for himself the subtlest and most heroic harmonies; and he is comforted for the illusions he has lost by being made incapable of desiring them.

We have seen that Shelley, being unteachable, could never put together any just idea of the world: he merely

collected images and emotions, and out of them made
worlds of his own. His poetry accordingly does not well
express history, nor human character, nor the constitution of nature. What he unrolls before us instead is, in
a sense, fantastic; it is a series of landscapes, passions,
and cataclysms such as never were on earth, and never
will be. If you are seriously interested only in what
belongs to earth you will not be ˋseriously interested
in Shelley. Literature, according to Matthew Arnold,
should be criticism of life, and Shelley did not criticise
life; so that his poetry had no solidity. But is life, we may
ask, the same thing as the circumstances of life on earth?
Is the spirit of life, that marks and judges those circumstances, itself nothing? Music is surely no description
of the circumstances of life; yet it is relevant to life
unmistakably, for it stimulates by means of a torrent
of abstract movements and images the formal and
emotional possibilities of living which lie in the spirit.
By so doing music becomes a part of life, a congruous
addition, a parallel life, as it were, to the vulgar one. I
see no reason, in the analogies of the natural world, for
supposing that the circumstances of human life are the
only circumstances in which the spirit of life can disport
itself. Even on this planet, there are sea-animals and
air-animals, ephemeral beings and self-centred beings,
as well as persons who can grow as old as Matthew
Arnold, and be as fond as he was of classifying other
people. And beyond this planet, and in the interstices
of what our limited senses can perceive, there are probably many forms of life not criticised in any of the books
which Matthew Arnold said we should read in order to

know the best that has been thought and said in the world. The future, too, even among men, may contain, as Shelley puts it, many " arts, though unimagined, yet to be." The divination of poets cannot, of course, be expected to reveal any of these hidden regions as they actually exist or will exist; but what would be the advantage of revealing them? It could only be what the advantage of criticising human life would be also, to improve subsequent life indirectly by turning it towards attainable goods, and is it not as important a thing to improve life directly and in the present, if one has the gift, by enriching rather than criticising it? Besides, there is need of fixing the ideal by which criticism is to be guided. If you have no image of happiness or beauty or perfect goodness before you, how are you to judge what portions of life are important, and what rendering of them is appropriate?

Being a singer inwardly inspired, Shelley could picture the ideal goals of life, the ultimate joys of experience, better than a discursive critic or observer could have done. The circumstances of life are only the bases or instruments of life: the fruition of life is not in retrospect, not in description of the instruments, but in expression of the spirit itself, to which those instruments may prove useful; as music is not a criticism of violins, but a playing upon them. This expression need not resemble its ground. Experience is diversified by colours that are not produced by colours, sounds that are not conditioned by sounds, names that are not symbols for other names, fixed ideal objects that stand for ever-changing material processes. The mind is fundamentally lyrical, inventive, redundant. Its visions are its own offspring, hatched

in the warmth of some favourable cosmic gale.   The
ambient weather may vary, and these visions be scattered;
but the ideal world they pictured may some day be
revealed again to some other poet similarly inspired;
the possibility of restoring it, or something like it, is
perpetual.   It is precisely because Shelley's sense for
things is so fluid, so illusive, that it opens to us emotionally what is a serious scientific probability; namely, that
human life is not all life, nor the landscape of earth
the only admired landscape in the universe; that the
ancients who believed in gods and spirits were nearer the
virtual truth (however anthropomorphically they may
have expressed themselves) than any philosophy or
religion that makes human affairs the centre and aim of
the world.   Such moral imagination is to be gained by
sinking into oneself, rather than by observing remote
happenings, because it is at its heart, not at its finger-
tips, that the human soul touches matter, and is akin to
whatever other centres of life may people the infinite.

For this reason the masters of spontaneity, the
prophets, the inspired poets, the saints, the mystics, the
musicians are welcome and most appealing companions.
In their simplicity and abstraction from the world they
come very near the heart.   They say little and help
much.   They do not picture life, but have life, and give
it.   So we may say, I think, of Shelley's magic universe
what he said of Greece; if it

> " Must be
> A wreck, yet shall its fragments re-assemble,
> And build themselves again impregnably
>   In a diviner clime,
> To Amphionic music, on some cape sublime
> Which frowns above the idle foam of time."

"Frowns," says Shelley rhetorically, as if he thought that something timeless, something merely ideal, could be formidable, or could threaten existing things with any but an ideal defeat. Tremendous error! Eternal possibilities may indeed beckon; they may attract those who instinctively pursue them as a star may guide those who wish to reach the place over which it happens to shine. But an eternal possibility has no material power. It is only one of an infinity of other things equally possible intrinsically, yet most of them quite unrealisable in this world of blood and mire. The realm of eternal essences rains down no Jovian thunderbolts, but only a ghostly Uranian calm. There is no frown there; rather, a passive and universal welcome to any who may have in them the will and the power to climb. Whether any one has the will depends on his material constitution, and whether he has the power depends on the firm texture of that constitution and on circumstances happening to be favourable to its operation. Otherwise what the rebel or the visionary hails as his ideal will be no picture of his destiny or of that of the world. It will be, and will always remain, merely a picture of his heart. This picture, indestructible in its ideal essence, will mirror also the hearts of those who may share, or may have shared, the nature of the poet who drew it. So purely ideal and so deeply human are the visions of Shelley. So truly does he deserve the epitaph which a clear-sighted friend wrote upon his tomb: *cor cordium*, the heart of hearts.

VI

THE GENTEEL TRADITION IN AMERICAN
PHILOSOPHY

*Address delivered before the Philosophical Union of the
University of California, August 25, 1911.*

LADIES AND GENTLEMEN,—The privilege of addressing
you to-day is very welcome to me, not merely for the
honour of it, which is great, nor for the pleasures of travel,
which are many, when it is California that one is visiting
for the first time, but also because there is something I
have long wanted to say which this occasion seems particularly favourable for saying. America is still a young
country, and this part of it is especially so; and it
would have been nothing extraordinary if, in this
young country, material preoccupations had altogether
absorbed people's minds, and they had been too much
engrossed in living to reflect upon life, or to have any
philosophy. The opposite, however, is the case. Not
only have you already found time to philosophise in
California, as your society proves, but the eastern
colonists from the very beginning were a sophisticated
race. As much as in clearing the land and fighting the
Indians they were occupied, as they expressed it, in
wrestling with the Lord. The country was new, but the
race was tried, chastened, and full of solemn memories.
It was an old wine in new bottles; and America did not

have to wait for its present universities, with their departments of academic philosophy, in order to possess a living philosophy—to have a distinct vision of the universe and definite convictions about human destiny.

Now this situation is a singular and remarkable one, and has many consequences, not all of which are equally fortunate. America is a young country with an old mentality: it has enjoyed the advantages of a child carefully brought up and thoroughly indoctrinated; it has been a wise child. But a wise child, an old head on young shoulders, always has a comic and an unpromising side. The wisdom is a little thin and verbal, not aware of its full meaning and grounds; and physical and emotional growth may be stunted by it, or even deranged. Or when the child is too vigorous for that, he will develop a fresh mentality of his own, out of his observations and actual instincts; and this fresh mentality will interfere with the traditional mentality, and tend to reduce it to something perfunctory, conventional, and perhaps secretly despised. A philosophy is not genuine unless it inspires and expresses the life of those who cherish it. I do not think the hereditary philosophy of America has done much to atrophy the natural activities of the inhabitants; the wise child has not missed the joys of youth or of manhood; but what has happened is that the hereditary philosophy has grown stale, and that the academic philosophy afterwards developed has caught the stale odour from it. America is not simply, as I said a moment ago, a young country with an old mentality: it is a country with two mentalities, one a survival of the beliefs and standards of the fathers, the other an expression of the instincts, practice, and discoveries of the younger generations. In all the higher things of the mind—in religion, in literature, in the moral emotions—it is the hereditary spirit that still prevails, so much so that Mr. Bernard Shaw finds that America is a hundred years behind the times. The truth is that one-half of the American mind, that not occupied intensely in practical affairs, has remained, I will not say high-and-dry, but slightly becalmed; it has floated gently in the back-water, while, alongside, in invention and industry and social organisation, the other half of the mind was leaping down a sort of Niagara Rapids. This division may be found symbolised in American architecture: a neat reproduction of the colonial mansion—with some modern comforts introduced surreptitiously—stands beside the sky-scraper. The American Will inhabits the sky-scraper; the American Intellect inhabits the colonial mansion. The one is the sphere of the American man; the other, at least predominantly, of the American woman. The one is all aggressive enterprise; the other is all genteel tradition.

Now, with your permission, I should like to analyse more fully how this interesting situation has arisen, how it is qualified, and whither it tends. And in the first place we should remember what, precisely, that philosophy was which the first settlers brought with them into the country. In strictness there was more than one; but we may confine our attention to what I will call Calvinism, since it is on this that the current academic philosophy has been grafted. I do not mean exactly the Calvinism of Calvin, or even of Jonathan Edwards; for in their systems there was much that was not pure philosophy, but rather faith in the externals and history of revelation. Jewish and Christian revelation was interpreted by these men, however, in the spirit of a particular philosophy, which might have arisen under any sky, and been associated with any other religion as well as with Protestant Christianity. In fact, the philosophical principle of Calvinism appears also in the Koran, in Spinoza, and in Cardinal Newman; and persons with no very distinctive Christian belief, like Carlyle or like Professor Royce, may be nevertheless, philosophically, perfect Calvinists. Calvinism, taken in this sense, is an expression of the agonised conscience. It is a view of the world which an agonised conscience readily embraces, if it takes itself seriously, as, being agonised, of course it must. Calvinism, essentially, asserts three things: that sin exists, that sin is punished, and that it is beautiful that sin should exist to be punished. The heart of the Calvinist is therefore divided between tragic concern at his own miserable condition, and tragic exultation about the universe at large. He oscillates between a profound abasement and a paradoxical elation of the spirit. To be a Calvinist philosophically is to feel a fierce pleasure in the existence of misery, especially of one's own, in that this misery seems to manifest the fact that the Absolute is irresponsible or infinite or holy. Human nature, it feels, is totally depraved: to have the instincts and motives that we necessarily have is a great scandal, and we must suffer for it; but that scandal is requisite, since otherwise the serious importance of being as we ought to be would not have been vindicated.

To those of us who have not an agonised conscience this system may seem fantastic and even unintelligible; yet it is logically and intently thought out from its emotional premises. It can take permanent possession of a deep mind here and there, and under certain conditions it can become epidemic. Imagine, for instance, a small nation with an intense vitality, but on the verge of ruin, ecstatic and distressful, having a strict and minute code of laws, that paints life in sharp and violent chiaroscuro, all pure righteousness and black abominations, and exaggerating the consequences of both perhaps to infinity. Such a people were the Jews after the exile, and again the early Protestants. If such a people is philosophical at all, it will not improbably be Calvinistic. Even in the early American communities many of these conditions were fulfilled. The nation was small and isolated; it lived under pressure and constant trial; it was acquainted with but a small range of goods and evils. Vigilance over conduct and an absolute demand for personal integrity were not merely traditional things, but things that practical sages, like Franklin and Washington, recommended to their countrymen, because they were virtues that justified themselves visibly by their fruits. But soon these happy results themselves helped to relax the pressure of external circumstances, and indirectly the pressure of the agonised conscience within. The nation became numerous; it ceased to be either ecstatic or distressful; the high social morality which on the whole it preserved took another colour; people remained honest and helpful out of good sense and good will rather than out of scrupulous adherence to any fixed principles.

They retained their instinct for order, and often created order with surprising quickness; but the sanctity of law, to be obeyed for its own sake, began to escape them; it seemed too unpractical a notion, and not quite serious. In fact, the second and native-born American mentality began to take shape. The sense of sin totally evaporated. Nature, in the words of Emerson, was all beauty and commodity; and while operating on it laboriously, and drawing quick returns, the American began to drink in inspiration from it æsthetically. At the same time, in so broad a continent, he had elbow-room. His neighbours helped more than they hindered him; he wished their number to increase. Good will became the great American virtue; and a passion arose for counting heads, and square miles, and cubic feet, and minutes saved—as if there had been anything to save them for. How strange to the American now that saying of Jonathan Edwards, that men are naturally God's enemies! Yet that is an axiom to any intelligent Calvinist, though the words he uses may be different. If you told the modern American that he is totally depraved, he would think you were joking, as he himself usually is. He is convinced that he always has been, and always will be, victorious and blameless.

Calvinism thus lost its basis in American life. Some emotional natures, indeed, reverted in their religious revivals or private searchings of heart to the sources of the tradition; for any of the radical points of view in philosophy may cease to be prevalent, but none can cease to be possible. Other natures, more sensitive to the moral and literary influences of the world, preferred to abandon parts of their philosophy, hoping thus to reduce the distance which should separate the remainder from real life.

Meantime, if anybody arose with a special sensibility or a technical genius, he was in great straits; not being fed sufficiently by the world, he was driven in upon his own resources. The three American writers whose personal endowment was perhaps the finest—Poe, Hawthorne, and Emerson—had all a certain starved and abstract quality. They could not retail the genteel tradition; they were too keen, too perceptive, and too independent for that. But life offered them little digestible material, nor were they naturally voracious. They were fastidious, and under the circumstances they were starved. Emerson, to be sure, fed on books. There was a great catholicity in his reading; and he showed a fine tact in his comments, and in his way of appropriating what he read. But he read transcendentally, not historically, to learn what he himself felt, not what others might have felt before him. And to feed on books, for a philosopher or a poet, is still to starve. Books can help him to acquire form, or to avoid pitfalls; they cannot supply him with substance, if he is to have any. Therefore the genius of Poe and Hawthorne, and even of Emerson, was employed on a sort of inner play, or digestion of vacancy. It was a refined labour, but it was in danger of being morbid, or tinkling, or self-indulgent. It was a play of intra-mental rhymes. Their mind was like an old music-box, full of tender echoes and quaint fancies. These fancies expressed their personal genius sincerely, as dreams may; but they were arbitrary fancies in comparison with what a real observer would have said in the premises. Their manner, in a word, was subjective. In their own persons they escaped the mediocrity of the genteel tradition, but they supplied nothing to supplant it in other minds.

The churches, likewise, although they modified their spirit, had no philosophy to offer save a new emphasis on parts of what Calvinism contained. The theology of Calvin, we must remember, had much in it besides philosophical Calvinism. A Christian tenderness, and a hope of grace for the individual, came to mitigate its sardonic optimism; and it was these evangelical elements that the Calvinistic churches now emphasised, seldom and with blushes referring to hell-fire or infant damnation. Yet philosophic Calvinism, with a theory of life that would perfectly justify hell-fire and infant damnation if they happened to exist, still dominates the traditional metaphysics. It is an ingredient, and the decisive ingredient, in what calls itself idealism. But in order to see just what part Calvinism plays in current idealism, it will be necessary to distinguish the other chief element in that complex system, namely, transcendentalism.

Transcendentalism is the philosophy which the romantic era produced in Germany, and independently, I believe, in America also. Transcendentalism proper, like romanticism, is not any particular set of dogmas about what things exist; it is not a system of the universe regarded as a fact, or as a collection of facts. It is a method, a point of view, from which any world, no matter what it might contain, could be approached by a self-conscious observer. Transcendentalism is systematic subjectivism. It studies the perspectives of knowledge as they radiate from the self; it is a plan of those avenues of inference by which our ideas of things must be reached, if they are to afford any systematic or distant vistas. In other words, transcendentalism is the critical logic of science. Knowledge, it says, has a station, as in a watch-tower; it is always seated here and now, in the self of the moment. The past and the future, things inferred and things conceived, lie around it, painted as upon a panorama. They cannot be lighted up save by some centrifugal ray of attention and present interest, by some active operation of the mind.

This is hardly the occasion for developing or explaining this delicate insight; suffice it to say, lest you should think later that I disparage transcendentalism, that as a method I regard it as correct and, when once suggested, unforgettable. I regard it as the chief contribution made in modern times to speculation. But it is a method only, an attitude we may always assume if we like and that will always be legitimate. It is no answer, and involves no particular answer, to the question: What exists; in what order is what exists produced; what is to exist in the future? This question must be answered by observing the object, and tracing humbly the movement of the object. It cannot be answered at all by harping on the fact that this object, if discovered, must be discovered by somebody, and by somebody who has an interest in discovering it. Yet the Germans who first gained the full transcendental insight were romantic people; they were more or less frankly poets; they were colossal egotists, and wished to make not only their own knowledge but the whole universe centre about themselves. And full as they were of their romantic isolation and romantic liberty, it occurred to them to imagine that all reality might be a transcendental self and a romantic dreamer like themselves; nay, that it might be just their own transcendental self and their own romantic dreams extended indefinitely. Transcendental logic, the method of discovery for the mind, was to become also the method of evolution in nature and history. Transcendental method, so abused, produced transcendental myth. A conscientious critique of knowledge was turned into a sham system of nature. We must therefore distinguish sharply the transcendental grammar of the intellect, which is significant and potentially correct, from the various transcendental systems of the universe, which are chimeras.

In both its parts, however, transcendentalism had much to recommend it to American philosophers, for the transcendental method appealed to the individualistic and revolutionary temper of their youth, while transcendental myths enabled them to find a new status for their inherited theology, and to give what parts of it they cared to preserve some semblance of philosophical backing. This last was the use to which the transcendental method was put by Kant himself, who first brought it into vogue, before the terrible weapon had got out of hand, and become the instrument of pure romanticism. Kant came, he himself said, to remove knowledge in order to make room for faith, which in his case meant faith in Calvinism. In other words, he applied the transcendental method to matters of fact, reducing them thereby to human ideas, in order to give to the Calvinistic postulates of conscience a metaphysical validity. For Kant had a genteel tradition of his own, which he wished to remove to a place of safety, feeling that the empirical world had become too hot for it; and this place of safety was the region of transcendental myth. I need hardly say how perfectly this expedient suited the needs of philosophers in America, and it is no accident if the influence of Kant soon became dominant here. To embrace this philosophy was regarded as a sign of profound metaphysical insight, although the most mediocre minds found no difficulty in embracing it. In truth it was a sign of having been brought up in the genteel tradition, of feeling it weak, and of wishing to save it.

But the transcendental method, in its way, was also sympathetic to the American mind. It embodied, in a radical form, the spirit of Protestantism as distinguished from its inherited doctrines; it was autonomous, undismayed, calmly revolutionary; it felt that Will was deeper than Intellect; it focussed everything here and now, and asked all things to show their credentials at the bar of the young self, and to prove their value for this latest born moment. These things are truly American; they would be characteristic of any young society with a keen and discursive intelligence, and they are strikingly exemplified in the thought and in the person of Emerson. They constitute what he called self-trust. Self-trust, like other transcendental attitudes, may be expressed in metaphysical fables. The romantic spirit may imagine itself to be an absolute force, evoking and moulding the plastic world to express its varying moods. But for a pioneer who is actually a world-builder this metaphysical illusion has a partial warrant in historical fact; far more warrant than it could boast of in the fixed and articulated society of Europe, among the moonstruck rebels and sulking poets of the romantic era. Emerson was a shrewd Yankee, by instinct on the winning side; he was a cheery, child-like soul, impervious to the evidence of evil, as of everything that it did not suit his transcendental individuality to appreciate or to notice. More, perhaps, than anybody that has ever lived, he practised the transcendental method in all its purity. He had no system. He opened his eyes on the world every morning with a fresh sincerity, marking how things seemed to him then, or what they suggested to his spontaneous fancy. This fancy, for being spontaneous, was not always novel; it was guided by the habits and training of his mind, which were those of a preacher. Yet he never insisted on his notions so as to turn them into settled dogmas; he felt in his bones that they were myths. Sometimes, indeed, the bad example of other transcendentalists, less true than he to their method, or the pressing questions of unintelligent people, or the instinct we all have to think our ideas final, led him to the very verge of system-making; but he stopped short. Had he made a system out of his notion of compensation, or the over-soul, or spiritual laws, the result would have been as thin and forced as it is in other transcendental systems. But he coveted truth; and he returned to experience, to history, to poetry, to the natural science of his day, for new starting-points and hints toward fresh transcendental musings.

To covet truth is a very distinguished passion. Every

philosopher says he is pursuing the truth, but this is seldom the case.   As Mr. Bertrand Russell has observed, one reason why philosophers often fail to reach the truth is that often they do not desire to reach it.   Those who are genuinely concerned in discovering what happens to be true are rather the men of science, the naturalists, the historians; and ordinarily they discover it, according to their lights.   The truths they find are never complete, and are not always important; but they are integral parts of the truth, facts and circumstances that help to fill in the picture, and that no later interpretation can invalidate or afford to contradict.   But professional philosophers are usually only apologists: that is, they are absorbed in defending some vested illusion or some eloquent idea. Like lawyers or detectives, they study the case for which they are retained, to see how much evidence or semblance of evidence they can gather for the defence, and how much prejudice they can raise against the witnesses for the prosecution; for they know they are defending prisoners suspected by the world, and perhaps by their own good sense, of falsification. · They do not covet truth, but victory and the dispelling of their own doubts. What they defend is some system, that is, some view about the totality of things, of which men are actually ignorant.   No system would have ever been framed if people had been simply interested in knowing what is true, whatever it may be.   What produces systems is the interest in maintaining against all comers that some favourite or inherited idea of ours is sufficient and right. A system may contain an account of many things which, in detail, are true enough; but as a system, covering infinite possibilities that neither our experience nor our logic can prejudge, it must be a work of imagination and a piece of human soliloquy. It may be expressive of human experience, it may be poetical; but how should any one who really coveted truth suppose that it was true?

Emerson had no system; and his coveting truth had another exceptional consequence: he was detached, unworldly, contemplative. When he came out of the conventicle or the reform meeting, or out of the rapturous close atmosphere of the lecture-room, he heard Nature whispering to him: " Why so hot, little sir? " No doubt the spirit or energy of the world is what is acting in us, as the sea is what rises in every little wave; but it passes through us, and cry out as we may, it will move on. Our privilege is to have perceived it as it moves. Our dignity is not in what we do, but in what we understand. The whole world is doing things. We are turning in that vortex; yet within us is silent observation, the speculative eye before which all passes, which bridges the distances and compares the combatants. On this side of his genius Emerson broke away from all conditions of age or country and represented nothing except intelligence itself.

There was another element in Emerson, curiously combined with transcendentalism, namely, his love and respect for Nature. Nature, for the transcendentalist, is precious because it is his own work, a mirror in which he looks at himself and says (like a poet relishing his own verses), " What a genius I am! Who would have thought there was such stuff in me? " And the philosophical egotist finds in his doctrine a ready explanation of what-

ever beauty and commodity nature actually has. No
wonder, he says to himself, that nature is sympathetic,
since I made it. And such a view, one-sided and even
fatuous as it may be, undoubtedly sharpens the vision
of a poet and a moralist to all that is inspiriting and
symbolic in the natural world. Emerson was particularly
ingenious and clear-sighted in feeling the spiritual uses
of fellowship with the elements. This is something in
which all Teutonic poetry is rich and which forms, I
think, the most genuine and spontaneous part of modern
taste, and especially of American taste. Just as some
people are naturally enthralled and refreshed by music,
so others are by landscape. Music and landscape make
up the spiritual resources of those who cannot or dare
not express their unfulfilled ideals in words. Serious
poetry, profound religion (Calvinism, for instance), are
the joys of an unhappiness that confesses itself; but
when a genteel tradition forbids people to confess that
they are unhappy, serious poetry and profound religion
are closed to them by that; and since human life, in its
depths, cannot then express itself openly, imagination
is driven for comfort into abstract arts, where human
circumstances are lost sight of, and human problems
dissolve in a purer medium. The pressure of care is thus
relieved, without its quietus being found in intelligence.
To understand oneself is the classic form of consolation;
to elude oneself is the romantic. In the presence of
music or landscape human experience eludes itself; and
thus romanticism is the bond between transcendental
and naturalistic sentiment. The winds and clouds come
to minister to the solitary ego.

Have there been, we may ask, any successful efforts to escape from the genteel tradition, and to express something worth expressing behind its back? This might well not have occurred as yet; but America is so precocious, it has been trained by the genteel tradition to be so wise for its years, that some indications of a truly native philosophy and poetry are already to be found. I might mention the humorists, of whom you here in California have had your share. The humorists, however, only half escape the genteel tradition; their humour would lose its savour if they had wholly escaped it. They point to what contradicts it in the facts; but not in order to abandon the genteel tradition, for they have nothing solid to put in its place. When they point out how ill many facts fit into it, they do not clearly conceive that this militates against the standard, but think it a funny perversity in the facts. Of course, did they earnestly respect the genteel tradition, such an incongruity would seem to them sad, rather than ludicrous. Perhaps the prevalence of humour in America, in and out of season, may be taken as one more evidence that the genteel tradition is present pervasively, but everywhere weak. Similarly in Italy, during the Renaissance, the Catholic tradition could not be banished from the intellect, since there was nothing articulate to take its place; yet its hold on the heart was singularly relaxed. The consequence was that humorists could regale themselves with the foibles of monks and of cardinals, with the credulity of fools, and the bogus miracles of the saints; not intending to deny the theory of the church, but caring for it so little at heart that they could find it infinitely amusing that it should be contradicted in men's lives and that no harm should come of it. So when Mark Twain says, " I was born of poor but dishonest parents," the humour depends on the parody of the genteel Anglo-Saxon convention that it is disreputable to be poor; but to hint at the hollowness of it would not be amusing if it did not remain at bottom one's habitual conviction.

The one American writer who has left the genteel tradition entirely behind is perhaps Walt Whitman. For this reason educated Americans find him rather an unpalatable person, who they sincerely protest ought not to be taken for a representative of their culture; and he certainly should not, because their culture is so genteel and traditional. But the foreigner may sometimes think otherwise, since he is looking for what may have arisen in America to express, not the polite and conventional American mind, but the spirit and the inarticulate principles that animate the community, on which its own genteel mentality seems to sit rather lightly. When the foreigner opens the pages of Walt Whitman, he thinks that he has come at last upon something representative and original. In Walt Whitman democracy is carried into psychology and morals. The various sights, moods, and emotions are given each one vote; they are declared to be all free and equal, and the innumerable commonplace moments of life are suffered to speak like the others. Those moments formerly reputed great are not excluded, but they are made to march in the ranks with their companions—plain foot-soldiers and servants of the hour. Nor does the refusal to discriminate stop there; we must carry our principle further down, to the animals, to inanimate nature, to the cosmos as a whole. Whitman became a pantheist; but his pantheism, unlike that of the Stoics and of Spinoza, was unintellectual, lazy, and self-indulgent; for he simply felt jovially that everything real was good enough, and that he was good enough himself. In him Bohemia rebelled against the genteel tradition; but the reconstruction that alone can justify revolution did not ensue. His attitude, in principle, was utterly disintegrating; his poetic genius fell back to the lowest level, perhaps, to which it is possible for poetic genius to fall. He reduced his imagination to a passive sensorium for the registering of impressions. No element of construction remained in it, and therefore no element of penetration. But his scope was wide; and his lazy, desultory apprehension was poetical. His work, for the very reason that it is so rudimentary, contains a beginning, or rather many beginnings, that might possibly grow into a noble moral imagination, a worthy filling for the human mind. An American in the nineteenth century who completely disregarded the genteel tradition could hardly have done more.

But there is another distinguished man, lately lost to this country, who has given some rude shocks to this tradition and who, as much as Whitman, may be regarded as representing the genuine, the long silent American mind—I mean William James. He and his brother Henry were as tightly swaddled in the genteel tradition as any infant geniuses could be, for they were born before 1850, and in a Swedenborgian household. Yet they burst those bands almost entirely. The ways in which the two brothers freed themselves, however, are interestingly different. Mr. Henry James has done it by adopting the point of view of the outer world, and by turning the genteel American tradition, as he turns everything else, into a subject-matter for analysis. For him it is a curious habit of mind, intimately comprehended, to be compared with other habits of mind, also well known to him. Thus he has overcome the genteel tradition in the classic way, by understanding it. With William James too this infusion of worldly insight and European sympathies was a potent influence, especially in his earlier days; but the chief source of his liberty was another. It was his personal spontaneity, similar to that of Emerson, and his personal vitality, similar to that of nobody else. Convictions and ideas came to him, so to speak, from the subsoil. He had a prophetic sympathy with the dawning sentiments of the age, with the moods of the dumb majority. His scattered words caught fire in many parts of the world. His way of thinking and feeling represented the true America, and represented in a measure the whole ultra-modern, radical world. Thus he eluded the genteel tradition in the romantic way, by continuing it into its opposite. The romantic mind, glorified in Hegel's dialectic (which is not dialectic at all, but a sort of tragi-comic history of experience), is always rendering its thoughts unrecognisable through the infusion of new insights, and through the insensible transformation of the moral feeling that accompanies them, till at last it has completely reversed its old judgments under cover of expanding them. Thus the genteel tradition was led a merry dance when it fell again into the hands of a genuine and vigorous romanticist like William James. He restored their revolutionary force to its neutralised elements, by picking them out afresh, and emphasising them separately, according to his personal predilections.

For one thing, William James kept his mind and heart wide open to all that might seem, to polite minds, odd, personal, or visionary in religion and philosophy. He gave a sincerely respectful hearing to sentimentalists, mystics, spiritualists, wizards, cranks, quacks, and im-postors—for it is hard to draw the line, and James was not willing to draw it prematurely. He thought, with his usual modesty, that any of these might have some-thing to teach him. The lame, the halt, the blind, and those speaking with tongues could come to him with the certainty of finding sympathy; and if they were not healed, at least they were comforted, that a famous professor should take them so seriously; and they began to feel that after all to have only one leg, or one hand, or one eye, or to have three, might be in itself no less beauteous than to have just two, like the stolid majority. Thus William James became the friend and helper of those groping, nervous, half-educated, spiritually dis-inherited, passionately hungry individuals of which America is full. He became, at the same time, their spokesman and representative before the learned world; and he made it a chief part of his vocation to recast what the learned world has to offer, so that as far as possible it might serve the needs and interests of these people.

Yet the normal practical masculine American, too, had a friend in William James. There is a feeling abroad now, to which biology and Darwinism lend some colour, that theory is simply an instrument for practice, and intelligence merely a help toward material survival. Bears, it is said, have fur and claws, but poor naked man is condemned to be intelligent, or he will perish. This feeling William James embodied in that theory of thought and of truth which he called pragmatism. Intelligence, he thought, is no miraculous, idle faculty, by which we mirror passively any or everything that happens to be true, reduplicating the real world to no purpose. Intelligence has its roots and its issue in the context of events; it is one kind of practical adjustment, an experimental act, a form of vital tension. It does not essentially serve to picture other parts of reality, but to connect them. This view was not worked out by William James in its psychological and historical details; unfortunately he developed it chiefly in controversy against its opposite, which he called intellectualism, and which he hated with all the hatred of which his kind heart was capable. Intellectualism, as he conceived it, was pure pedantry; it impoverished and verbalised everything, and tied up nature in red tape. Ideas and rules that may have been occasionally useful it put in the place of the full-blooded irrational movement of life which had called them into being; and these abstractions, so soon obsolete, it strove to fix and to worship for ever. Thus all creeds and theories and all formal precepts sink in the estimation of the pragmatist to a local and temporary grammar of action; a grammar that must be changed slowly by time, and may be changed quickly by genius. To know things as a whole, or as they are eternally, if there is anything eternal in them, is not only beyond our powers, but would prove worthless, and perhaps even fatal to our lives. Ideas are not mirrors, they are weapons; their function is to prepare us to meet events, as future experience may unroll them. Those ideas that disappoint us are false ideas; those to which events are true are true themselves.

This may seem a very utilitarian view of the mind; and I confess I think it a partial one, since the logical force of beliefs and ideas, their truth or falsehood as assertions, has been overlooked altogether, or confused with the vital force of the material processes which these ideas express. It is an external view only, which marks the place and conditions of the mind in nature, but neglects its specific essence; as if a jewel were defined as a round hole in a ring. Nevertheless, the more materialistic the pragmatist's theory of the mind is, the more vitalistic his theory of nature will have to become. If the intellect is a device produced in organic bodies to expedite their processes, these organic bodies must have interests and a chosen direction in their life; otherwise their life could not be expedited, nor could anything be useful to it. In other words—and this is a third point at which the philosophy of William James has played havoc with the genteel tradition, while ostensibly defending it—nature must be conceived anthropomorphically and in psychological terms. Its purposes are not to be static harmonies, self-unfolding destinies, the logic of spirit, the spirit of logic, or any other formal method and abstract law; its purposes are to be concrete endeavours, finite efforts of souls living in an environment which they transform and by which they, too, are affected. A spirit, the divine spirit as much as the human, as this new animism conceives it, is a romantic adventurer. Its future is undetermined. Its scope, its duration, and the quality of its life are all contingent. This spirit grows; it buds and sends forth feelers, sounding the depths around for such other centres of force or life as may exist there. It has a vital momentum, but no predetermined goal. It uses its past as a stepping-stone, or rather as a diving-board, but has an absolutely fresh will at each moment to plunge this way or that into the unknown. The universe is an experiment; it is unfinished. It has no ultimate or total nature, because it has no end. It embodies no formula or statable law; any formula is at best a poor abstraction, describing what, in some region and for some time, may be the most striking characteristic of existence; the law is a description *a posteriori* of the habit things have chosen to acquire, and which they may possibly throw off altogether. What a day may bring forth is uncertain; uncertain even to God. Omniscience is impossible; time is real; what had been omniscience hitherto might discover something more to-day. "There shall be news," William James was fond of saying with rapture, quoting from the un-published poem of an obscure friend, "there shall be news in heaven!" There is almost certainly, he thought, a God now; there may be several gods, who might exist together, or one after the other. We might, by our con-spiring sympathies, help to make a new one. Much in us is doubtless immortal; we survive death for some time in a recognisable form; but what our career and transformations may be in the sequel we cannot tell, although we may help to determine them by our daily choices. Observation must be continual if our ideas are to remain true. Eternal vigilance is the price of knowledge; perpetual hazard, perpetual experiment keep quick the edge of life.

This is, so far as I know, a new philosophical vista; it is a conception never before presented, although implied, perhaps, in various quarters, as in Norse and even Greek mythology. It is a vision radically empirical and radically romantic; and as William James himself used to say, the visions and not the arguments of a philosopher are the interesting and influential things about him. William James, rather too generously, attributed this vision to M. Bergson, and regarded him in consequence as a philosopher of the first rank, whose thought was to be one of the turning-points in history. M. Bergson had killed intellectualism. It was his book on creative evolution, said James with humorous emphasis, that had come at last to " *écraser l'infâme.*" We may suspect, notwithstanding, that intellectualism, infamous and crushed, will survive the blow; and if the author of the Book of Ecclesiastes were now alive, and heard that there shall be news in heaven, he would doubtless say that there may possibly be news there, but that under the sun there is nothing new—not even radical empiricism or radical romanticism, which from the beginning of the world has been the philosophy of those who as yet had had little experience; for to the blinking little child it is not merely something in the world that is new daily, but everything is new all day.

I am not concerned with the rights and wrongs of that controversy; my point is only that William James, in this genial evolutionary view of the world, has given a rude shock to the genteel tradition. What! The world a gradual improvisation? Creation unpremeditated? God a sort of young poet or struggling artist? William James is an advocate of theism; pragmatism adds one to the evidences of religion; that is excellent. But is not the cool abstract piety of the genteel getting more than it asks for? This empirical naturalistic God is too crude and positive a force; he will work miracles, he will answer prayers, he may inhabit distinct places, and have distinct conditions under which alone he can operate; he is a neighbouring being, whom we can act upon, and rely upon for specific aids, as upon a personal friend, or a physician, or an insurance company. How disconcerting! Is not this new theology a little like superstition? And yet how interesting, how exciting, if it should happen to be true! I am far from wishing to suggest that such a view seems to me more probable than conventional idealism or than Christian orthodoxy. All three are in the region of dramatic system-making and myth to which probabilities are irrelevant. If one man says the moon is sister to the sun, and another that she is his daughter, the question is not which notion is more probable, but whether either of them is at all expressive. The so-called evidences are devised afterwards, when faith and imagination have prejudged the issue. The force of William James's new theology, or romantic cosmology, lies only in this: that it has broken the spell of the genteel tradition, and enticed faith in a new direction,

which on second thoughts may prove no less alluring than
the old. The important fact is not that the new fancy
might possibly be true—who shall know that?—but that
it has entered the heart of a leading American to conceive
and to cherish it. The genteel tradition cannot be dis-
lodged by these insurrections; there are circles to which
it is still congenial, and where it will be preserved. But
it has been challenged and (what is perhaps more insidious) it has been discovered. No one need be brow-
beaten any longer into accepting it. No one need be
afraid, for instance, that his fate is sealed because some
young prig may call him a dualist; the pint would call the
quart a dualist, if you tried to pour the quart into him.
We need not be afraid of being less profound, for being
direct and sincere. The intellectual world may be
traversed in many directions; the whole has not been
surveyed; there is a great career in it open to talent.
That is a sort of knell, that tolls the passing of the genteel
tradition. Something else is now in the field; something else can appeal to the imagination, and be a thousand times more idealistic than academic idealism, which
is often simply a way of white-washing and adoring
things as they are. The illegitimate monopoly which the
genteel tradition had established over what ought to be
assumed and what ought to be hoped for has been broken
down by the first-born of the family, by the genius of the
race. Henceforth there can hardly be the same peace
and the same pleasure in hugging the old proprieties.
Hegel will be to the next generation what Sir William
Hamilton was to the last. Nothing will have been disproved, but everything will have been abandoned. An

honest man has spoken, and the cant of the genteel tradition has become harder for young lips to repeat.

With this I have finished such a sketch as I am here able to offer you of the genteel tradition in American philosophy. The subject is complex, and calls for many an excursus and qualifying footnote; yet I think the main outlines are clear enough. The chief fountains of this tradition were Calvinism and transcendentalism. Both were living fountains; but to keep them alive they required, one an agonised conscience, and the other a radical subjective criticism of knowledge. When these rare metaphysical preoccupations disappeared—and the American atmosphere is not favourable to either of them —the two systems ceased to be inwardly understood; they subsisted as sacred mysteries only; and the combination of the two in some transcendental system of the universe (a contradiction in principle) was doubly artificial. Besides, it could hardly be held with a single mind. Natural science, history, the beliefs implied in labour and invention, could not be disregarded altogether; so that the transcendental philosopher was condemned to a double allegiance, and to not letting his left hand know the bluff that his right hand was making. Nevertheless, the difficulty in bringing practical inarticulate convictions to expression is very great, and the genteel tradition has subsisted in the academic mind for want of anything equally academic to take its place.

The academic mind, however, has had its flanks turned. On the one side came the revolt of the Bohemian temperament, with its poetry of crude naturalism; on the other side came an impassioned empiricism, welcoming popular religious witnesses to the unseen, reducing science to an instrument of success in action, and declaring the universe to be wild and young, and not to be harnessed by the logic of any school.

This revolution, I should think, might well find an echo among you, who live in a thriving society, and in the presence of a virgin and prodigious world. When you transform nature to your uses, when you experiment with her forces, and reduce them to industrial agents, you cannot feel that nature was made by you or for you, for then these adjustments would have been pre-established. Much less can you feel it when she destroys your labour of years in a momentary spasm. You must feel, rather, that you are an offshoot of her life; one brave little force among her immense forces. When you escape, as you love to do, to your forests and your sierras, I am sure again that you do not feel you made them, or that they were made for you. They have grown, as you have grown, only more massively and more slowly. In their non-human beauty and peace they stir the sub-human depths and the superhuman possibilities of your own spirit. It is no transcendental logic that they teach; and they give no sign of any deliberate morality seated in the world. It is rather the vanity and superficiality of all logic, the needlessness of argument, the relativity of morals, the strength of time, the fertility of matter, the variety, the unspeakable variety, of possible life. Everything is measurable and conditioned, indefinitely repeated, yet, in repetition, twisted somewhat from its old form. Everywhere is beauty and nowhere permanence, everywhere an incipient harmony, nowhere an intention, nor a responsibility, nor a plan. It is the irresistible suasion of this daily spectacle, it is the daily discipline of contact with things, so different from the verbal discipline of the schools, that will, I trust, inspire the philosophy of your children. A Californian whom I had recently the pleasure of meeting observed that, if the philosophers had lived among your mountains their systems would have been different from what they are. Certainly, I should say, very different from what those systems are which the European genteel tradition has handed down since Socrates; for these systems are egotistical; directly or indirectly they are anthropocentric, and inspired by the conceited notion that man, or human reason, or the human distinction between good and evil, is the centre and pivot of the universe. That is what the mountains and the woods should make you at last ashamed to assert. From what, indeed, does the society of nature liberate you, that you find it so sweet? It is hardly (is it?) that you wish to forget your past, or your friends, or that you have any secret contempt for your present ambitions. You respect these, you respect them perhaps too much; you are not suffered by the genteel tradition to criticise or to reform them at all radically. No; it is the yoke of this genteel tradition itself that these primeval solitudes lift from your shoulders. They suspend your forced sense of your own importance not merely as individuals, but even as men. They allow you, in one happy moment, at once to play and to worship, to take yourselves simply, humbly, for what you are, and to salute the wild, indifferent, non-censorious infinity of nature. You are admonished that

what you can do avails little materially, and in the
end nothing. At the same time, through wonder and
pleasure, you are taught speculation. You learn what
you are really fitted to do, and where lie your natural
dignity and joy, namely, in representing many things,
without being them, and in letting your imagination,
through sympathy, celebrate and echo their life. Because
the peculiarity of man is that his machinery for reaction
on external things has involved an imaginative transcript
of these things, which is preserved and suspended in his
fancy; and the interest and beauty of this inward landscape, rather than any fortunes that may await his body
in the outer world, constitute his proper happiness. By
their mind, its scope, quality, and temper, we estimate
men, for by the mind only do we exist as men, and are
more than so many storage-batteries for material energy.
Let us therefore be frankly human. Let us be content
to live in the mind.

PLATONISM
AND THE SPIRITUAL LIFE

I

INTELLECTUAL anarchy is full of lights; its
blindness is made up of dazzling survivals,
revivals, and fresh beginnings. Were it not
for these remnants or seeds of order, chaos
itself could not exist; it would be nothing.
Without demanding from the men of to-day
anything final or solid we may be grateful to
them for those glimpses of great things past
and of great things possible, which flash
through their labouring minds. One of these
great things past is Platonism, and one of the
great things always possible is spiritual life.
There is, or there seems to be, a certain affinity
between these two, as if deep called unto deep.
Yet I am not sure that everything in Platonism,
or even its first principles, can be called
spiritual; nor is it easy to discern what the
essence of spirituality may be, entangled as its
manifestations have always been with all sorts
of accidental traditions and prejudices.

In this perplexity I find a list of points

common to Platonism and to "spiritual religion" drawn up by the competent hand of the Dean of St. Paul's.[1] These points are "a firm belief in absolute and eternal values as the most real things in the universe—a confidence that these values are knowable by man—a belief that they can nevertheless be known only by whole-hearted consecration of the intellect, will, and affections to the great quest —an entirely open mind towards the discoveries of science—a reverent and receptive attitude to the beauty, sublimity, and wisdom of the creation, as a revelation of the mind and character of the Creator—a complete indifference to the current valuations of the worldling." This faith " is distinguished, among other things, by its deep love of this good and beautiful world, combined with a steady rejection of that same world whenever it threatens to conceal, instead of revealing, the unseen and eternal world behind. The Platonist loves . . . Nature, because in Nature he perceives Spirit creating after its own likeness. As soon as the seen and the unseen worlds fall apart and lose connection with each other, both are dead." " Values are

---

[1] Cf. *The Platonic Tradition in English Religious Thought*, the Hulsean Lectures at Cambridge, 1925-6, by William Ralph Inge, Dean of St. Paul's, etc., Longmans, Green and Co., London, 1926. All the phrases quoted are drawn from this book.

for the Platonist not only ideals but creative powers."

This, of course, is the language of a modern. Dean Inge is not quoting Plato or Plotinus, but expressing what he believes to be substantially their view in words natural to a man of his own country and religion. We must, therefore, puzzle a little and hazard a guess before we can recall the Platonic tenets to which some of these phrases may refer. The term " value " in particular is subjective, imageless, and in a manner evasive. It may be taken as a neutral term fairly representing the common quality of what Plato called the good and the beautiful, before these were hypostatized; but then to hypostatize not only such values, but all natural types and logical concepts, was the very soul of Platonism; and when the good and the beautiful have been hypostatized and have become God or the One, the Ideas, the Demiurgus, or the Soul of the World, they are no longer values, but independent beings, existing long before the need or the admiration of mortals could attribute any value to them. Value is something relative, a dignity which anything may acquire in view of the benefit or satisfaction which it brings to some living being. If God or the Ideas were mere values, as are pleasure or health, they would be unsubstantial, and only a desired or achieved perfection in something else. They might, indeed, have value in their own eyes, but only if they were alive. A man, or a god, cannot prize his existence before he exists. An automatic harmony must be established in his life before he can distinguish its direction, suffer at its diminution, or conceive and desire its greater perfection. This harmony itself is a good only because the spirit which it creates so regards it.

II

IF I were a theologian, or even a bishop, I might be innocently led to ask Dean Inge what he means by a value. Is it anything that anybody values, or only that which some other person thinks we ought to value? Is it the fact that some satisfying aspect is found in things, or rather a magic necessity providing that such an aspect shall be found there? Or, as we gather from other Cambridge philosophers,[1] is this necessity not magical but natural and omnipresent in things, so that whenever a wave rises and bursts into foam, or a snowflake takes shape in the air, or any other form trembles for a moment in the flux of existence, the realization of this visiting essence is intrinsically a value, whether it be watched and prized by any spirit or not? Or on the contrary are values existing supernatural beings, by their influence compelling or inclining nature often to reproduce these satisfactory aspects? And I might even like to ask, going a little deeper, whether such supernatural beings, granting that they exist, work in nature towards the production of values of any

[1] For instance, in Whitehead's *Science in the Modern World*.

223

and every sort—as the law of the survival of the fittest might work to produce harmony between each sort of animal and its habitat, but to make their forms and their pleasures more and more diverse—or whether these supernatural beings are biassed in favour of certain natural forms and certain values to the exclusion of others; and finally, whether it is this congenital bias in supernatural powers that we should understand by the eternal reality of values.

In the modern notion—a very hazy one—that values themselves might be forces there is a contradiction, or at least an ellipsis. In any single instance, indeed, a mind disinclined to look for the causes or origins of things may find in an actual value a final and satisfying fact. Felt values reconcile the animal and moral side of our nature to their own contingency: if anything is well, we neglect to ask why it happens. The inner connivance and peace of our will explain it sufficiently. But when values are supposed to sustain themselves in being through a long tangle of circumstances, and to reassert themselves intermittently by their own strength, we are not merely content not to inquire why they arise, but we profess to explain their occasions and causes by their future presence: a position not only impossible to defend, but impossible to conceive clearly, and one that can be held only under cover of half-thoughts and cant phrases. Perception carves out its conventional units, and final causes insinuate themselves into the survey of facts, when their patient genesis is ignored or untraceable. Life on the whole is a proof of the possibility of life; each sort of life is a proof that circumstances made that sort of life inevitable. A vigorous and courageous animal assumes that fortune will not fail him. Did he not assume it, how should he be able to live? This sense of safety may be expressed and justified intellectually by finding the facts or habits of nature which support our own habits, and so bring the customary values about in the round of our experience. If these favouring circumstances are dominant in our world we shall be as safe in fact as we feel ourselves to be by instinct. This situation might then be expressed elliptically, by saying that the good is certain to prevail, or that values are powers: the justification for such an expression being that our assurance of safety and good fortune rests on a substantial harmony between our interests and our circumstances. But when this harmony becomes audible, when for a moment some value is realized, all potentiality and material efficacy are left far behind: we are in the realm of actuality, of music, of spirit; and the value actualized lives and ends in itself. The promise which often lies in it, as well as the disillusion or disaster that may

ensue, will not be due to that value in its moral nature, to that living and immaterial good; it will be due to the organization of nature beneath. All moral functions have their material organs and their material effects; in that context they are powers, or rather vehicles of power—for as the Moslems say, there is no power but Allah. Goods are, in their material ground, an integral part of the flux of events; and the healthy habit in nature which creates them once may repeat them and perfect them, if the season is favourable and the fates allow.

III

FOR my purpose, however, it is fortunately unimportant to dispel these ambiguities, dear to half-hearted philosophies, because the Platonic doctrine at least is clear. If for the Platonist goods and evils are everlastingly fixed and distinct, this moral dogmatism in him is no accident of temperament, no mere lack of moral elasticity, as in the bigot. If he is sure that some goods often passionately loved are nevertheless false goods, it is only because he attributes a definite and unchangeable constitution to the material world and to human nature. Life, he thinks, has been kindled and is alone sustained by the influence of pre-existing celestial models. It is by imitating these models in some measure that we exist at all, and only in imitating, loving, and contemplating them that we can ever be happy. They are our good. In themselves, however, they are inviolate beings, serenely shedding, like the stars, an everlasting radiance, and no doubt happy beings, if they are living and self-contemplative: but they are by no means mere goals which this nether world sets freely for itself, or perfections which it might enjoy intrinsically. God and the Ideas could be ruling powers, because they were existing beings, definite in their character and influence. They exercised a miraculous, magnetic control over formless matter, inducing in it here and there an inward striving to imitate their forms. They therefore had the greatest value for the creature whose life was directed upon them and who invincibly loved them; but this value in them remained relative to the aspiration of their lover, and variable in so far as his nature might change; so that St. Thomas Aquinas goes so far as to say that to the sinner God becomes an evil—the Christian God, he means, for I suppose the reprobate might still find a divine friend in Bacchus or Venus. It was never the actual values found in the world that were separated from it, either in Platonism or in Christianity, and conceived to compose an eternal world behind it. The powers that were creative, substantial, and permanent were not values at all, but the *underpinning* which values required if they were to arise; and although this substructure had to be in itself physical or metaphysical, the discovery of it had momentous consequences for morals, in that it enabled the enlightened believer to distinguish possible attainable goods from the impossible happiness after which the heathen seek. Those goods which the nature of things or the will of God assures and sanctions are the " eternal values "; the others are " the current valuations of the worldling." Thus religion or philosophy was the great arbiter of true values, the guide of life; it justified the sense of sin and the hope of salvation. The distinction between true goods and false goods can never be established by ignorant feeling or by conscience not backed by a dogmatic view of the facts: for felt values, taken absolutely and regarded as unconditioned, are all equally genuine in their excellence, and equally momentary in their existence. The distinction hangs on the system of forces, natural or supernatural, believed to produce and sustain these various goods, some for a moment, others for ever. *Some* constitution the cosmos must have, and must disclose to our faith or science, if ever we are to decide which of our pleasures or affections reveal " the unseen and eternal world behind," and which of them threaten to conceal it.

IV

THIS separation of the Platonic Ideas from the things which manifested them has been much blamed, yet it goes with another doctrine which is much prized, often by the same critics. The precious consequence of this abhorred dualism was that the Ideas, if separate, might be powers, creative forces that generated their expressions. Separation is a pre-requisite to causal connection: a thing cannot be derived from a part of itself. If Ideas were only values, if they were immanent in things, as the form of a poem or its peculiar beauty is immanent in that poem, there would be no sense in saying that the beauty or the form was a power that had produced the poem. Not only would each be dead without the other, as Dean Inge says, but each would be nothing; the poem arises by taking that form, and the form is merely that precise arrangement of words and images. The beauty of a thing is an essence which it manifests spontaneously, a pure quality of being revealed there, and perhaps never to be revealed again. The natural causes that produce the thing and bring it to notice produce also this manifestation of beauty in it; both spring into existence together out of a complex of circumstances and impulses among which it is impossible to place that homeless essence, the form of beauty thereby revealed; yet this form is their only value for the spirit, a value which that precise conjunction of causes was needed to realize.

There is a sense—a somewhat esoteric sense —in which such essences as beauty may be called " the most real things in the universe." They are the ultimate characters by which one thing can be distinguished from another in the flux of nature, or one thought from another in the mind; and if the word " real " be used sentimentally, to mean whatever is most clear or important or nearest to the heart, such values will be not only " most real " but even the only " reality," because their presence or absence, their purity or contradiction, make up the spiritual sum of life, all that matters in it, without which no one would care to raise his head from the pillow of non-being. If, however, by " most real " we understand most primitive or fundamental physically, the roots of existence, it is clearly impossible that the most real things should be values. Values presuppose living beings having a direction of development, and exerting themselves in it, so that good and evil may exist in reference to them. That the good should be relative to actual natures and simply their innate ideal, latent or realized, is essential to its being truly a good. Otherwise the term " good " would be an empty title applied to some existing object or force for no assignable reason.

The good may nevertheless be called absolute in several senses proper to current speech. The good is by no means relative to opinion, but is rooted in the unconscious and fatal nature of living beings, a nature which predetermines for them the difference between foods and poisons, happiness and misery. The moralist may speak for others with authority when he knows them better than they know themselves, but not otherwise. Moreover, their natural good may be absolute in the sense of being fixed and unalterable, so long as the living beings concerned and the circumstances in which they flourish remain constant in type. That human nature and the world are unchangeable was an assumption of classic times which survives often in modern moralists, without its dogmatic justification. Finally, the good may be called absolute in the sense of being single and all-sufficient, filling the whole heart, and leaving nothing in the rest of the universe in the least tempting, interesting, or worth distinguishing. It is in this sense that lovers and mystics proclaim the absoluteness of the good with which they are united, and when the thing is true as a confession it would be frivolous and ungracious to quarrel with it as a dogma.

V

IF then the Ideas were immanent in things, as
the beauty of a poem is immanent in it, they
could not conceivably be powers producing
their occasional manifestation. The beauties
intrinsic to the tragedy of Hamlet could not
have caused Shakespeare to compose that play
since those values could not possibly come to
existence until the play had already composed
itself in his fancy, and burst into just those
beauties. In order to maintain seriously the
efficacy of Ideas and to conceive matters in the
orthodox Platonic way, we must make a different supposition. Suppose Hamlet had been a
living prince, like the present Prince of Wales,
and that Shakespeare, with his company of
players, had happened to appear at this
prince's court, and had conceived for him a
passionate Platonic attachment, such as he
seems to have conceived for the W.H. of the
Sonnets: and suppose further that, by the
prodigious inspiration of this passion, Shakespeare had been led to imagine episodes and
phrases that might in part express so tender,
intellectual, and profound a character as that
living Prince seemed to him to possess; then
indeed a most real Hamlet, with a pre-existing
power and charm, might have been the " only

begetter " of the play. In exactly this way the
Platonic Ideas, the Christian God, or the
Christ of devout Christians, may be conceived
to be the causes of their temporal manifestations in matter or in the souls of men. Evidently a play written in such circumstances
might have the same intrinsic value as one
purely imaginary; but it would not be this
literary value that would constitute the model
or the creative influence which had produced
the play; this literary value would have been
begotten, like the play itself and inseparably
from it, by the influence radiating from the
living Hamlet, a prince having his existence
apart, who by chance had come for a moment
within the poet's orbit.

This separation between the creator and the
created is not only the condition of derivation,
contact, and causal influence, but it is also
the condition of a genuine worship; because
then that which is expression in the poet is at
the same time homage in the lover, as it could
not be except fatuously and by a poetic
affectation if the being loved did not exist
separately. And " only begetter " is the right
phrase to indicate the relation between such a
creative influence and its work. A Platonic
Idea could never be the whole cause of its
temporal expressions; a material or feminine
element is involved that may receive that
influence and make it fruitful; a fact which

would also explain the many variants and the many imperfections which things might exhibit in response to the same unchanging virtue of their divine model.

When the matter is so conceived all force departs from the contention that if we separate God or the Ideas from the temporal world, " both are dead." God and the Ideas, like the living Prince Hamlet, would remain exactly as they were, with all their intrinsic warmth and virtue; and the temporal world, like the Shakespearean tragedy, would also remain just as it is, with all its literary values. The only difference would be that the living prince would have inspired no poet, and that the self-inspired poet would have celebrated no living prince. Shakespeare's Hamlet would be reduced to what, in fact, he is, an object of occasional imagination, a pure essence, and not a power. Meantime the inexhaustible powers which, if a divine life existed, would certainly lie in it, would have continued to radiate un-manifested, like those many rays of the sun which are dissipated in space, not being by chance reflected or absorbed and made temporally fruitful by any speck of an earth.

Platonism accordingly would be entirely stultified and eviscerated if it were not suffered to be all that modern criticism, inspired as it is by a subjective and psychological philosophy, most thoroughly dislikes; I mean, super-

naturalistic, realistic, and dualistic. This is
only another way of saying that, according to
the Platonic doctrine, God and the unseen
world really exist in themselves, so that they
can precede, create, attract, and survive their
earthly emanations.

VI

Is this to say that Aristotle and all the other critics of Platonism have had no reason on their side? Far from it: their criticism was amply justified by the facts of nature, and their only defect was perhaps not to have felt its full force, and to have still attributed power to those very Ideas to which they denied separate existence.[1] The Platonic system is mythological: if taken literally and dogmatically, it can seem to cold reason nothing but a gratuitous fiction, as all systems of religion or metaphysics necessarily seem to the outsider. Of course they are not inwardly gratuitous; they are the fervent expression and product of the deepest minds; and anyone capable of sharing the inspiration which prompted them will know them to be inevitable, persuasive, and morally coherent. Thus Dean Inge says that those who think Platonism dualistic have simply not understood; that is (if I myself understand him), they have not understood it from within, genetically, historically, emotionally; they have not recovered the experience

[1] I have elsewhere ventured to suggest that perhaps Aristotle himself was not guilty of this inconsistency. Cf. *Dialogues in Limbo: the Secret of Aristotle*, pp. 181-193.

and the immanent logic which, as a matter of fact, held the Platonic dualism in solution. This dualism appears only in the dogma precipitated and left, as it were, as a sediment; and the most sympathetic modern critic can hardly take such dogma seriously. He cannot receive it as a revelation, like a humble catechumen, drinking-in the marvellous supernatural facts from the lips of the masters. Platonism, like Christianity, cannot now produce in him the illusion which it was its early mission to produce. When he turns back to the origin of such a faith, he cannot, for all his sympathy, share the prophetic impulse which carried the Fathers from their first intuitions to the full expression of the same in consistent and final dogmas. Truth for him means historical, psychological truth; and the whole force of his learning and imagination is spent in dissolving those dogmas dramatically into their subjective components, and showing them to be but verbal expressions for certain radical ambient values. This is what, in fact, they were, or something of that kind: and he may be assured of this not merely by the naturalistic philosophy (perhaps unconsciously inspiring him) which proclaims such dogmas to be nothing else, but by the study of the surviving documents. Plato's writings in particular show clearly that the eventual Platonic system was but a moral and poetic fable.

The Ideas originally were really nothing but values. Socrates had conceived them as forms of the good, and this good itself was identical with the useful, beneficent, or advantageous. In the *Republic* we learn that anything—a shepherd or a ruler, a bridle or a bed—is good when it fulfils its natural function. Fitness to control a horse for the purposes of war, commerce, or sport would be the Idea (or value) of a bridle, and fitness to induce sound and comfortable sleep would be, I suppose, the Idea of a bed; and as to the eternal Idea of a ruler or shepherd, what should it be but to protect and conduct his sheep or his people, and in due season to shear them? This homely Socratic wisdom may seem not far removed from " the current valuations of the worldling "; it rested on no revelation, private or public, and had no principle save the reasonableness of the simplest mortal when forced by shrewd questions to disentangle his prejudices and to discover what he really wants. But great is the power of logic, when the mind is single and the heart open. In a trice it will bring the humblest judgements into the clarifying presence of the highest good. Socrates was a plain man, but fearless; he was omnivorous, playful, ironical, but absolutely determined. His one purpose was to be rational, to find and do what was best. If Anaxagoras would tell him what profit men might draw from the sun and moon, he would listen gladly; but if it was only a question of the substance or motions of those bodies, he would turn his back on Anaxagoras and laugh. This cobbler's wisdom was the same that almost made saints of the Cynics; it reappeared in the monks; it may reappear any day in some popular prophet. A fervid utilitarianism has a strangely revolutionary force: in squeezing the world to get every drop of pure good out of it, it leaves the world worthless, and has to throw it away: nothing remains but the immediate good of the spirit, the naked soul longing to be saved.

VII

In Plato and in his followers this revolution took more time and a larger sweep. Plato's mind was more accomplished and less consecrated than that of his master: that of his followers was more dogmatic and single than his own. Idealism, as it moves away from its origins, may easily become idolatrous: while leaving earthly things dry and empty, it may worship the pure forms which these things would have had if they had been perfect. In criticizing and condemning this world the prophet will find himself in the presence of another world, its sublimated image. The gift of thinking in myths, once native to the Greeks, was not altogether lost; it could still fuse the forms seen with a life unseen; it could transform definition of terms into intuition of Ideas; it could personify the functions of things and turn their virtues into patron deities animating those things and causing them to shine with a strength and beauty alien to their earthly substance. In the unclouded, synthetic, believing mind of Plotinus this chastened mythology crystallized into the most beautiful of systems.

An inexhaustible divine energy—so the system ran—poured perpetually down into the chaos of matter, animating and shaping it as well as that torpid substance would permit. At the bottom or centre there was little life, but it stirred more actively and nobly at each successive level, somewhat as the light of the sun floods the ether absolutely, the air variously, the sea dubiously, and the earth only darkly, with a shallow warmth. Hence the hierarchy of created goods, which is itself a good; and as to the defeats and confusions involved in being other than the highest, and other than one's own Idea, they were due to the inopportune inertia of matter, or to blind accident, or to a diabolical soul intervening and poisoning the fountains of divine grace. All levels of being were good in some measure, each after its kind. Consistently, and yet perhaps only with an effort and against the spirit of his times, Plotinus defended the excellence of the material world against the Gnostics, and the worthiness of the state and of the traditions of Hellenism, so that an emperor and even an empress might be his auditors without offence; and his philosophy remained Socratic in principle, a mythical underpinning to morals, and not a view of nature founded on observation, like those of the Stoics and the Epicureans. Yet in the five or six hundred years since Socrates, moral life itself had changed its centre. The good of the soul and her salvation had taken the place of domestic, military, and political goods; so that while the various spheres of being, like the terraces of Dante's Purgatorio, were all permanent and divinely appointed, the spirit now moved through them without rest. Its abiding-place was beyond. They were but the rounds of a Jacob's ladder by which the soul might climb again to her native heaven, and it was only " *there*," above, that she truly lived and had been blessed from all eternity.

Platonism, as Dean Inge observes, has no tendency to become pantheistic. Its first principle is the difference between good and evil. Its final dogmas describe a half-astronomical, half-dramatic setting for the phases of spiritual life. The divine spirit burned with such an intense and concentrated fire, it was so rich in its inner being, it overflowed into a celestial hierarchy of so many choirs, all superior to man, even on earth it found so many marvellous and amiable non-human manifestations, that man, with his two-footed featherlessness and his political artifices, lost his ancient Hellenic dignity: it was almost a disgrace for the soul to be expressed in a body or a body in a statue. Thus the imagined universe which was to shelter morality threatened to outgrow its original office. Man and his earthly fortunes began to seem to the contemplative mind but incidents in the barnyard. The only ambition worthy of a philosopher was to transcend and transfigure his human nature, and to pass unsullied through this nether world in adoration of the world above.

VIII

PLOTINUS professed to be, and actually was, an orthodox Platonist; and yet this dominant sense in him of the spiritual life was perfectly foreign to Socrates and Plato. I say this without forgetting the dialogues on love or the almost Roman religiosity of the *Laws*. After having been very poetical Plato became very austere; but his philosophy remained political to the end. To this descendant of Solon the universe could never be anything but a crystal case to hold the jewel of a Greek city. Divine as the heavens were, they were but a mothering and brooding power: in their refined materiality and mathematical divinity they circled about the earth, at once vivifying it and rebuking it by the visible presence of an exemplary good. The notion of the heavenly spheres was no mere optical image, the dream of a philosopher who, on a clear night, could measure the radius of the universe with the naked eye: this image was a moral parable. The realm of ethics will always be a set of concentric circles. Life necessarily radiates from centres; it stirs here, in the self; from here it looks abroad for supports and extensions, in the family, the nation, the intellectual world, the parent and subject universe. Wide as it may seem, this prospect is homely, and taken from the hearth of Vesta.

If the theology of Socrates and Plato was in this way domestic, the remnant of traditional religion in them was doubly so. Their attachment to ancient piety was childlike and superstitious when it remained personal, but more often it was expressly political and politic: they saw in religion a ready means of silencing dangerous questions and rebuking wickedness. It was a matter of moral education and police, and in no sense spiritual.

As to the Socratic philosophy of love, there is an obvious spiritual tendency in it, inasmuch as it bids the heart turn from the temporal to the eternal; and it does so not by way of an arid logic but by a true discipline of the affections, sublimating erotic passion into a just enthusiasm for all things beautiful and perfect. This is the secret of Platonism, which makes it perennial, so that if it were ever lost as a tradition it would presently be revived as an inspiration. It lives by a poignant sense of eternal values—the beautiful and the good— revealed for a moment in living creatures or in earthly harmonies. Yet who has not felt that this Platonic enthusiasm is somewhat equivocal and vain? Why? Because its renunciation is not radical. In surrendering some particular hope or some personal object of passion, it preserves and feeds the passion itself; there is no true catharsis, no liberation, but a sort of substitution and subterfuge, often hypocritical. Pure spiritual life cannot be something compensatory, a consolation for having missed more solid satisfactions: it should be rather the flower of all satisfactions, in which satisfaction becomes free from care, selfless, wholly actual and, in that inward sense, eternal. Spiritual life is simple and direct, but it is intellectual. Love, on the contrary, as Plotinus says, is something material, based on craving and a sense of want. For this reason the beautiful and the good, for the Platonic enthusiast, remain urgent values; he would cease to be a true Platonist or a rapt lover if he *understood*, if he discounted his illusions, rose above the animal need or the mental prejudice which made those values urgent, and relegated them to their relative station, where by their nature they belong. Yet this is what a pure spirit would do, one truly emancipated and enlightened.

IX

HERE, at the risk of parting company with Dean Inge and even with Plato, I come to a radical conclusion. Spiritual life is not a worship of " values," whether found in things or hypostatized into supernatural powers. It is the exact opposite ; it is *disintoxication* from their influence. Not that spiritual insight can ever remove values from nature or cease to feel them in their moral black and white and in all their aesthetic iridescence. Spirit knows these vital necessities : it has been quickened in their bosom. All animals have within them a principle by which to distinguish good from evil, since their existence and welfare are furthered by some circumstances and acts and are hindered by others. Self-knowledge, with a little experience of the world, will then easily set up the Socratic standard of values natural and inevitable to any man or to any society. These values each society will disentangle in proportion to its intelligence and will defend in proportion to its vitality. But who would dream that *spiritual life* was at all concerned in asserting these human and local values to be alone valid, or in supposing that they were especially divine, or bound to dominate the universe for ever ?

In fact, the great masters of the spiritual life are evidently not the Greeks, not even the Alexandrian Greeks, but the Indians, their disciples elsewhere in the East, and those Moslems, Christians, and Jews who have surrendered precisely that early, unregenerate claim to be enveloped in a protecting world designed for their benefit or vindication, a claim of which Platonism after all was but a refined version. To cling to familiar treasures and affections is human, but it is not particularly spiritual; to hypostatize these home values into a cosmic system especially planned to guarantee them, certainly expresses an intelligible passionate need for comfort and coddling in the universe, but with spirituality it has nothing to do. If such confidence may be called faith, it may also be called fatuity and insolence; an insolence innocent in a spirited child, but out of place in a philosopher. Spirituality comes precisely of surrendering this animal arrogance and this moral fanaticism and substituting for them pure intelligence: not a discoursing cleverness or scepticism, but perfect candour and impartial vision. Spirit is merciful and tender because it has no private motive to make it spiteful; yet it is unflinchingly austere because it cannot make any private motive its own. It need have no scientific or artistic pretensions; it appears quite adequately in straight seeing of simple things; these, to pure spirit, are speculative enough and good to whet its edge upon; the proudest dreams of science or theology are no better for the purpose. The spirit is content with the widow's mite and a cup of cold water; it considers the lilies of the field; it can say with literal truth: Inasmuch as ye did it unto the least of these, ye did it unto me.

As the spirit is no respecter of persons, so it is no respecter of worlds: it is willing to put up with any of them, to be feasted in one or to be martyred in another. And while it is allowed to live—a point that concerns the world it lives in rather than the spirit itself—it looks with a clear and untroubled sympathy on such manifestations of being as happen to be unrolled before it. As it loves the non-human parts of nature, so it loves the human parts, and is in no way hostile to the natural passions and to the political and religious institutions that happen to prevail. If spirit was to be incarnate and to appear in existence at all, it had to be born in one odd world or another: why should it quarrel with its earthly cradle? This is not to say that all circumstances are equally favourable to the spiritual life. On the contrary, most circumstances exclude it altogether; the vast abysses of nature seem to be uninhabited; and even where spirit feebly appears, it is in order to be, very often, stifled at once, or long tormented. Almost always its world is too much with it; the spirit is so deeply engaged and distracted by current events that it cannot realize its proper function, which is to see such things as come in its way under the form of eternity, in their intrinsic character and relative value, in their transitiveness and necessity, in a word, in their truth. This contemplative habit evidently finds a freer course in solitude than in society, in art than in business, in prayer than in argument. It is stimulated by beautiful and constant things more than by things ugly, tedious, crowded, or uncertain. For this reason it is more prevalent and freer in the East than in the West, among Catholics than among Protestants, among Moslems than among Jews. For the same reason the Platonic system, up to a certain point, is sympathetic to the spirit. Its universe was compact and immortal; the oscillations of fortune on earth could not disturb its unchangeable order. If nature were conceived to be, as in fact she is, barbarous and in indefinite flux, giving rein to anything and everything, there would seem hardly to be time to reach perfection on any level of being before the soil was undermined and the budding Idea was lost and dissipated. The great merit of an unchanging world is that all its inhabitants can be adapted to it. If they ever fall out of tune the cause will be but a passing disease and an accidental slackness in the strings; it will be easy to screw up the pegs, to renew a snapped cord, and to restore the harmony. Such a world offers an immovable basis and sanction for the good: it establishes an orthodox morality. Imperfection enters it only below the circle of the moon, like bad manners below stairs; and even here, on earth, evil is but an oscillation and dizziness in matter which nature perpetually calls back to the norm, as the motion of a top rights it in its gyrations.

X

I AM not confident, however, that a pure spirit
would feel safe in such a seven-walled celestial
castle, or would prize the sort of safety which,
if it were real, it would afford. Existence is
contingent essentially. As things might just
as well have been different, so they might just
as well prove to be inconstant; and since they
cannot manifest their groundlessness by now
being other than they happen to be, they may
manifest it by being other at other times and
places. No existing being can have the means
of knowing that it will always exist or prosper
in the universe: the neatest cosmos and the
most solitary god might collide with something
unsuspected; or the unsuspected thing might
exist in its own preserves without being discovered or coming into collision. Yet that
undiscovered world, for the spirit, would be as
real and as interesting as this world. Ignorance
cannot justify any negative prophecy: but
existence, while it is the home of particular
certitudes, is also a cage in which an inevitable
and infinite ignorance sings and dies imprisoned.
Existence is self-centred, limited in character
by the character which it chances to have,
and in duration by the crawling fact that it
exists while it is found existing. There is no

necessary and all-comprehensive being except the realm of essence, to which existence is irrelevant: for whether the whole exist or only a part, or even if no part existed, the alternative fact would always be knocking at the door; and nothing in the actual facts could ever prove that the door would not suddenly open and let the contrary in. Like people living on the slopes of volcanoes, we ignore these possibilities, although a catastrophe is rapidly approaching each of us in the form of death, and who knows how soon it may overtake the whole confused life of our planet? Nevertheless, except in the interests of detachment and freedom, spirit has no reason for dwelling on other possible worlds. Would any of them be less contingent than this one, or nearer to the heart of infinite Being? And would not any of them, whatever its character, lead the spirit inexorably *there*? To master the actual is the best way of transcending it. Those who know but one language, like the Greeks, seem to find language a purer and more transparent vehicle than those of us who notice its idiosyncrasies and become entangled in its meshes. So it is the saints most steeped each in his traditional religion who are nearest together in spirit; and if nature caused them to change places, it is they that, after a moment's pause to get their bearings, would be most at ease in one another's skins. No one is

more unspiritual than a heretic, or more grace-
less and wretched than an unfrocked priest;
yet the frock of the faithful is but an earthly
garment; it melts into the clouds which, in
their ascension, they leave behind them.

XI

IN what places the spirit shall awake, and how long and how freely it shall be suffered to flourish are evidently questions of mundane physics and politics: it is the world's business to call down spirit to dwell in it, not the spirit's business to make a world in which to dwell. The friends of spirit, in their political capacity, will of course defend those forms of society in which, given their particular race and traditions, spirit may best exist: they will protect it in whatever organs and instruments it may already have appeared, and will take care that it pursues its contemplative life undisturbed in its ancient sanctuaries. Spirituality has material conditions; not only the general conditions of life and intuition (for a man must exist before he can become a spiritual man), but subtler and more special conditions such as concentration of thought, indifference to fortune and reputation, warmth of temperament (because spirit cannot burn clear except at a high temperature) disciplined into chastity and renunciation. These and other such conditions the master of novices does well to consider; but spirit itself, when once aroused, does not look back in that direction. Many Christian saints have qualified their spirituality with too much self-consciousness; it was no doubt their religious duty to examine their consciences and study to advance in holiness; but the holiness really did not begin until they forgot themselves in the thought of God. So with those who were consumed with zeal for the Church, the conversion of sinners, and other works of charity. These are moral interests or duties accruing to men as members of some particular society; they are political cares. They may be accompanied by spiritual insight, if it be really salvation or spiritualization of souls that preoccupies the missionary, and not some outward change of habit or allegiance, that may make other people more like himself and ensure the dominance of his home traditions. Political zeal even in the true friends of spirit is not spiritual; a successful apostle must have rather a worldly mind, because he needs to have his hand on the pulse of the world; his appeal would not be intelligible if it were not threatening or spectacular or full of lewd promises. It will be only afterwards, perhaps, when people have been domesticated in the new faith, that the spirit will descend upon them. The spirit itself is not afraid of being stamped out here, or anxious to be kindled there; its concern is not about its instances or manifestations; it is not essentially learned or social; its kingdom is not of this world. It leaves propaganda to those who call themselves its friends but probably know nothing of it, or are even its enemies, and only the agents of some worldly transformation ultimately quite nugatory.

Nor has the world, on its side, any obligation to cultivate the spiritual life. Obligations are moral; they presuppose a physical and social organism with immanent spontaneous interests which may impose those obligations. The value and opportuneness of spiritual life, in any of its possible forms, must be adjudged by reason in view of the moral economy for which, in any instance, reason may speak. All values fall within the purview of ethics, which is a part of politics. Spirituality is the supreme good for those who are called to it, the few whose intellectual thirst can be quenched only by impartial truth and the self-annihilating contemplation of all Being. The statesman and the father of a family may not always welcome this disposition; it may seem to them wasteful and idle. Just as the value of an artist must be judged by the world, in view of all the interests which his art affects or subserves, while the artist himself lives only in his own labour, irresponsible, technical, and visionary; so the value of spiritual life in general, or in any of its incidental forms, must be judged morally by the world, in view of its own ambitions, while the spirit, standing invisibly at its elbow, judges the world and its ambitions spiritually.

XII

It is impossible that spirit in a living creature
should ever be wholly freed from the body and
from the world; for in its inwardness it would
have ceased to follow and enact the fortunes
of that creature; it would either have been
absorbed in the contemplation of pure Being
and become virtually omniscient, or at least
it would contemplate its special objects equably
under the form of eternity, and not in the
perspectives determined by the station of its
body in time and place. Pure Being, or these
special essences and truths, would evidently
gain nothing by the fact that this new mind
had been lost in them; and this mind, in
gaining them, would have lost itself; it would,
in fact, have ceased to exist separately. Meantime the body of that creature might go on
living automatically; the mind which it had
previously fed, as a lamp feeds its flame, would
have evaporated, gone up into the sun, and
ceased to light the precincts and penumbra of
that particular vessel, or to be a measure of its
little oil. But a living automaton is by nature
conscious: the lamp has not been materially
extinguished: the creature is accordingly still
breeding a faithful if flickering mind, which
feels and notes its further vicissitudes. Evi-

dently this fresh mind is the true continuation of that creature's experience; it is again continuously cognizant of that body in that world. The effort to liberate souls from their bodies or to transport them beyond their world has therefore a rather ironical result: the redeemed soul ceases to be anybody's soul, and the body continues to have a soul that is quite personal and unregenerate.

The difference between the life of the spirit and that of the flesh is itself a spiritual difference: the two are not to be divided materially or in their occasions and themes so much as in the quality of their attention: the one is anxiety, inquiry, desire, and fear; the other is intuitive possession. The spirit is not a talebearer having a mock world of its own to substitute for the humble circumstances of this life; it is only the faculty—the disenchanting and re-enchanting faculty—of seeing this world in its simple truth. Therefore all the worldly hatred of spirit—and it is very fierce—can never remove the danger that, after a thousand persecutions and a long conspiracy of derision, a child of the spirit should be born in the bosom of the worldly family. The more organic and perfect the life of the world becomes, the more intelligent it will be: and what shall prevent intelligence from asking what all this pother is about and driving the moneychangers from the house of prayer? Spirit must have some organ; but when once aroused it does not look in the direction of its organ or care at all about preserving it. It looks rather, as we see in Indian philosophy, to a realm anterior to all worlds, and finds there a comprehensive object which in one sense includes all worlds, since it is infinite Being, but for that very reason excludes the enacted existence of any one of them, since they can be enacted, as the moments of time are enacted, only by excluding and ousting one another. *This* world, for a speculative mind, is exactly analogous to *this* moment. It seems alone real to those who inhabit it, but its preeminence is relative and egotistical: if maintained dogmatically it becomes at once illusory and absurd.

XIII

NOT that the existence of a particular world—perhaps its exclusive existence—is an evil. If the lovers of pure Being are ever tempted to say so, it is only in their human capacity, because some rude fact may have wounded their feelings. These feelings are a part of the world which they condemn, inevitable as this world is inevitable, and unnecessary in the sense in which this world is unnecessary. The contradiction or self-dislike which they betray in that world is, no doubt, a defect from the point of view of the parts in it which are quarrelling, each of which would wish to have it all its own way. But this fact does not render that world, or the conflicts in it, evil absolutely. Evil can arise only within each world when it becomes faithless to some Idea which it has begun to pursue, or is crossed in the pursuit of it either by some external enemy (if any) or by the inward contradiction and complexity of its impulses, which allow it only to drift towards uncertain, tragic, and romantic issues. But, as we see in some desperately romantic philosophers, this very disorder may please an imagination which is stirred by that stimulus more deeply than by any impulse towards harmony and fixity of form. Some impulse towards form, some initial essence or essences, a world must preserve so long as it exists, else it would dissolve into chaos or into that metaphysical non-entity, matter without form: but this modicum of form may be composed by the perpetual defeat of every particular endeavour, and the greatest evil of the greatest number of souls may fulfil the romantic ideal. The theologians who have maintained that the damnation of the great majority is no evil in the sight of God, and leaves his intrinsic holiness and glory unsullied, have understood the matter speculatively; and although the ferocity of the Calvinists was not spiritual, and their notion of " an angry God " was grotesque, there was spirituality in their elevation above the weak judgements of the flesh and even of the heart; only that the speculative sword really cuts both ways, and their sense for the superhuman should also have dissolved their moral fanaticism. Pure Being is infinite, its essence includes all essences; how then should it issue particular commands, or be an acrimonious moralist?

The two-edged sword falls again here. If it be true that the world can be evil only in its own eyes and therefore only partially and pro- visionally, until the eyes are closed or are hardened like the eagle's to that wounding light, so it is true also that it can be good in its own eyes only: and more, that the spiritual life and the pure Being to which its contemplation is addressed, can be good only in relation to the living souls that may find their good there. Plotinus and many other mystics have admitted that the One, though habitually called good, is not properly so called. It is the good of religion, because religion is a conversion from one object of pursuit to another, under the form of the good: but in the One itself, or in attainment, the pursuit is absent, and the category of the good no longer has any application. The title may be retained, in human parlance, to indicate that the attainment really satisfies the aspiration which preceded, and does not disappoint it; for to end there, to end absolutely, was the very aim of that aspiration. The case is like that of a man building his tomb, or bequeathing his property to his son; the result is a good for him in that he desired it, but not in that he survives to enjoy it. So is the peace that passeth understanding, that annuls desire, and that excludes the gasping consciousness of peace.

XIV

SPIRIT, which is ultimately addressed to pure
Being, is not itself this pure Being. It is the
gift of intuition, feeling, or apprehension: an
overtone of animal life, a realization, on a
hypostatic plane, of certain moving unities in
matter. So, at least, I understand the word;
but its original meaning was a breath or wind,
and hence, often, an influence. In this last
sense it is used in Christian theology; the Holy
Ghost is not the Father nor the Son, but proceeds from them and animates the world, or at
least the souls of the elect. It is the fountain
of grace. We also read in the gospel that God
is a spirit, to be worshipped in spirit and in
truth. Here the word evidently bears more
than one sense; the spirit in which God is
worshipped is a disposition of the mind, whereas God himself, we may presume, is a spirit in
the mighty sense in which Jehovah swept the
void, a breath or a word, bringing order out of
chaos; the same voice that spoke to Job out
of the whirlwind, with the sheer authority of
power. Spirit thus seems to be sometimes a

creative energy, sometimes a sanctifying influence.   So in the Latin hymn:

Veni creator Spiritus
corda tuorum visitans
imple supernâ gratiâ
quae tu creasti pectora.

This double function of spirit, if we investigated its origin, would bring back the double source of Christian doctrine, here Hebraic and there Platonic: a profound dualism which custom scarcely avails to disguise or theology to heal.   Creative power and redeeming grace point in opposite directions; but a complete religion needs to look both ways, feeding piously at the breast of nature, yet weaning itself spiritually from that necessary comfort to the contemplation of superhuman and eternal things.   The object of piety is necessity, power, the laws of life and prosperity, and to call these things spirit is pure mythology; they are indeed a great wind, sometimes balmy, sometimes terrible; and it is the part of wisdom to take shelter from it, or spread wings or sails in it, according as it lists to blow.   But to what end?   To live, to have spirit, to understand all these things.

There is also a conventional modern sense in which we speak of the spirit of an age, a place, or a book, meaning some vague tendency or inspiration either actually dominating that thing or suggested by it to the mind of a third person. This is a verbal survival of myth, poetry become cant: spirit here means those characters of a thing which a myth-making mind would have attributed to a spirit.

In contrast to all these uses I am employing the word spirit to mean something actual; indeed, the very fact of actuality, the gleam of intuition or feeling. But this gleam ordinarily serves only to light up material life and the perspectives in which it moves in time and in space: an incessant sketchy sense of the affairs of the body and of its world. The digestion and preparation of action (as the behaviourists have shown) is a physical matter. In that business the spirit is entirely superfluous. The behaviourists even affect to deny its existence, on the ground that it is invisible and would be a useless luxury in nature: excellent economy, as if a man, the better to provide for his future, should starve himself to death. The spirit in us is that which, morally, we actually are: if anything is to be expunged from the complex face of reality it might rather be our material and social setting and all the strange and incoherent stories told us in history and science. Certainly all these apparent or reported facts would be perfectly vain, if they did not create the spirit, and teach it to observe and enjoy them. So we are brought back to the immediate revelation of things, which is also their ultimate value: we are

brought back to the spirit. Its life is composed
of feelings and intuitions, in many stages and
degrees; and when spirit is free and collected
it has no life but this spiritual life, in which the
ultimate is immediate. All the experiences of
the spirit, until they are so exorcized and
appropriated—so enshrined in pure Being—are
sheer distraction.

XV

WERE any world perfect, as the Platonists thought that this world was in its upper parts, its spirit would view it with the same contemplative satisfaction with which it views any pure essence that spontaneously engages its attention. It would not, in respect to that perfect world, be harassed by remorse, as it must be in an imperfect world when it counts the cost of existence and considers the dreadful sufferings which plagued it like a nightmare, before something beautiful and good could appear even for a moment. I say *remorse*, because such is the feeling that comes over me when I remember the travail which, at least in man, the spirit has had to endure in bringing its better life to birth : but the spirit itself has no guilt in the matter ; it was caught in a vice ; and it may accept and overlook that terrible gestation when at last it reaches the open and rewards itself with an hour of freedom and gladness. These are its natural notes : it is born out of an achieved harmony, only in creatures already formed and in some measure fit to live : contradiction and torment are inexplicable to it, and danger a cause of laughter. How should spirit, the very essence of radiance, ever become morose ? It runs and sparkles wherever it may, the free child of nature. It has no grudge against its fostering world; on the contrary, nothing but delighted wonder. It has no native enmity towards the flesh—that comes to it afterwards from the sad flesh itself; it has no disinclination to folly. The difference between folly and wisdom, between crime and piety, is not naturally known to spirit; it is a lesson learned by experience, in view of the conditions of material life; spirit would of itself gladly take a turn with the devil, who is also a spirit. Yet all this innocent joy and courage native to spirit bind it to the world with no tie. That which is tied, that which cannot live save in its home climate and family nest, is only the mortal psyche, the poor, absurd, accidental human person. The psyche in each of us is like Vesta, the goddess of the Hearth, mother of the Promethean flame, mother of spirit; and she needs to learn the difficult unselfishness of the parent—or of the foster-parent: for her child is of another race. She must be content to be abandoned, revisited only in haste on some idle holiday, with a retrospective piety; and even as she embraces her full-grown over-topping son he will seem a stranger to her, and she will catch sight of his eyes, gazing over her head into a far country.

At the same time this homelessness of spirit is not romantic; it is not impatience of this and longing for that; it is not the snobbery of learning and culture so characteristic of intellectual people who are not spiritual. No: the homelessness of spirit comes from detachment, detachment no less from the grander thing which the snob respects and pretends to know as from this humbler thing which he despises. Anything is enough if it be pure; but purity itself comes to things from the simplicity of the spirit which regards them, not indeed with indifference, rather with joy, but without any *ulterior* interest; in other words, purity comes of detaching the thing seen and loved from the world that besets and threatens it and attaching it to the spirit to which it is an eternal possession. But this thing eternally possessed by the spirit is not the thing as the world knows and prizes it; it is not the person, or nation, or religion as it asserts and flaunts itself, in a mortal anxiety to be dominant; it is only that thing in its eternal essence, out of which the stress and the doubt of existence have wholly passed. It is that thing dead, immortal, its soul restored, as Plotinus would have said, to the soul of the universe where, together with all other souls, it has always been contained in its purity and perfection. But the truth of it *there* is not the fact of it *here*; and therefore the world, though the spirit loves it far more truly and tenderly than it loves itself, is chilled and rebuked by that look of divine love, which, if it were heeded, would transmute its whole life and change it from what it so passionately and cruelly is, in time, into that which the spirit sees it to be in eternity.

XVI

THE human heart is full of political, religious, metaphysical ambition; it hugs all sorts of pleasant projects in art and in fortune. These are moral interests and, if not misguided, may bring hidden or future facts before the mind, and broaden the basis for rational action. So the Platonic philosophy sets the scene in one way for the play, the Christian system in a way somewhat different, and modern science, if we make a naturalistic system out of it, in still another. I will not say that the question which of these is true, or truer, is indifferent to the spirit; its fortunes and temper will evidently vary if it is bred in one or another of these climates. But if the facts were discovered, whatever they might turn out to be, the spirit would be equally ready and able to face them. It is not in the least bound up with the supposition, whatever it may mean exactly, that any " values are the most real things in the universe." What should the spirit care if moralistic metaphysics ceased to invade the field of natural philosophy, venturing there upon some guesses flattering to human vanity? What if the most real—that is, I suppose, the most fundamental and dynamic—things in the universe were utterly inhuman? Would spirituality be thereby prevented from being spiritual, from seeing and judging whatever world happened to exist in the light of spirit?

When I say the *light of spirit* I might as well say *light* simply; for what is spirit but the act of making light actual, of greeting, observing, questioning, and judging anything and everything? Spirit is awareness, intelligence, recollection. It requires no dogmas, as does animal faith or the art of living. Human morality, for the spirit, is but the inevitable and hygienic bias of one race of animals. Spirit itself is not human; it may spring up in any life; it may detach itself from any provincialism; as it exists in all nations and religions, so it may exist in all animals, and who knows in how many undreamt-of beings, and in the midst of what worlds? It might flourish, as the Stoics felt, even in the face of chaos, except that chaos could not sustain the animal life, the psyche, which spirit requires for its organ. From the existence of spirit a psychologist may therefore argue back to the existence—at least local and temporary—of some cosmos of organized matter: but this dependence of mind on body is a lesson taught by natural philosophy, when natural philosophy is sound; it is not a free or evident requirement of spirit in its first deliverance. On the contrary, the body which is the matrix and cradle of spirit in time, seems a stumbling-block to it in its spontaneous career; and a rather long discipline and much chastening hardly persuade this supernatural nursling that it is really so domestic, and that it borrows its existence from a poor, busy, precarious animal life; or that the natural rhythms, pauses, and synthetic reactions of that life are the ground of its native affinity with the eternal. Yet such is the fact: spirit, as I have said, is a hypostatic unity which makes actual and emotional the merely formal unities or harmonies of bodily life; and since the living psyche is in flux, any actual existence which bridged its processes and relations would have to transcend time in its survey, and not be attached or confined to any of the moments which it overlooked and spanned. Therefore spirit is essentially dateless, and its immediate terms are essences in themselves eternal; which is not to say that one form of spirit does not continually replace another in the world. There is a continual variation in themes, and there may be intermittences in intuition itself; but each of these themes is an essence overarching a part of the existential flux, and each moment or node in intuition looks out of its narrow window upon a vista which, whether broad or confined, is not anchored in the place of any of its sundry objects.

To this organ and to this temporal basis spirit can accommodate itself perfectly when once it has discovered them. Naturalism has its modest way of doing the spirit honour. In whatever manner natural forces may operate, if ever they issue in life, it can be only because they already have established rhythms, such as day and night, favourable to that life, to its renewal and inheritance. Any world, any society, any language has a natural inertia or tendency to continue; it satisfies and encourages the spirit which it creates. It fits the imagination because it has kindled and moulded it, and it satisfies its resident passions because these are such, and such only, as could take root and become habitual in precisely that world. This natural harmony between the spirit and its conditions is the only actual one: it is the source of every ideal and the sole justification of any hope. Imperfect and shifting as this harmony must be, it is sufficient to support the spirit of man; and if this spirit be clear and open, it is sufficient to unroll before it all the proper objects of its contemplation in their invincible beauty and eternity. That the vision, considered as an event in history, must change and pass is indifferent. It is not because other people love what I love that, if I am a free spirit, I love it, nor because I have always loved it or must always love it in future, but because it is lovely as I see it now. Such is the assurance that is proper to life, to actuality, to intuition: the rest is weariness of spirit, and a burden to the flesh. But the animal in man is wretched unless he can imagine that his language, nation, arts, and sentiments are destined to be supreme in the world for ever; he is hardly content to suppose that he may not rise again to take part in celebrating some final, yet unending, victory; and he demands eternity not for the lovely essences which he may have beheld, which have eternity in themselves already, but for the manifestation of those essences, which cannot have it.

XVII

SINCE spirit is an emanation of natural life there would be impiety on its part in flouting or denying its own source: yet this has always been a temptation for spirit when self-conscious and self-contained: hence the pride of Lucifer, the mock independence of the Stoic sage, the acosmism and absoluteness of the Indian mystic, and the egotism of German philosophy, thinking to create and recreate its world in its flight through nothingness. The trouble with such forced attitudes is that they attempt to divorce spirituality from piety, which is the other half, and the fundamental half, of a sound religion. In Platonism and Christianity this divorce has been avoided, but without establishing a happy and stable marriage; because the object of piety is the power, whatever it may be, on which life depends; and it is not true piety to invent or posit other sources for life or welfare than those which experience shows to exist: piety is wisdom. Nor does the spiritual life profit in the end by trespassing in this way on the preserves of a sober piety and a sober science; because the spirit is thereby entangled in the fanatical defence of fantastic dogmas, as if these were indispensable to its life; so that its peace is poisoned, and its wings are clipped. What folly to suppose that ecstasy could be abolished by recognizing the true sources of ecstasy! Yet ecstatic, and not addressed to matters of fact, the spirit is in its essence, whenever it arises at all. It actualizes, in an intuition which is through and through poetical and visionary, various movements, rhythms, potentialities, and transcendent relations which physical life involves but which are not parts or moments of its moving substance, and remain merely formal facts for the external observer.

The attachment of spiritual minds to some particular system of cosmology, Platonic, Christian, Indian, or other, is, therefore, a historical accident—a more or less happy means of expression, but a treacherous article of faith. The truth of any of these systems is a question for science, not at all a postulate of the spiritual life. Accordingly, as Dean Inge says, " an entirely open mind towards the discoveries of science " would be characteristic of a purely spiritual religion. But it is not possibly characteristic of a convinced Platonist or a convinced Christian. In Platonism, as in Christianity, the spiritual life is not pure, but incarnate in a particular body of dogma, historical and cosmological: both systems are pledged to the magic ascendancy of certain supernatural powers, posited in order to guarantee certain particular human values. No such system, giving an unnatural fixity, in a special cosmos, to a special morality or civilization or to a private personality, can look upon the hypotheses of a free science with anything but terror, perhaps mitigated by contempt: terror, because it has laid up its treasure in an eventual material heaven, which it feels in its bones to be mythical; and perhaps contempt, because free science is but human discourse, in which one shaky hypothesis is always replacing another; whereas the dogmas of an allegorical religion, for the very reason that they express elementary human feelings and fancies, can appeal to the heart so long as the heart is human. To cultivate this contempt for free science, and to endure that terror with fortitude, aided by hypnotic ritual influences and the contagion of many voices crying in unison, must be the policy of any such system; it must stand by its guns. It can cultivate its own learning and arts and philosophy, but with free science it can have nothing to do. It is not to-day or yesterday, as Dean Inge seems to think, that science has discredited these mythical dogmas. Science is but a name for consecutive observation and understanding, and science had amply disproved those dogmas before they arose: a fact which did not prevent them from arising and from prevailing exceedingly.

The interests which these dogmas expressed

and sanctioned were respectable interests, political, moral, and emotional. The civilized mind is still very much more at home in such a cosy world than in the universal flux of nature, which not only opens material immeasurable abysses on every side of our human nest, but threatens us with an indefinite flux in our own being, in our habits, institutions, affections, and in the very grammar and categories of our thought. Yet neither science nor spirituality share this classic dislike or fear of the infinite. Science, although its occasion is the description and manipulation of the field of action, is heartily willing to describe it and manipulate it in any convenient way. It is perhaps the best sign of a scientific, as distinguished from a doctrinaire, temper not to lay great store on science itself, that is, on its forms, language, and theories, but to keep it plastic in the presence of its existing subject-matter, and of the spontaneity of human fancy, which, at any moment, may suggest new methods of notation, new abbreviations, new syntheses. As to spirit, it has a far deeper reason than science for eluding every convention and not regarding institutions, whether political, ecclesiastical, or intellectual, with more than a resigned courtesy. Such things must needs be: it would be foolish to reject them instead of profiting by them. The body, which is an institution of nature, is the indispensable organ of spirit in man; political and religious institutions are organs necessary also for certain kinds of spiritual life; and if the cosmos, too, is a permanent institution, the spirit can very well acknowledge that accidental fact and submit, *here*, to the limitations thereby imposed upon it. But it would be, for spirit, a limitation; its proper field is *there*, in the world which is eternal by inward necessity and essence, not by a longevity presumed to be perpetual; a world which for the same reason is infinite, as a world of change, even if endless, cannot be, since it expressly excludes any order of events other than the one which it happens to realize.

XVIII

THE Platonists, like all typical Greeks, shuddered at the infinite and hardly thought of it, even in the optical form of infinite space. This is of itself a sufficient proof that they were fundamentally political philosophers, moralists, humanists, and not men living primarily in the spirit. They thought the infinite formless—a conception which is possible only in the absence of concentration upon that idea; for, when considered intently, the infinite is seen to contain all forms: it is the realm of essence. This observation, if they had stopped to make it (and it requires no special intelligence, only pause) would have dispelled any aesthetic dislike which they may have had of the infinite; yet it would not have changed their radical indifference to it. The Greeks were not aesthetes; their love of form and their approach to perfection in it were not aesthetic but moral, political, hygienic: like noble animals they were proud and content in their own bodies, faculties, and loves; words could not express their indifference to what was not human; and when some divine shaft rent those bodies and blackened that mind, the cry of their mourning was brief but absolute. Their love of finitude was vital; it was the love of existence, and of perfection in existence ; and for that reason, not for any idle aestheticism, they were clear discerners of beauty. Aestheticism is incapable of producing the beautiful or, in the end, even of loving or discerning it ; it has cut off the vital and moral roots of form which render one form more beautiful than another, and which, deeper still, give unity of form to objects at all. These vital roots of form were alive in the Greeks : they flowered into sundry finite perfections ; and evidently they could not flower into forms contrary to these particular perfections, rooted in a particular living seed, limited to the play of a particular animal body and its appropriate mind. The infinite was valueless : and from the moral point of view, from the point of view of some natural organism striving to be free and perfect, valueless the infinite certainly is.

But spirit is a terribly treacherous inmate of the animal soul ; it has slipped in, as Aristotle says, from beyond the gates : and its home is the desert. This foreignness is moral, not genealogical : spirit is bred in the psyche because the psyche, in living, is obliged to adjust herself to alien things : she does so in her own interest : but in taking cognizance of other things, in moulding a part of her dream to follow their alien fortunes, she becomes intelligent, she creates spirit ; and this spirit overleaps the pragmatic function of physical

sensibility—it is the very act of overleaping it
—and so proves itself a rank outsider, a child
rebellious to the household, an Ishmael ranging
alone, a dweller in the infinite.

This infinite is the infinite of forms, the
indestructible and inevitable infinite that contains everything, but contains it only in its
essence, in that eternal quality of being in
which everything is a companion and supple-
ment to everything else, never a rival or a contradiction. These essences, when thought considers any of them without knowing whether
they describe any earthly object or not, may
be called ideal; but they are not ideal intrinsically, either in the sense of being figments of
thought or of being objects of aspiration. They
become ideal, or enter into an external moral
relation to the animal soul, when this soul
happens to conceive them, or to make them
types for the objects of its desires. A perfectly
free spirit (if it could exist) would not consider
eternal beings in their ideal capacity, because
it would no longer refer them to the fancies or
hopes of some living creature, but would consider them in themselves, ranging from one to
another quite speculatively, that is, guided by
the intrinsic formal relations of similarity or
inclusion which obtain between them. It
would therefore virtually traverse the infinite,
its path not being hedged in by pre-existing
irrelevant interests in one form of being rather

than in another. But evidently this perfect impartiality is not human; it is contrary to the initial status of spirit, as the hypostatic synthetic expression and realization of some discursive phase of animal life—some adventure, some predicament, some propensity, some preoccupation. It is therefore natural that the intrinsic infinity of Being should remain in the background, even in the spiritual life, and that essences should be contemplated and distinguished rather as ideals for the human imagination than as beings necessary in themselves.

XIX

FOR this reason the Platonic philosophy opens a more urbane and alluring avenue towards spiritual enlightenment than does the Indian, although the latter runs faster towards the goal and attains it more perfectly. The limitation of the divine intellect, or the Ideas, to the types of earthly or celestial bodies, and to the values proper to their lives, leaves the afterglow of passion upon them; the eternal profits by the interest which its worshippers have in the temporal. This accommodation is also conspicuous in the Catholic tradition: it seems doubtful sometimes whether that other world is a liberation from this one, or a reduplication of it, with all its temporal, moral, social, and diplomatic business extended indefinitely. This is the price which the spiritual life has to pay for being made amiable. A universe is composed on purpose to facilitate it; life there becomes so easy and natural, it retains so many human values, that it threatens to be choked in a system of anxious hopes and adjustments, worse than those involved in mundane life, because inescapable. In this world, at least, the spirit can flee to solitude, to nature, to play, to the delicious irony of despising the passions which one is forced to

share; but from heaven, ennobled and sancti-
fied as it would be by so many immortal personages, so many high maxims, marvellous
dogmas, and moral exclusions, whither should
the spirit flee? Of course the spiritual sense
for those celestial facts might be recovered;
even in heaven one might be a philosopher.
The other world would be but a second touchstone for the spirit if, like this world and its
moral order, it were a fact existing in itself.
In the Catholic, as in the Platonic, kingdom,
the spirit must still blaze its own trail; the
carpets spread accommodatingly before its
feet, leading to the celestial courts, will never
lead it, of themselves, to spiritual liberation.

Consider the universe of Plotinus: a process
of emanation from the One through the Ideas
to the Soul of the World, whence, like rays
from different stars, human and animal souls
descend on occasion to animate material
bodies. This system was designed to encourage
the spirit to rise from its animal prison—
prison was the word—reversing that emanation
until it recovered the primal bliss of contemplative union with pure Being. But what is
there in the system, if we accept it as describing
the facts, to compel or even to invite the spirit
to rise at all? The cosmology of Plotinus
might almost be adopted by a Hegelian interested only in evolution and not in the least in
redemption; he might behold with rapture the

successive embodiment of linked Ideas in the thoughts and institutions of men; far from wishing to reverse the process in his heart, and renounce all these endless transformations, conflicts, and cumulative cares, his only joy might be to share them, to be the first to announce them, and at every turn in the battle to drop the cry of yesterday in order to pick up that of to-morrow. Since it was the nature of things to emanate from the One, he would hasten to emanate with them. All his angels would be seen descending Jacob's ladder, and none ascending. Yet only the ascent concerns the spiritual life. The descent is the creation of the world and the work of the world, by which the spirit, when it awakes at last, finds itself entangled in animal passions and foolish ambitions. Starting from whatever facts and predicaments may seem to envelop it, its function is then to detach itself from them one by one, escaping the flux and urgency which they have in the realm of existence, unravelling and synthesizing their temporal perspectives, in order to transpose them all into the realm of truth, where they form an eternal picture; and then to let this picture itself recede into its setting in the realm of essence, where it is but one form of being, which this world by chance has manifested, amid the countless forms of being which perhaps have not been manifested anywhere. The angels, even in their descent, will then be messengers to the philosopher from an eternal world, to which, in ascending again, they carry up his heart; whereas if the angels were born in transit and lived only in their apparition in time, he might have perhaps a pleasanter casual environment, but no heavenly treasure; and his attitude would be that of a lover and gloating denizen of this world, not that of the spirit. Even from the best world the spirit must depart. Beauty calls it away no less than confusion; and happiness is only a more amiable sacrament than suffering to carry it to the impassible Being which infinitely outruns all these accidents of existence.

XX

SPIRIT, since its essence is to aspire, comes to
life at the foot of the ladder; it lives by contemplation, by knowing the thing above it.
It is not its own object, as the Platonic Ideas
seemed to become in Aristotle's theology, when
they were identified with a cosmic intellect
eternally contemplating its own structure.
Spirit might indeed attain to such a condition
if its natural organ were, as Aristotle supposed,
some perfectly harmonious and immortal revolution of the heavens. Even then spirit would
properly be the rapt aspiration towards those
Ideas, the immortal love of them, which kept
the moving spheres constant in their round:
for the soul of each sphere was intently fixed
upon the Idea (or, as we might say, the
formula) which it was to realize by its motion
and to turn into a sustained note in the
celestial symphony. Even in this astronomical
theology spirit would be the third person of the
Trinity rather than the second; it would be the
Soul of the World looking towards the Ideas,
rather than the Ideas looking towards the One.
This One, if we may identify it with the Brahma
of the Indians, would be infinite Being; it
would not be any longer conformable or proper
to any particular cosmos or to any particular

moral life. Relevance to nature would begin with the divine intellect or the sphere of the Platonic Ideas: they would be finite in number and exclusive in type; they would compose the morphology of this world. The third person or hypostasis in the eternal, would be the divine spirit, the love or attention by which those particular forms were made the theme of an actual life. This divine spirit looks towards the Ideas; it is hardly different from the God of Aristotle; and it may be said to descend (although inwardly still wholly attentive to the beings above it) and to animate the world, in the sense in which heavenly souls may be said to descend to animate our bodies; namely, in that an echo or imitation of them or obedience to them keeps the world or the body alive. The immortal soul of the world could never itself look downwards or be troubled by the vicissitudes of the matter which imitates its form: no more could the immortal soul of any man be compromised by the imperfections of its earthly shadow.

We are here in the region of speculative fiction; souls have become so perfect in their eternal abode that other souls have to take their places in living bodies. Indeed, an organic inherited soul, a principle of material growth and action, is no spirit; spirit is first generated in it when it awakes to some actual feeling or thought. Such a spirit evidently can

never envisage pure Being, or the realm of
essence, in its infinite fullness and detail; the
essences which will appear to it will be such,
and such only, as its material organ evokes by
its quite special processes and contacts. But
quantity is not a category important to spirit;
as it is indifferent to duration, because it lives
in the eternal, so it is indifferent to the endless
multiplicity of things, existing or not existing,
which may lie beyond its ken. It is not
anxious, like an animal soul hounded by
curiosity and fear, to dominate and possess
everything, lest by overlooking some secret
enemy it should live in a fool's paradise, and
to-morrow be ruined. The limitations of
experience, when experience is spiritual, are
not invidious; what it possesses it cannot lose;
what it leaves out is not denied or condemned
or demanded. As Dante says, there is no envy
in these spheres. The sense that the rest is
there (since all essences are implied in infinite
Being) suffices to give the spirit room, to
detach it from all partiality, from all unjust
affection; while the essential eternity of that
which is manifested suffices to wed the spirit
to it with an absolute confidence, without the
least ignoble hankering to look beyond. Spirit
differs from animal intelligence less in material
scope than in inward quality; its distinctive
object is not pure Being in its infinity, but
finite being in its purity.

XXI

EVEN in rare moments of attainment, when the human spirit has seemed to be united or even identified with the supreme Being, the reports which reach us of that ecstasy indicate that the chasm has never really been bridged. These reports are avowedly inadequate; words cannot render what has been seen, nor would it be lawful, perhaps, to reveal it. Ultimate insights have a tendency to undermine the orthodox approaches by which they have been reached. The saint pulls his ladder up with him into his private heaven; and the community of the faithful, on whose sturdy dogmatic shoulders he has climbed, must not be deprived of the means of following his example. Hence any dissolving culmination of the religious life must be kept a secret, a mystery to be divulged only to the few whom the knowledge of it can no longer scandalize or discourage. Besides this prudence and this consideration for the weaker brethren, there is a decisive reason for silence: the revelation has been essentially a revelation of the illusion inherent in all language, in all experience, in all existence. It cannot be communicated save by being repeated.

Doubtless the state of being achieved in ecstasy is intrinsically immensely positive, but it is the negation of every human wish and idea ; there are, and can be, no human words to express its nature. So true is this, that if the mystic uses this very suspension of thought, this ecstasy itself, as a true rendering of his ultimate object of contemplation, he falls into a worse error than the animal and worldly mind. For at least, in current experience, scattered and accidental manifestations of being appear ; they are illusions if taken for more than appearances, relative to particular animal organs and interests ; they are trivial and competitive ; yet they are distinct, and each of them, by its positive character, enriches that revelation of essence to spirit which animal life necessarily affords, in spite of its distraction. It would suffice to suspend the urgency of the animal will (as sometimes happens to children and poets in their simplicity) in order to disinfect this sensuous revelation of its distraction and illusion ; it would not reveal much, but it would reveal something of pure Being. In poets and children this is but play ; they revert from it at once to what the world thinks serious interests and sound knowledge of facts. When on the contrary the same disillusion is attained laboriously, by a long spiritual discipline, the adept attempts to maintain and propagate his insight ; and then there is trouble, for in the very act of defending this insight, he is likely to lose it. In so far as the objects of his contemplation are familiar to everyone and have accepted names, these names will carry animal faith with them, and when he uses them they will conceal or even contradict the new quality of pure being which things have acquired in his eyes; to him they have become eternal essences, to his hearers they will still be temporal facts. Meantime, in that realm of essence which he now envisages, vistas may have opened to him into all sorts of regions which are not of this world, which have no names at all in human discourse; how should he be able to express or even to remember their intricate and unearthly nature? Even in ordinary dreams, composed as they are, presumably, out of bits of earthly imagery and puffs of animal anxiety, there are many marvels and vicissitudes, momentous to themselves, which we cannot recover in the light of day: how much harder the vision must be to recompose if its elements were original or its mood sublime! If spiritual attainment could ever be complete and infinite Being could reveal itself (which I do not believe) in its entirety, evidently the disproportion would be overwhelming between the number and variety of things to report and the human means of reporting them.

Silence is therefore imperative, if the mystic has any conscience; he cannot have perceived, and he cannot retain, the fullness of his ultimate

object. This fullness came to him, and remains
in him, merely as a *sense* of fullness, the brilliancy of a blinding light, without any specifica-
tion of the infinity of essences which were there
to be lighted up. He therefore can only assure
us that it was a great revelation, freeing him
from the oppression of ordinary existence and
thought; it was peace, it was bliss, it was
virtual knowledge; but beyond that his powers
of perception and retention could not go.

XXII

HERE the mystic—he who feels he has passed beyond the veil and seen things not to be uttered—if he lacks humility and discipline, may fall, and may lead us, into a sad illusion. He may take his dazzled feeling itself, the blinding glory of mere light, for the supreme reality, or for the true description of its nature. He may say that infinite Being is itself simply feeling, or intensity without quality or distinctions, or the pure light of spirit falling, not on everything, but only on itself. He would then be confusing his own incapacity with the object which infinitely exceeds it. The glass dome, far from creating the many colours of infinite Being, fuses and neutralizes them into a white light—the blurred effect of a rude and summary vision. This unitary feeling, rather than a revelation of pure Being, is the customary sense of one's own bodily existence. The words existence and being are often used interchangeably, and this verbal ambiguity serves to obscure the infinite difference between the realm of essence—pure Being in all its eternal modes—and the pressure of external things and of internal change in a living organism. This sense of existence, essentially transitive and restless, may sometimes be lulled into a simmering warmth and voluminous comfort, a pleasant animal trance in which spirit dives as deep as it can into the life of the matter. This feeling has a true depth of its own, a kinship with universal substance. Brahma is sometimes likened to deep sleep, and Nirvana to nothingness; and in modern philosophy we are sometimes told that the true reality is pure duration or pure sentience. These expressions ignore pure Being, and even the presumable substance of the natural world, which must somehow be diversified and unevenly distributed; but they describe fairly enough the sentiment which the presence of overwhelming things inspires, or the trail which their passage leaves in the animal mind. Persons far advanced in the spiritual life often use language of this kind, as they use pious or erotic language; but their language must not be taken amiss; they use, like all of us, the words they find. To the true mystic even things are symbols; how should he worship words? The Spanish mystic, for instance, San Juan de la Cruz, represents all virtues and graces as by-paths diverging from the straight but difficult way, the name of which is Nothing, Nothing, Nothing. In the end the spirit indeed claims nothing, posits nothing, and is nothing in its own eyes, but empties itself completely into the Being which it contemplates; but if this Being itself were said to be nothing, our mysticism would evidently have slipped into a bad heresy, not to speak of the flat contradiction. So Nirvana may be called annihilation in that it annihilates personality, desire, and temporal existence; yet the "Buddha teaches that all beings are from eternity abiding in Nirvana"[1] so that far from being nothing Nirvana embraces the whole realm of essence—pure Being in its infinite implications—from which, of course, existence is excluded; because since existence is necessarily in flux and is centred in some arbitrary moment, it itself exists only by exclusion and with one foot in the grave. Existence is that realm of Becoming which combines Being and Non-Being so much to Hegel's satisfaction, and which generates those unstable but "current valuations of the worldling" to which the spirit, according to Dean Inge, is so completely indifferent.

[1] Dasgupta, *History of Indian Philosophy.*

XXIII

THE spiritual life, then, is distinguished from worldly morality and intelligence not so much by knowledge as by disillusion: however humble may be its career, it lifts those few and common adventures into the light of eternity. This eternal aspect of things summons spirit out of its initial immersion in sensation and in animal faith and clarifies it into pure spirit. This eternal aspect of things is also their immediate aspect, the dimension in which they are not things but pure essences; for if belief and anxiety be banished from the experience of any object, only its pure essence remains present to the mind. And this aspect of things, which is immediate psychologically, ontologically is ultimate, since evidently the existence of anything is a temporary accident, while its essence is an indelible variation of necessary Being, an eternal form. The spirit lives in this continual sense of the ultimate in the immediate. Mortal spirits, the spirit in animals, cannot possibly survey pure Being in its infinity; but in so far as they free themselves from false respect for the objects of animal faith and animal passion, they may behold some finite being in its purity. For this reason, established morality and religion, by protecting the eye from too much distraction and fixing it on noble objects, may make a better soil for spirit than does wayward living. Not that spirit may not crop out marvellously in the sinner, as it may in the child or the poet. It notoriously does so; and even in the saint it remains profoundly indifferent to the occasion that may have kindled its flame, be this occasion religious faith or sensuous vision, be it passion, study, or practical dominion over the world. All is grist for the mill, if only there be force of intellect actually to grind that experimental substance and reduce it to some pure essence on which contemplation can feed. But moralities and religions, if they merely extend or exaggerate the pressure of circumstance on the soul, are as dreadful an incubus on the spirit as ever was the animal search for food, love, or safety; indeed, they are but a monstrous and terrifying shadow of these radical compulsions cast needlessly on the screen of heaven.

I ask myself sometimes, is not morality a worse enemy of spirit than immorality? Is it not more hopelessly deceptive and entangling? Those romantic poets, for instance, whose lives were often so irregular—were they not evidently far more spiritual than the good people whom they shocked? Shelley, Leopardi, Alfred de Musset were essentially children of the spirit: they were condemned to flutter on broken

wings only for lack of measure and discipline;
they were spiritual waifs, untaught to see the
relativity and absurdity of their proud passions.
The perfect spirit must be a patient hearer, a
sober pupil, not an occasional automatic skylark. Yet when spirituality, as in Words-
worth, has to struggle instead against a black
coat and a white choker, it seems to be more
sadly and decisively stifled, buried alive under
a mountain of human alarms and a heavy
tombstone of sanctimony. The world, he
sighed, is too much with us; but the hills and
even the mock Tritons blowing their wreathed
horns were not able to banish the world from
his conscientious concern. Nothing is able to
banish the world except contempt for the
world, and this was not in him. It would even
have been contrary to his Protestant religion
—that so unspiritual determination to wash
the world white and clean, adopt it, and set it
up for a respectable person. The world is not
respectable; it is mortal, tormented, confused,
deluded for ever; but it is shot through with
beauty, with love, with glints of courage and
laughter; and in these the spirit blooms
timidly, and struggles to the light among the
thorns.

Such is the flitting life of this winged thing,
spirit, in this old, sordid, maternal earth. On
the one hand, in its innocence, spirit is happy
to live in the moment, taking no thought for

the morrow; it can enjoy the least gift as gladly as the greatest; it is the fresh, the pure voice of nature, incapable of learned or moral snobbery. It ignores its origin, so buoyant is it; its miraculous light seems to it a matter of course. Its career is everywhere conditioned and oppressed from without, yet it passes through the fire with a serene incredulity, an indomitable independence. On the other hand, the eye of spirit, in its virtual omniscience, sees the visible in its true setting of the invisible; it is fixed instinctively on the countless moments that are not this moment, on the joys that are not this sorrow and the sorrows that are not this joy, on the thousand opinions that are not this opinion and beauties that are not this beauty; understanding too much to be ever imprisoned, loving too much ever to be in love. Spirit chills the flesh and is itself on fire; thought, as Dean Inge says, " becomes passionate, the passions become cold "; or rather they are confronted and controlled by a profound recollection, in which laughter and tears pulse together like the stars in a polar sky, each indelibly bright, and all infinitely distant.

XXIV

IF with these considerations in mind I turn
back to the characteristics of Dean Inge's
" Platonic tradition in religious thought " I find
that some of these characteristics belong to the
spiritual life everywhere, but not to the
Platonic system. Such is openness to science,
or (what this openness implies) tolerance of any
dogmatic conception, and readiness to accept
any kind of world. Other characteristics are
indeed proper to Platonism, but irrelevant to
the spiritual life; such is the mythical cosmology meant to secure the perpetual prevalence of particular human or divine goods, in a
particular Hellenic universe. Still other characteristics seem to belong both to the spiritual
life and to Platonism; but I find on closer
inspection that these qualities are ambiguous,
and are not assignable to both in the same
sense. Of these apparently common properties
the most important is the gift of seeing the
eternal in the temporal. But what is the
eternal? For pure spirit the eternal means the
timeless; all images of sense and all events in
time offer eternal themes for contemplation
and are themselves eternal in the realm of truth.
This spiritual insight has been frequent among
Platonists, and may indeed have been at the

root of that trance-like vision of essences which enabled Plato to turn the general terms of Socratic logic into individual and immortal beings. But, if his sense for the eternal had been absolutely direct and pure, he would have seen the eternal in the figments of sense, no less than in those of logic or ethics: for all forms equally are essences, and all essences equally are eternal.

It is true that " things seen are temporal," if by " seeing " we understand that animal reaction by which we turn towards material objects which affect our eyes, so that we are prompted to grasp them or to get out of their way. This animal sensibility is what has usually been understood by sense, so that sense has been conventionally regarded as revealing matter, and a man immersed in sense as a materialist. But this kind of " seeing," if it be more than a bodily reaction, is also more than a pure intuition: it is a belief. Sense thereby engages the spirit in the observation and pursuit of material things; and these obviously are temporal. But in this belief and pursuit pure intuition must have intervened to supply the terms of the experience; and this pure intuition is no vision of material things, but of the essences which we call and think to be the qualities of material things, or of whatever else we think about; and these essences in themselves are eternal forms of

Being. One whose attention was wholly absorbed in them would be an extreme idealist, a poet or dreamer not suspecting that he was living in a material world, falling into every pit, and hugging every ghost to his bosom, as the most solid of possible realities. And though the world would laugh at him, the angels would not; for after life is done, and the world is gone up in smoke, what realities may the spirit of a man boast to have embraced without illusion, save the very forms of those illusions by which he has been deceived? These, and not the things which he thought he saw, were his eternal discoveries.

In the Platonic system, however, the eternal also has another signification; it may mean the everlasting. This system was cosmological and quasi-scientific; it sought for the substances and the permanent shapes of existing things. God, the Ideas, and the Soul of the World, though invisible, were in a wide sense physical, since they were powers at work in nature. Like the laws of modern physics they were presumed to be unchangeable; but this persistence of their expression in matter was evidently an entirely different sort of eternity—a presumptive eternity—from that intrinsic to them as essences. Yet the same word *eternal* designates now the pure objects of the contemplative faculty and now certain special objects of scientific presumption, belief in which is unnecessary, audacious, and, to be frank, superstitious. That anything existent should be eternal in the spiritual sense is logically impossible, because existence has to verify itself from moment to moment and must always remain temporal, no matter how long it lasts. That any recognizable existing thing should last for ever seems improbable and contrary to all the analogies of nature. It is contrary, too, to that profound natural philosophy of Heraclitus which Plato had adopted and which, by a happy counterblast, had quickened his sense for the truly eternal—for the inviolate and super-existential being of forms.

If this hazardous belief in permanent natural powers were abandoned the comfortable moral assurances of Platonism would also lapse. It would cease to be popular with tender minds, and a nest of sentimental fancies. The beauty and goodness actually found in the world would no longer be alleged to reveal the forces at work in it more truly than do its ugliness and confusion. It would become impossible to maintain that goodness and beauty are somehow intentional in the world, and their opposites interlopers. Values would be seen not to be powers, but harmonies—the very thing which Plato, in his purely moral wisdom, had made the first and highest principle of the good. Indeed, that superstitious belief, with

which he thought to buttress the crumbling
virtues of antiquity, is useless to human morals.
Human morals draw their vigour from earthly
economy, and find their sanction there. Nor
is that superstitious belief helpful to the
spiritual life or even compatible with it at
bottom. For while to accept and love the
constituted order of nature and society is easy
for a pure spirit, which is without prejudices
or claims, for this same reason it is impossible
for spirit to deny or detest the other forms of
being which nature or society for the moment
does not happen to manifest.

XXV

THE manner of combining unworldliness with the love of nature and of man is another point not understood in the same sense in Platonism and in the spiritual life. Platonism is moralistic: it will love in man and in nature so much as conforms to the patterns which its mathematical physics, its zoology, and its political idealism prescribe for things: all that deviates from these norms will seem to it sad, unaccountable, terrible, and dangerous. In fact, the love of nature and of man, though the beauty of order and harmony in both was still felt in the Greek manner, does not seem to me conspicuous in Platonism. It was a censorious, puritan, prescriptive love; it was not spontaneous, it was not sympathetic, it was not love of nature at all, but of a political, human good, and of so much in nature as might illustrate or sanction it. Free spirit would be more generous. When the renunciation of the world, and of existence itself, has been hearty and radical, the love of nature can be universal; I will not say unqualified by sadness, because the spirit, having itself suffered, recognizes in many an alien form of existence a maimed effort and a lost glory analogous to its own; but a love unqualified by prejudice, by envy, by fear of being outshone or discountenanced by the marvels which nature or society may elsewhere bring to light. It is of the essence of spirit to see and love things for their own sake, in their own nature, not for the sake of one another, nor for its own sake.

Meantime it is a question for scientific speculation, on which pure spirit remains ignorant and impartial, whether there are in existence organisms so vast (measured by the human scale) as the Platonic cosmos, with its deity or deities animating its concentric spheres. If so, spirit would have for its habitation and organ other bodies larger and more long-lived than the bodies of men or of kindred animals: and the concert of so many happier spirits would certainly be sublime, singing in their Pythagorean symphony so calmly together. Yet even then, we should remember that the human scale is relative, and that this Platonic cosmos (or the Christian cosmos which, though historical rather than astronomical, is not very different in principle) is vast only in that perspective. Seen from without, and beyond, it might be infinitesimal, and an insignificant ingredient in some greater world. Its longevity, too, would be relative; and the traditional attribution of eternity to it must be regarded as a rhetorical hyperbole, expressing the sense that its duration is incalculable in terms of human chronology; but true eternity, as I have said, is not of that kind. In the end such a universe, floating like a bubble in the flux of things, would almost certainly dissolve. It is not there that an enlightened heart would lay up its treasure. The flood itself is a nobler companion, and the spirit moves at ease upon the waters.